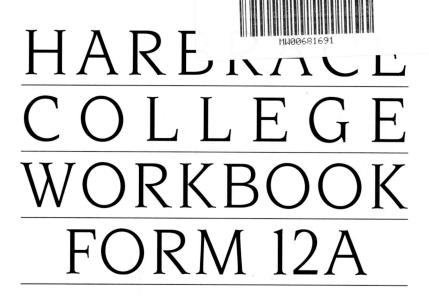

HARBRACE
COLLEGE
WORKBOOK
FORM 12A

Larry G. Mapp

Middle Tennessee State University

HARCOURT
BRACE

Harcourt Brace College Publishers

Fort Worth Philadelphia San Diego New York Orlando Austin San Antonio
Toronto Montreal London Sydney Tokyo

Publisher • Ted Buchholz
Developmental Editor • Sarah Helyar Smith
Project Editor • Nancy Lombardi
Production Manager • Erin Gregg
Senior Book Designer • Don Fujimoto
Project Management • Tripp Narup, Monotype Editorial
Services Group

Address for Editorial Correspondence: Harcourt Brace College Publishers, 301 Commerce Street, Suite 3700, Fort Worth, TX 76102

Address for Orders: Harcourt Brace & Company, 6277 Sea Harbor Drive, Orlando, FL 32887. 1-800-782-4479, or 1-800-433-0001 (in Florida).

Library of Congress Catalog Card Number, Student Edition: 93-78227

ISBN, Student Edition: 0-15-501237-1

Printed in the United States of America

3456789012   039   987654321

TO THE INSTRUCTOR

The three forms of the *Harbrace College Workbook* are designed to be used either independently or in conjunction with the twelfth edition of the *Harbrace College Handbook.* Each form is unique, however, because each develops a particular theme throughout its examples and exercises. Form 12A examines the lives and writings of culturally diverse writers in America. Form 12B explores nature, and Form 12C focuses on writing for the world of work. For Form 12A all exercises and examples have been extensively rewritten.

Arrangement   The materials in Form 12A are arranged in chapters that parallel the chapters in the *Harbrace College Handbook,* Twelfth Edition. The numbers and letters denoting subdivisions within the chapters also correspond to those of the Handbook.

Chapter **1** of Form 12A covers the main points of grammar and punctuation; it is, in other words, a practical minicourse in the grammar and punctuation of sentences. Some students may be able to move directly from chapter **1** to the later chapters that treat word choice and sentence effectiveness (chapters **20** through **30**) or even to chapters that go beyond the sentence to longer units of composition (chapters **31** through **33**). Other students will need additional review of basic areas—such as agreement, tense, and the uses of the comma and apostrophe—that is supplied in the intervening chapters (**2** through **19**). Of course, the needs of the class or the individual student will determine how much time is devoted to chapters **2** through **19** and how many of the exercises in each chapter are assigned.

Exercises   The exercises and examples cover nineteenth-century women writers, especially a group of African American women writers whose work is only recently being rediscovered. The exercises and examples discuss their lives as they struggled to become accepted as writers, all the while not being accepted because they were black and because they were women. There also is much material by immigrant writers. The exercises and examples provide some insight into the writing by Asian Americans, Hispanics, and Europeans who have used writing to help them sort out the vast American experience. Another voice that is heard in the exercises and examples is that of the Native American, voices as varied as those of Black Elk and William Least Heat Moon. As students read this varied and rich material they will learn something about the literary heritage which this country possesses and something about the connection between literature and the lives of women, immigrants, and Native Americans. I hope that first encounter with some of these writers will inspire students to seek out other writing and other writers and to become life-long students of American writing.

Writing Form 12A includes chapters on writing paragraphs (**32**) and essays (**33**). There is enough material in the examples and exercises within each of the chapters to provide a starting point for student writing. Students might be asked to respond to particular questions raised by their reading, perhaps even doing parallel reading in other sources to gather extra material, or they could be encouraged to respond to what they have read in less structured, more expressive writing.

The Dictionary   Use of the dictionary is stressed throughout Form 12A: in the study of nouns, adjectives, adverbs, and verbs, and in the chapters on capitalization, abbreviations, italics, and numbers. Unless each member of the class is already familiar with the dictionary, the best place to begin teaching and learning dictionary skills might be chapter **19**, "Good Usage."

Spelling   Although most students receive little formal instruction in spelling after elementary school, correct spelling is important to success in college and in other work. Form 12A does not presume to be a complete spelling manual, but it does emphasize throughout the use of the dictionary to avoid various kinds of misspellings and it covers all major spelling rules. In addition, it presents a list of words that are frequently misspelled in professional writing. Perhaps even more important, the "Individual Spelling List" at the end of the Workbook offers a chart on which students can record the words they misspell in their writing assignments and the reasons for the misspellings.

Note: Each of the forms of the *Harbrace College Workbook* is available in an Instructor's Edition as well as a Student Edition. The Instructor's Edition is an exact replica of the Student Edition, with answers overprinted in red.

Acknowledgments   I am grateful to the staff of Harcourt Brace College Publishers for their help in preparing this book, especially Sarah Helyar Smith who has been a supportive and encouraging editor.

I also offer thanks to my family: Ann, Anna, and Sarah. They are constant and loving supporters of all that I do.

Larry G. Mapp

TO THE STUDENT

You learn how to write chiefly by revising your own work. Corrections made for you are of comparatively little value. Therefore the instructor points out the problem but allows you to make the actual revision for yourself. The instructor usually indicates a necessary correction by a number (or a symbol) marked in the margin of your paper opposite the error. If a word is misspelled, the number **18** (or the symbol **sp**) will be used; if there is a sentence fragment, the number **2** (or the symbol **frag**); if there is a faulty reference of a pronoun, the number **28** (or the symbol **ref**). Consult the text (see the guides on the inside covers), master the principles underlying each correction, and make the necessary revisions in red. Draw one red line through words to be deleted, but allow such words to remain legible in order that the instructor may compare the revised form with the original.

The Comma   After the number **12** in the margin you should take special care to supply the appropriate letter (**a, b, c, d,** or **e**) from the explanatory sections on the comma to show why the comma is needed. Simply inserting a comma teaches little; understanding why it is required in a particular situation is a definite step toward mastery of the comma. (Your instructor may require that you pinpoint each of your errors by supplying the appropriate letter after every number written in the margin.)

Specimen Paragraph from a Student Theme

Marked by the Instructor with Numbers

18	Most people only see the problems that come with landfeels.
	Communities have been very concerned about leakage of leechate
6	into their drinking water. Leechates is created when rain filters
12, 3	through the layers of garbage to create a toxic black chemical, it
28	is a dangerous contaminant for sources of drinking water. They
	must monitor the landfill and the drinking water supply to prevent
2	contamination. All of this requiring constant testing of water and
	landfill.

Marked by the Instructor with Symbols

sp   Most people only see the problems that come with landfeels.

Communities have been very concerned about leakage of leechate

agr   into their drinking water. Leechates is created when rain filters

p, cs through the layers of garbage to create a toxic black chemical, it

ref is a dangerous contaminant for sources of drinking water. They

must monitor the landfill and the drinking water supply to prevent

frag contamination. All of this requiring constant testing of water and

landfill.

Corrected by the Student

18   Most people only see the problems that come with land~~feels~~ fills.

Communities have been very concerned about leakage of leechate

6   into their drinking water. Leechates ~~is~~ are created when rain filters

12, 3 through the layers of garbage to create a toxic, black chemical; it

28 is a dangerous contaminant for sources of drinking water. ~~They~~ Communities

must monitor the landfill and the drinking water supply to prevent

2   contamination. All of this requir~~ing~~es constant testing of water and

landfill.

CONTENTS

GRAMMAR

MECHANICS

PUNCTUATION

SPELLING AND DICTION

EFFECTIVE WRITING

GRAMMAR

SENTENCE SENSE   ss 1

1

Develop your sentence sense.

You probably have more sentence sense than you realize. As proof, what is your response to this group of words?

> When the first African women arrived in America in 1619.

Probably you will say, almost without thinking, that something is missing from the sentence.

What would you write instead of "When the first African women arrived in America in 1619"? Maybe you would add words.

> When the first African women arrived in America in 1619, they were sold as indentured servants.

In that case your sentence sense tells you to add another subject (*they*) and another verb (*were sold*). Or maybe you would simply omit a word.

> The first African women arrived in America in 1619.

Your instinct tells you that without the word *when,* a subordinator, the group of words is a sentence. Whether you add another subject and verb or omit the subordinator, you are responding to your sense of what is needed to make the group of words into a complete thought.

As you have learned to speak and write, you have become aware of what a sentence is. But to develop this awareness fully, you must know the basic parts of a sentence and how they can be put together in clear and varied patterns. An understanding of this section, then, is necessary to the study of almost all the other parts of this text.

Almost all sentences have a *subject,* someone or something spoken about, and a *predicate,* something said (predicated) about the subject.

SUBJECT	+	PREDICATE
Phillis Wheatley	+	lived in Massachusetts.

The predicate may be subdivided into two parts: the *verb* and the *complement.* The verb states an action, an occurrence, or a state of being; and the complement receives the action of the verb or expresses something about the subject.

SUBJECT   +   VERB   + COMPLEMENT
Phillis Wheatley + wrote +   poetry.
[The complement receives the action of the verb.]

Phillis Wheatley + was +   famous.
[The complement expresses something about the subject.]

1

Most of the sentences that we write have all three of these basic parts: Subject–Verb–Complement (S–V–C). In the examples that follow, the subject is underlined once, the verb twice, and the complement three times. (This is the pattern that you will be asked to follow when working the exercises in this section of the Workbook.)

S-V-C   We studied Phillis Wheatley.

But some sentences have only the subject and the verb.

S-V   Lucy Terry came to America before Phillis.

To write clearly and simply, we make most of our sentence patterns follow the normal order—that is, Subject–Verb–Complement or Subject–Verb. But sometimes, for variety or for emphasis, we vary from the usual order.

NORMAL ORDER

S-V-C   Phillis Wheatley was famous in England.

EMPHATIC ORDER

C-V-S   Famous in England was Phillis Wheatley.

We also vary from normal order when we write most questions.

V-S-V-C   How can we study her poetry?

C-V-S-V   How much effect did her poetry have on America?

And we vary from normal order when we write a sentence that begins with *there* or *it*.

V-S   There remains one poem by Lucy Terry.

V-S   It is not surprising that Phillis Wheatley and Lucy Terry are still read.

[When *it* introduces a sentence, the subject is usually more than one word. Here the subject is a clause, a structure discussed in **1b** and **1c**.]

Each of these basic sentence parts, along with the modifiers that may accompany them, is fully discussed in the following pages.

Basic Sentence Parts   Exercise 1–1

NAME _____ SCORE _____

DIRECTIONS   In the following sentences, the subject is underlined with one line, the verb with two lines, and the complement, when there is one, with three lines. Decide whether or not the sentence parts follow normal order. Write 1 in the blank if they do and 2 if they do not. When you have finished, try writing in normal order three of the sentences that you have labeled 2. (To do so, you will have to change a question into a statement or omit a "there.")

EXAMPLES
Phillis Wheatley published a volume of poetry in 1773.   1

Have you read Wheatley's poetry?   2

1. A slave trader brought Wheatley to Boston in 1761.   1

2. There she was bought by John and Susannah Wheatley.   1

3. There were few opportunities for slaves to become educated.   2

4. Only seven years old, Phillis quickly learned to read and write.   2

5. Fortunately, there was a tutor for Phillis in the Wheatley
   household.   2

6. Mary, the eighteen-year-old daughter, became Phillis's tutor.   1

7. What did Phillis read first?   2

8. Within sixteen months Phillis could read the Bible well.   1

9. What other texts did she read at an early age?   2

10. She read classical writers, such as Virgil and Ovid.   1

11. In the eighteenth century few slaves had such a good education.   1

12. Indeed, there were few well-educated women in the eighteenth
    century.   2

13. At this early age Phillis studied the poetry of Alexander Pope.   1

14. What did she take as the subject of her poetry?   2

15. She often wrote about the births and deaths among the citizens of
    Boston.   1

3

16. Her first published <u>poem</u>, in 1770, <u>honored</u> the <u>death</u> of the minister George Whitefield.   *1*

17. There <u>were</u> many social and literary circles in Boston.   *2*

18. <u>Phillis</u> soon <u>became</u> the honored <u>guest</u> at meetings of those groups.   *1*

19. Self-confident and eloquent, <u>Phillis</u> <u>blended</u> easily into this environment.   *1*

20. <u>We</u> <u>find</u> few <u>reminders</u> in her writing or behavior of her slavery.   *1*

REVISIONS

1.

2.

3.

1a Learn to recognize verbs.

Although the verb is usually the second main part of the sentence, you should master it first because the verb is the heart of the sentence. It is the one part that no sentence can do without. Remember that a trainer can communicate with a dog using only verbs: *Sit. Stay. Fetch.*

Function   The verb, as the heart of the sentence, says something about the subject; it expresses an action, an occurrence, or a state of being.

ACTION   Phillis Wheatley *wrote* all her life.

OCCURRENCE   She *considered* Christianity to be her greatest blessing.

STATE OF BEING She *seems* to have been a strong woman.

The verb also determines what kind of complement the sentence will have: either a word or words that will receive the action of the verb or a word or words that will point back to the subject in some way. If the verb is *transitive,* it transfers or passes along its action to a complement called a *direct object.*

TRANSITIVE   Phillis described personal experiences.

                [The transitive verb *described* passes its action along to its complement, the direct object, *experiences.*]

If the verb is *intransitive,* it does not pass its action along to a complement. One kind of intransitive verb is complete in itself; it has no complement.

INSTRANSITIVE   The images soared.

                [The verb *soared* is complete; it does not need a complement.]

Another type of intransitive verb is the *linking verb,* which links the subject with a complement that refers back to the subject. The most common linking verbs are *be* (*is, are, was, were, has been, have been, will be,* and so on), *seem,* and *appear,* as well as those that are related to the senses, such as *feel, look,* and *taste.*

INSTRANSITIVE   The images seem original.

                [The linking verb *seem* calls for a complement that refers back to the subject.]

Position   The verb (underlined twice) is usually the second main part of the sentence, but in questions, emphatic sentences, and sentences that begin with *there* or *it,* the verb may come first or before the subject (underlined once).

USUAL ORDER	Ethnographers can write the history of a culture.
QUESTION	Have ethnographers described your culture?
EMPHATIC	Rare is the unstudied culture.
THERE	There are resemblances between our cultures.

Always look for the verb first when you are trying to match it with its subject. This practice will help you to avoid agreement errors (the use of a plural verb with a singular subject and vice versa). If you look for the subject first, you may easily choose the wrong word in a sentence like this: "The historians in the research institute (is, are) studying the records at Jamestown." You are much less likely to choose "institute" as the subject if you first locate the verb (is, are) *studying* and then determine who or what the verb is speaking about: the institute is not studying; the *historians* are studying.

Form   The verb may be recognized not only by its function and its position but also by its endings in the third person. Verbs ending in *-s* or *-es* are singular in number: he tries, she jumps, it requires. Verbs ending in *-d* or *-ed* are in the past tense: he tried, she jumped, it required. (Sometimes, however, the verb changes its form altogether in the past tense: he rides, he rode; she lies down, she lay down; it comes, it came.)

Auxiliaries (Helping Verbs)   The verb may be one word or several words. The main part of the verb—the word that actually expresses the action, occurrence, or state of being—may be accompanied by auxiliaries or helping verbs—words like *has, have, should,* and *can* and forms of *be* (see the Appendix for a list of auxiliary verbs). This cluster of verbs is referred to as a *verb phrase.* Often the parts of the verb phrase are separated.

Many immigrants did not find life easy in America.

[*Not* often comes between the auxiliary and the main verb; it is a modifier, not a part of the verb, even when it appears in contractions like *don't.*]

Do you know your ethnic heritage?

[In a question the parts of the verb phrase are usually separated.]

Phrasal Verbs   The main verb may also be accompanied by a word like *up, down,* or *in* that functions as a part of the verb. This part of the verb is called a *particle;* the particle usually changes or adds to the meaning of the main verb.

VERB	I passed an Ethiopian restaurant near the park.
VERB WITH PARTICLE	I passed up a chance to eat at an Ethiopian restaurant near the park.

The particle ordinarily follows immediately after the main verb, but it may sometimes be separated from the main verb.

I passed the restaurant up.

SUMMARY

Function   The verb expresses an action (*throw, run, talk*), an occurrence (*prevent, criticize, modify*), or a state of being (*be, seem, appear, become*).

Position   The verb is usually the second main part of the sentence ("We *photographed* the old buildings."), but it may come elsewhere, especially in questions ("*May* we *copy* the records?").

Form   In the third person (*he, she, it*), the verb shows singular number by an *-s* or *-es* ending (feed*s*, come*s*, carrie*s*) and past tense by a *-d* or *-ed* ending (solve*d*, walk*ed*, carri*ed*). Sometimes, however, the verb changes form completely in the past tense: *run, ran; buy, bought; choose, chose.* The verb may be only one word (*turned*) or several words (*has turned, will be turning, should turn in*).

7

Verbs in Simple Sentences

Exercise 1–2

NAME _____ SCORE _____

DIRECTIONS   In the following sentences, the subject, which is usually the first main part of the sentence, is underlined once. Underline the verb twice and enter the word or words that make up the verb in the blank. Notice that a singular verb is used with a singular subject and a plural verb with a plural subject.

EXAMPLE
Many scholars name Lucy Terry as the first African

American poet.   *name*

1. Lucy Terry lived in Massachusetts as a slave for over
two decades.   *lived*

2. During those years she was strongly affected by her
Christian beliefs.   *affected*

3. In 1746, as an impressionable sixteen year old, Lucy
wrote her first and only known poem.   *wrote*

4. In nearby Deerfield, Indians had massacred two
families.   *had massacred*

5. Lucy's ballad honored the victims of the massacre. *honored*

6. The original manuscript of the poem has been lost. *has been*

7. Fortunately, oral historians of Deerfield preserved the
poem.   *preserved*

8. During her long life Lucy was highly respected by the
people of Massachusetts.   *was*

9. Abijah Prince, a former slave, married Lucy in 1756. *married*

10. Abijah soon bought Lucy's freedom.   *bought*

11. Lucy's ability as a raconteur made her locally popular. *made*

12. Young people were especially eager to gather at her
house to hear her talk.   *were*

SENTENCE SENSE

13. In 1760 Lucy and Abijah moved to Guilford, Vermont,
    home to a number of writers.   _moved_

14. Lucy's spirit soon gained her fame in Vermont.   _gained_

15. For example, she fought hard, but in vain, to have one
    of her sons admitted to Williams College.   _fought_

16. Lucy's one poem still reminds us of her passion and
    ability to empathize.   _reminds_

17. In it she names several of the victims, "brave and
    bold."   _names_

18. The images often are realistic and graphic.   _are_

19. Modern readers may find it unremarkable poetry.   _may_

20. However, it still stands as the first effort in African
    American literature.   _stands_

Verbs in Simple Sentences

Exercise 1–3

NAME _____ SCORE _____

DIRECTIONS   Fill in the blank with one of the verbs listed before the exercise. If the verb that you list has an auxiliary (helping verb) or a particle already as a part of the sentence, underline that word or words. Then write the complete verb in the blank at the right.

EXAMPLE

In her poems Phillis Wheatley <u>wrote</u> about her Christian
faith.

wrote about

affected ✓	rejects ✓	gives ✓	celebrates ✓	established ✓
criticize ✓	objected ✓	reprint ✓	describes ✓	invited ✓
look ✓	wrote ✓	treated ✓	visited ✓	published ✓

1. Phillis Wheatley's poems do not directly *Describe* slavery.

Describe

2. For this reason, many readers have *objected* to her work.

objected

3. However, in subtle language she *celebrates* the dignity and equality of the African American.

celebrates

4. Anthologies of American literature often *reprint* her poem, "On Being Brought from Africa to America."

reprint

5. In that poem she *gives* thanks for her Christian faith.

gives

6. In one image she *treated* African Americans as finally part of God's "angelic train."

treated

7. With that image Wheatley *rejects* any differences between the races.

rejects

8. *Criticize* up the text of the poem in an anthology.

Criticize

9. Wheatley's relationship with her white owners greatly *affected* her poetry.

affected

10. They *look to* her as a friend and a member of the family.

look to

SENTENCE SENSE

11. Phillis even _has visited_ England in the company of the
    Wheatley's son.

                                                    has visited

12. In 1773, during her visit to England her only book of
    poetry was _published_.

                                                    published

13. In 1775, Phillis _wrote_ George Washington a letter
    and poem.

                                                    wrote

14. Washington _invited_ her to visit him in Cambridge.   _invited_

15. She had been _Established_ as the "African poetess " of
    America.

                                                    Had been established

1b(1) Learn to recognize subjects of verbs.

All sentences except those that issue commands have a stated subject. And even in a command, the subject—*you*—is understood.

[You] Write a paper about Phillis Wheatley.

Function   The subject is who or what the sentence is about. Once you have located the verb in the sentence, you need only to ask who or what is *doing, occurring,* or *being.* Your answer will be the complete subject. To find the simple subject, ask specifically who or what the verb is talking about.

Everyone in our class is writing a paper about Phillis Wheatley.

[Who is writing? *Everyone in our class.* Who specifically is writing? Not *in our class* but *everyone.*]

My topic, unlike the others, has been assigned by the instructor.

[What has been assigned? *My topic, unlike the others.* What specifically has been assigned? Not *my* or *unlike the others* but *topic.*]

As in these examples, a word or group of words usually comes before and/or after the simple subject. Do not confuse one of these other words with the subject. If you do, you may fail to make the subject and the verb work together well; you may use a singular subject with a plural verb or vice versa. As was suggested in the discussion of verbs, always identify the verb before you try to locate the subject to avoid this kind of agreement mistake.

The students in our class are studying Phillis Wheatley.

[The verb, *are studying,* is plural; therefore the subject must be plural too. *Students,* not *class,* is the plural subject; it is the word that answers the question "Who is studying?"]

Position   In most sentences the subject is the first main part of the sentence. But in questions, emphatic sentences, and sentences that begin with *it* or *there,* the subject follows the verb or comes in the middle of the verb phrase.

USUAL ORDER   Students carefully research Phillis Wheatley's career.

QUESTION   Do students keep notes on their research?

EMPHATIC   Very detailed are the students' notes.

THERE   There are very careful notes about Phillis Wheatley.

Form   Because the subject tells who or what the sentence is about, it must be either a *noun* or *pronoun*—the two parts of speech that name people and things—or a cluster of words that functions as a noun or pronoun. (Word clusters that may be substituted for a noun or pronoun are explained in section **1d**.)

Nouns are words that name individuals or classes of people (*Maya Angelou, tribe, jury*), places (*Nashville, rivers, Venus*), things (*Pampers, candy, watch*), activities (*Little League, soccer, festival*), and concepts (*divine right of kings, endurance, conclusion*). Pronouns are words used in the place of nouns; they take their meaning from the nouns that they replace.

> NOUNS   The *students* brought *books* to the *library*.
>
> PRONOUNS   *They* brought *them* to *it*.   [*They* replaces *students*; *them* replaces *books*; *it* replaces *library*.]

Some pronouns—such as *we, he,* and *who*—refer only to people; some—such as *it, something,* and *which*—refer only to things; and some—such as *each, many,* and *some*—refer to either people or things.

Like verbs, nouns have certain endings that help you identify them. But unlike verbs, nouns show the plural by an *-s* or an *-es* ending (keys, caves, tomato*es*). Some nouns completely change their form when they are made plural (*man→men; leaf→leaves; child→children*). Nouns may also be recognized by the articles that frequently accompany them (*a* chair, *an* error, *the* person) and by their ability to form the possessive (child*'s* shoe, people*'s* choice, boys*'* dates).

Somewhat like verbs, nouns may consist of more than one word, but all the words are necessary to name the person, place, or thing being spoken of: *space shuttle, Whoopi Goldberg, Smithsonian Institution.*

SUMMARY

Function   The subject is who or what the sentence is about. Thus when we ask who or what specifically is responsible for the action, the occurrence, or the state of being that the verb expresses, the answer will be the simple subject.

Position   The subject is usually the first main part of the sentence (*Phillis Wheatley* was an early American writer.); however, in questions, emphatic sentences, and sentences that begin with *there* or *it*, it may come after the verb or in the middle of the verb phrase (When did *Phillis Wheatley* publish her poetry?).

Form   Most nouns and pronouns that function as subjects undergo various changes to show plural number (*hurdle → hurdles; woman → women; I → we*). Noun subjects are frequently preceded by articles (*a* stone, *an* essay, *the* ledger), and both noun and pronoun subjects are often followed by words that limit their meaning (a poem *without a title*; each of *the women*; someone *in our class*). A noun subject is often made up of more than one word, especially if the noun is naming a particular person, place, or thing (*Annie Dillard, Puget Sound, Halley's Comet*).

Subjects in Simple Sentences

Exercise 1–4

NAME _____ SCORE _____

DIRECTIONS   In the following sentences the verb is underlined twice. Underline the subject once and write the word or words you have underlined in the blank at the right. (Remember that a simple subject is sometimes made up of two or more words, which are usually capitalized, such as *Ms. Kingston, Cape Hatteras,* or *Fourth of July.*)

EXAMPLE

In 1862 Charlotte Forten Grimke was the first African

Amerian teacher to help to educate freed slaves.

Charlotte Forten Grimke

1. In 1859 the first novel by an African American was

   published in Boston.

   novel

2. The author of this first novel was Harriet Wilson.

   Harriet Wilson

3. Historians of African American literature have

   researched Wilson's life.

   Historians

4. Her life is best revealed in her fiction.

   Her life

5. The central character in Wilson's fiction is Alfrado.

   the central character

6. As the daughter of a poor white woman and a black

   man, Alfrado becomes an indentured servant.

   daughter

7. Does your dictionary give a good definition of

   "indentured"?

   dictionary

8. Can you give a good definition of "demonic"?

   definition

9. Alfrado is abandoned at the home of the Bellmonts.

   Alfrado

10. Many readers label Mrs. Bellmont as a demonic

    character.

    Many readers

11. Mrs. Bellmont overworks the young Alfrado.

    Mrs. Bellmont

12. Mrs. Bellmont's chief ally in her mistreatment of

    Alfrado is her daughter, Mary.

    Mary

13. Other <u>members</u> of the family <u>prove</u> more kind.   *members of the family*

14. Mr. Bellmont often <u>rescues</u> <u>Alfrado</u> from her tormenters.   *Alfrado*

15. Upon reaching the age of eighteen <u>Alfrado</u> <u>is</u> free to leave.   *Alfrado*

16. <u>Life</u> as a free African American woman in the North <u>proves</u> difficult.   *life*

17. In poor health and unable to work <u>she</u> <u>lives</u> in a succession of charity homes.   *she*

18. Her <u>experience</u> <u>parallels</u> Wilson's experience.   *experience*

19. Like Wilson, <u>Alfrado</u> <u>writes</u> a book about northern mistreatment of freed slaves.   *Alfrado*

20. Both <u>authors</u> <u>hoped</u> to help their families with the money from the sale of their books.   *authors*

Subjects and Verbs in Simple Sentences

Exercise 1–5

NAME _____   SCORE _____

DIRECTIONS   Here are ten sentences about African American women writers, all written without people-related subjects. Rewrite each sentence with a person or people (or a personal pronoun like *he, she,* or *they*) as the subject. Underline the subject of your revised sentence with one line and the verb with two lines. When you have finished revising the sentences, decide which version you think is easier and more interesting to read.

EXAMPLE
The first novel by an African American woman was written by Harriet E. Wilson.

<u>Harriet E. Wilson</u> <u>wrote</u> the first novel by an African American woman.

1. The autobiographical account was written in the guise of fiction.

2. Before the Civil War southern racism was constantly attacked by northern abolitionists.

    Northern abolitionists constantly attacked Southern racism before the Civil War.

3. The novel was Wilson's attempt to point out the North's hypocrisy.

4. Personal experience had revealed to her the racism of the North.

5. Her biography has been uncovered by the diligent scholarship of modern scholars.

6. The most important scholarship on Wilson has been done by Henry Louis Gates.

7. Testimony by Wilson's contemporaries also helped confirm the autobiographical nature of her fiction.

8. However, relatively little is still known about Wilson's life.

9. Much of our information about Wilson's life has been inferred from the plot of the novel.

10. The plot of the novel has been compared to the plot of a Dickens novel.

1b(2) Learn to recognize objects and other kinds of complements.

Not every sentence has a complement.

> The character abruptly died.

> The novel ended fittingly.

Sometimes a complement is implied.

> The public applauded.

> [A complement, though it is not stated, may be added because the verb, *applauded,* is a transitive verb: "The public applauded Emma Kelley's novel, *Megda.*"]

If the sentence has a complement, it can be found by following the subject and verb with "who," "whom," or "what."

> The book was a success. [The book was what? *Success* is the complement.]

> It tells the story of Megda's Christian conversion. [It tells what? *Story* is the complement.]

> Kelley published this first novel in 1891. [Kelley published what? *Novel* is the complement.]

> *Megda* ends with Megda married to a minister.

> [There is no word to answer the "Who?" "Whom?" or "What?" Thus the sentence has no complement, only a prepositional phrase following the verb.]

Function   Following a transitive verb, a complement (or complements) is a word (or words) to which the action of the verb is transferred or passed along. Three types of complements may follow transitive verbs: *direct objects, indirect objects,* and *object complements.* The direct object is the most common type of complement following a transitive verb. Sometimes it is accompanied by either an indirect object, which precedes it, or an object complement, which follows it.

> DIRECT OBJECT   The writer tells the story of Megda's faith.

> [The action of the verb is passed along to the direct object, *story.*]

INDIRECT OBJECT AND	The story gives readers a moral lesson.
DIRECT OBJECT	[The action of the verb is passed along to both the indirect object, *readers,* and the direct object, *lesson.* An indirect object follows a verb like *give, send, bring, buy, sell* and shows to whom or for whom the verb is doing something.]

DIRECT OBJECT AND	Readers call the novel an inspiration.
OBJECT COMPLEMENT	[The object complement, *inspiration,* is another name for the direct object, *novel.* An object complement follows a verb like *name, elect, make,* or *consider.*]

DIRECT OBJECT AND	Readers consider the novel inspirational.
OBJECT COMPLEMENT	[Here the object complement, *inspirational,* is an adjective that describes the direct object, *novel.*]

Note: One test for a direct object is to make the active verb passive—that is, to add a form of *be* to the main verb. The word that is the object of the active verb then becomes the subject of the passive verb.

ACTIVE	Readers identified several plots in *Megda.*

PASSIVE	Several plots in *Megda* were identified by readers.

[Note that *readers,* the subject of the active verb, now follows the passive verb and is the object of the preposition *by.*]

ACTIVE	The novel gave many readers a new context in which to view their faith.

PASSIVE	Many readers were given by the novel a new context in which to view their faith.

[*Novel,* the subject of the active verb *gave,* now follows the passive verb and is the object of the preposition *by.*]

A complement (or complements) following a linking verb (forms of *be* and verbs like *seem, feel, appear,* and *look*) points back to the subject of the sentence; it either describes the subject or renames it in some way. Such complements are called *subject complements.* A complement that renames the subject is either a noun or pronoun; it is often referred to as a *predicate nominative* or a *predicate noun.* A complement that describes the subject is an adjective; it is often referred to as a *predicate adjective.*

PREDICATE NOMINATIVE   Reverend Stanley Arthur is Megda's husband.

[The subject complement, *husband,* more or less renames the subject; the husband is the same person as Reverend Stanley Arthur.]

PREDICATE ADJECTIVE   Megda seems contented as the minister's wife.

[The subject complement, *contented,* describes something about the subject, *Megda.*]

Position   The complement is usually the third main part of the sentence, but it may appear first in a question or in an emphatic sentence. There is no complement in a sentence that begins with the expletive *there* or *it.*

USUAL ORDER   Megda seems an unlikely heroine for Kelley's novel.

QUESTION   Why does Megda seem an unlikely heroine for Kelley's novel?

EMPHATIC   Surprising indeed is the heroine of Kelley's first novel.

Form   The form of the noun complement, whether it is an object or a subject complement, is the same as the form of the subject. It can be distinguished from the subject only by its position in the sentence as the third main part of the basic formula.

SUBJECT   Young female *characters* dominate this novel.

OBJECT   A concern for religion dominates the young female *characters* in this novel.

Pronoun subject complements have the same form as pronoun subjects: *I, he, she, we, they,* and *who.* However, many pronouns used as objects have distinct forms: *me, him, her, us, them,* and *whom.*

SUBJECT COMPLEMENT The writer is she.

[Compare "*She* is the writer." The subject complement has the same grammatical form that the subject would have.]

OBJECT   No one ignored her.

[Compare "*She* ignored everyone." The object differs in form from the subject.]

Some pronouns, like nouns, have the same form whether they are subject complements or objects—for example, *you, it, each, some, many,* and *one.*

23

SUBJECT COMPLEMENT The last person to read the novel was *you*.

OBJECT The others beat *you*.

Adjectives have the same form whether they are subject complements or object complements.

SUBJECT COMPLEMENT Jennifer was *lucky*.

OBJECT COMPLEMENT Jennifer considered herself *lucky*.

SUMMARY

Function Asking the question "Who?" "Whom?" or "What?" of the subject and its verb reveals whether or not a sentence has a complement. Complements function either as objects—direct or indirect—or object complements that receive the action of transitive verbs ("She wrote the *novel*.") or as subject complements that rename or describe the subjects of linking verbs ("The writer was *she*.").

Position The complement is usually the third main part of the sentence ("Jennifer was *lucky*."), but in questions and emphatic sentences the complement may be stated first ("*Lucky* was Jennifer.").

Form Nouns have the same form whether they are used as subjects, as objects, or as subject complements. Most personal pronouns have different forms as objects (*me, him, her, us, them, whom*) than they do as subject complements (*I, he, she, we, they, who*). Some pronouns have the same form whether they are used as objects or as subject complements (*you, it, each, one, some, many*, for example). Adjectives have the same form whether they are used as subject complements ("The novel was *dull*.") or as object complements ("The class called the novel *dull*.").

Subjects, Verbs, and Complements in Simple Sentences Exercise 1–6

NAME _____ SCORE _____

DIRECTIONS   In the following sentences underline the simple subject once, the verb twice, and the simple complement or complements three times. Write *subject* in the blank if the complement (or complements) refers back to the subject; write *object* if the complement (or complements) receives the action of the verb. If there is no complement, leave the blank empty.

EXAMPLE

In recent years scholars have rediscovered the work of many

early African American writers.   *object*

1. In 1861 Harriet Jacobs published an account of her former life as a slave.   _____

2. Jacobs's work received little attention at its publication.   _____

3. Since that time few people have read her narrative.   _____

4. Now, however, literary scholars have drawn attention to Jacobs.   _____

5. They recognize Jacobs's important contribution to American literature.   _____

6. She is an important African American woman writer of the nineteenth century.   _____

7. In her narrative Jacobs tells the story of Linda Brent.   _____

8. Brent suffers abuse at the hands of her master and his family.   _____

9. Jacobs also tells of Flint's sexual advances toward Brent.   _____

10. Flint's wife is jealous of his interest in Brent.   _____

11. She adds to the abuse of Brent.   _____

12. Jacobs very effectively portrays the special hardships of life for a female slave.   _____

13. Sexual oppression of slaves was not often discussed in the nineteenth century.   _____

14. After the Civil War many writers explored this aspect of slavery. _____

15. Like Jacobs, other recently freed slaves viewed themselves as only partially free. _____

16. By writing about their past, they sought complete freedom. _____

17. They found support in a variety of organizations. _____

18. African American churches, newspapers, and benevolent organizations were most supportive. _____

19. Many African American writers published their work in the *Anglo-African,* a journal based in New York. _____

20. We can admire now the courage and honesty of many of those early writers. _____

1c Learn to recognize the parts of speech.

Now that you have learned about the basic structure of a sentence, you are ready to begin working with all the elements that combine to give a sentence its meaning. The following chart lists the various functions words can perform in a sentence and the types of words that perform each function.

Function	*Kinds of Words*
Naming	Nouns and Pronouns
Predicating (stating or asserting)	Verbs
Modifying	Adjectives and Adverbs
Connecting	Prepositions and Conjunctions

The next chart summarizes the parts of speech that you will study in detail in the rest of this section (except for interjections).

Parts of Speech	*Uses in Sentences*	*Examples*
1. Verbs	Indicators of action, occurrence, or state of being	Andy *wrote* the report. The students *studied* the essay. They *are* seniors.
2. Nouns	Subjects and objects	*Karen* gave *James* the *list* of stories.
3. Pronouns	Substitutes for nouns	*He* will return *it* to *her* later.
4. Adjectives	Modifiers of nouns and pronouns	The *horror* story is the *interesting* one.
5. Adverbs	Modifiers of verbs, adjectives, other adverbs, or whole clauses	presented *clearly* a *very* interesting study *entirely* too long *Indeed,* we are ready.

Parts of Speech	Uses in Sentences	Examples
6. Prepositions	Words used before nouns and pronouns to relate them to other words in the sentence	*in* a hurry *with* no thought *to* them
7. Conjunctions	Connectors of words, phrases, or clauses; may be either coordinating or subordinating	lyric poems *and* ballads before the reading *or* after it *since* the signing of the contract
8. Interjections	Expressions of emotion (unrelated grammatically to the rest of the sentence)	*Good grief!* *Ouch!* *Well,* we tried.

1d Learn to recognize phrases and subordinate clauses.

A phrase is a series of related words (words grouped together) that lack either a subject or a verb or both. You are already familiar with phrases that may function as the verb of a sentence—the main verb with one or more auxiliaries (*will be writing*) and the verb with a particle (*put up with* [**1a**]). Other phrases may function as the subject or object (**1d[1]** below) or as modifiers (**1d[2]**).

1d(1) Learn to recognize phrases and subordinate clauses used as subjects and objects.

The main types of word groups that function as subjects and as objects are verbal phrases and noun clauses.

Verbal Phrases   The verbal phrase is the kind of phrase that most frequently functions as a subject or object. The main part of the verbal phrase is the verbal itself—a word that shows action, occurrence, or a state of being as a verb does but that cannot function as the verb of a sentence.

VERB   Harriet Wilson *published* her novel in 1859.

VERBALS   *publishing, to publish, having published*

Notice that none of these verbals can substitute for the verb *published* in a sentence.

Harriet Wilson *publishing* her novel in 1859 [a fragment]
Harriet Wilson *to publish* her novel in 1859 [a fragment]
Harriet Wilson *having published* her novel in 1859 [a fragment]

But such verbals, alone or with other words in verbal phrases, can function as subjects or objects just as individual nouns or pronouns can.

NOUN	The *history of minority writers* reveals some surprising facts. [subject]
VERBAL PHRASE	*Studying the history of minority writers* reveals some surprising facts. [subject]
VERBAL PHRASE	*To study the history of minority writers* is a worthy goal. [subject]
VERBAL PHRASE	*Having studied the history of minority writers* makes one more appreciative of minorities in general. [subject]
NOUN	I enjoy the *history of minority writers*. [object]
VERBAL PHRASE	I enjoy *studying the history of minority writers*. [object]
VERBAL PHRASE	I plan *to study the history of minority writers*. [object]
VERBAL PHRASE	I will never regret *having studied the history of minority writers*. [object]

Noun Clauses   A clause is a series of related words (words grouped together) that has both a subject and a verb. One kind of clause, referred to as a *main clause* or *independent clause,* can stand alone as a sentence. The other, called a *subordinate clause* or *dependent clause,* may function as a noun—either a subject or object—or as a modifier in a sentence. (**1d[2]** discusses the use of phrases and subordinate clauses as modifiers. In fact, they are more commonly used as modifiers than as subjects or objects.) As nouns, subordinate clauses usually are introduced by one of these words: *who, whom, whose, which, that, whoever, whomever, what, whether, how, why,* or *where.* These introductory words are clause markers; they are printed in boldface in the following examples.

NOUN	Our *discovery* surprised us. [subject]
NOUN CLAUSE	**What** *we discovered about early American writers* surprised us. [subject]
NOUN	We reported our *discovery*. [object]
NOUN CLAUSE	We reported **what** *we discovered about early American writers.* [object]
NOUN CLAUSE	**Whoever** *studies early American writers* will learn **that** *many of them are women.* [subject and object]

Verbal Phrases and Noun Clauses as Subject Complements   Verbal phrases and noun clauses can replace nouns and pronouns not only as subjects and objects but also as subject complements.

NOUN	His passion was *poetry*.
VERBAL PHRASE	Her passion was *studying poetry.*
VERBAL PHRASE	His ambition was *to study poetry.*
NOUN CLAUSE	Her opinion was *that everyone should write poetry.*

Verbal Phrases and Noun Clauses as Subjects,
Direct Objects, and Subject Complements

Exercise 1–7

NAME _____ SCORE _____

DIRECTIONS   Each of the following sentences contains one or more verbal phrases or noun clauses functioning as subject, direct object, or subject complement. First, underline such verbal phrases and/or noun clauses. Then write in the blank (1) *S* for a phrase or clause functioning as the subject of the sentence, (2) *DO* for a phrase or clause functioning as a direct object, or (3) *SC* for a phrase or clause functioning as a subject complement. If you write two or more things in the blank, use dashes between them. (Be sure to look for the main verb of the sentence before you try to identify the subject, direct object, and subject complement.)

EXAMPLE
We hope to study American women writers.   _DO_

1. That most early American writers were men is a common misconception.   _____

2. Discovering the work of those women writers often requires some detective work.   _____

3. Editors of *The Anglo-African,* a New York journal, began to publish African American writers in 1859.   _____

4. Publishing in *The Anglo-African* built the fame of A. E. Chancellor.   _____

5. We now know that Chancellor was the most famous African American woman writer of the 1850s.   _____

6. Reading the work of Frances Ellen Watkins Harper still inspires us.   _____

7. We know that she was a famous abolitionist.   _____

8. We also know that she published the first African American short story in 1859.   _____

9. Most of these early writers tried to support the antislavery movement.   _____

10. The writing seems to have inspired the movement.   _____

11. That many of these slave narratives were written by whites is ironic. _____

12. Many former slaves had to dictate their stories to whites. _____

13. They had never learned to read or to write. _____

14. Literary historians tell us that slave narratives were published until well into the twentieth century. _____

15. Telling their slave narratives helped to build the fame of Harriet Tubman and Sojourner Truth. _____

1d(2) Learn to recognize words, phrases, and subordinate clauses used as modifiers.

A modifier is a word or word cluster that describes, limits, or qualifies another, thus expanding the meaning of the sentence. Adjectives are the modifiers of nouns or pronouns; adverbs are the modifiers of verbs, adjectives, other adverbs, and sometimes whole sentences. The function of an adjective or an adverb can be fulfilled by a single word, a phrase, or a subordinate clause, as the following sentences demonstrate.

            1   **2**   **3**

ADJECTIVES *One* example *of an early African American writer who wrote without a model*

of her own was Mary Cary.

[All three adjectival modifiers (a word, a prepositional phrase, and a subordinate clause, in that order) qualify the subject *example.*]

            1   **2**   **3**

ADVERBS *In 1854,* Cary traveled, wrote, and lectured *in America, while she planned to*

                                              4   **5**

establish a Canadian antislavery newspaper because there blacks had more

freedom.

[The first adverbial modifier (a prepositional phrase) qualifies the whole sentence. The second (a prepositional phrase) and third (a subordinate clause) modify the verbs *traveled, wrote,* and *lectured.* The fourth (a subordinate clause) modifies the verbal, *to establish.* The fifth (a word) modifies the verb, *had,* of the subordinate clause.]

Single-Word Modifiers Some authorities consider articles (*a, an,* and *the*), number words (*some, few, many,* and so on), and possessive pronouns (*my, its, your,* and so on) to be modifiers, while others call these words "noun determiners." Clearly, all three normally signal that a noun is to follow.

Many men of *the* nineteenth century would not support *the* idea of *a* woman devoting

her energies to *a* career outside *the* home.

Other single-word modifiers describe some quality of or set some kind of limitation on the words they refer to.

After the Civil War many *recently freed African American* women *quickly* seized the

opportunity to tell the *harrowing* stories of their years in bondage.

[*Recently* qualifies *freed, freed* and *African American* describe *women, quickly* describes *seized,* and *harrowing* modifies *stories.*]

Except when they are used as subject complements, adjective modifiers, by their very nature, are almost always found near the nouns or pronouns that they refer to. In emphatic word order, an adjective modifier may follow the noun or pronoun that it qualifies, but in usual word order the adjective precedes the word that it modifies.

USUAL ORDER   The *sentimental, romantic* novels were published.

EMPHATIC   The novels, *sentimental* and *romantic,* were published.

Adverb modifiers usually are not as clearly tied to the words that they modify and may move around more freely in the sentence, as long as their location does not cause awkward or difficult reading.

> *Undeniably,* the novels were popular.
> The novels, *undeniably,* were popular.
> The novels were *undeniably* popular.
> The novels were popular, *undeniably.*

Phrases as Modifiers A phrase, as you may remember, is a word cluster that lacks either a subject or a verb or both. The two types of phrases that function as modifiers are verbal phrases and prepositional phrases.

Verbal Phrases   The key word in the verbal phrase is the verbal itself (see **1d[1]**). Participles, which usually end in *-ing, -ed,* or *-en* and are often preceded by *having,* can function only as adjective modifiers.

The participial phrase, which consists of the participle and sometimes a modifier and an object that are part of the participle's word cluster, is frequently used to expand the basic formula of a sentence. The use of a participial phrase often avoids a series of short, choppy sentences.

SHORT, CHOPPY   The novel was never published. It told a predictable story of a romance.

PARTICIPIAL PHRASE   *Never published,* the novel told a predictable story of a romance.

OR

                     The novel, *never published,* told a predictable story of a romance.

An infinitive phrase may function as a modifier too. Unlike a participial phrase, however, it may be used as either an adjective or adverb.

ADJECTIVAL   The desire *to produce a publishable manuscript* has kept him writing for years. [The infinitive phrase modifies the subject *desire.*]

ADVERBIAL   Not every writer is able *to produce a publishable manuscript.* [The infinitive phrase modifies the predicate adjective (subject complement) *able.*]

Sometimes the verbal has its own subject. It is then called an *absolute phrase* because it does not modify a single word in the sentence but rather the entire sentence (see also **12d**). Although an absolute phrase is not a sentence, it does have a greater degree of independence from the sentence than an ordinary verbal phrase does.

PARTICIPIAL PHRASE
: The manuscript, *rejected by several publishers*, disappeared for nearly fifty years. [The verbal, *rejected,* modifies the subject, *manuscript,* and must stand near it in the sentence.]

ABSOLUTE PHRASE
: *Her first efforts encouraged by brisk sales*, the author began a lecture tour. [The verbal, *encouraged,* has its own subject, *efforts;* thus the meaning of the phrase is clear wherever it is placed in the sentence.]

Like a participial phrase, an absolute phrase can be used effectively to combine short, choppy sentences.

SHORT, CHOPPY
: Her first novel was published serially in *Harper's* magazine. She found herself famous almost overnight.

ABSOLUTE PHRASE
: *Her first novel having been published serially in* HARPER'S *magazine*, she found herself famous almost overnight.

Prepositional Phrases   A prepositional phrase begins with a preposition—a word like *in, of, to,* or *with*—and ends with an object, either a noun or pronoun. The preposition is the word that connects the whole phrase to one of the main parts of the sentence, to another modifier, or to the object of another prepositional phrase. (A prepositional phrase often rides piggyback on a preceding prepositional phrase.)

    1   2   3   4
In the first chapter of this novel she introduces the themes *of religion* and *of traditional morality*

        5   6   7   8   9
that she developed *in all of her later work. With the success of this first novel behind her,*

          10
she began a trilogy that was based *on the Civil War.*

[The first prepositional phrase (adverbial) explains the verb, *introduces;* the second (adjectival) modifies the object of the first phrase, *chapter;* the third and fourth (adjectival) modify the direct object, *themes;* the fifth phrase (adverbial) modifies the verb, *developed;* the sixth modifies the object of the preceding phrase, *all.* In the second sentence, the seventh phrase modifies the verb, *began;* the eighth and ninth phrases modify the object of the preceding phrase, *success;* and the tenth phrase modifies the verb, *was based.*]

Often, as in the case of *with the success,* the prepositional phrase does not immediately follow the word it modifies. When you see a preposition (such as *with*), you know that an object ("with the unexpected *success*") and perhaps a modifier of the object ("with the *unexpected* success") follow.

There are so few prepositions that you can easily memorize a list of the most common ones (see the Appendix). But the prepositions that we do have we use again and again. We write few sentences that do not include at least one prepositional phrase. Notice how incomplete the meaning of the following sentences would be without the prepositional phrases that qualify the meanings of the words they modify.

35

The income *from her first novel* paid her daughter's college tuition.

[Without the prepositional phrase the sentence reads "The income paid her daughter's college tuition."]

The biggest reward *from publishing the novel* came *with her daughter's graduation.*

[Without the prepositional phrases the sentence reads "The biggest reward came."]

Word and Phrase Modifiers:
Adjectives and Adverbs

Exercise 1–8

NAME _____ SCORE _____

DIRECTIONS   In each of the following sentences, the word in italics is qualified by one or more single-word and/or phrase modifiers. First underline these modifiers; then draw an arrow from each one to the italicized word. Do not underline or draw an arrow from the articles—*a, an,* and *the.* Write *adj.* in the blank if the modifier or modifiers are functioning as adjectives and *adv.* if the modifier or modifiers are functioning as adverbs. Notice how the modifiers make the italicized words more exact in meaning.

EXAMPLES

The best *report* in the class was presented by Sarah.   *adj.*

Professor Kirkman obviously *expected* Sarah's report to be good.   *adv.*

1. Several reports examined nineteenth-century African American

    women *writers.*   _____

2. The writing *careers* of these women amaze me.   _____

3. For example, *think* about the career of Pauline Hopkins.   _____

4. At the age of fifteen, in 1874, she *won* a prize of ten dollars for an

    essay on the evils of intemperance.   _____

5. William Wells Brown, the first African American *novelist,*

    presented her prize.   _____

6. Hopkins began her writing pursuits by composing a

    four-act musical *drama* about the underground railroad.   _____

7. Hopkins' first short story *was published* in May 1900 in a periodical

    for African American writers.   _____

8. By this time Hopkins *was respected* as a speaker and lecturer.   _____

9. Later in 1900 she published a romantic historical *novel* written in

   the manner of earlier African American novels.   _____

10. The story examines the *problems* of the post-Reconstruction era.   _____

11. It is a *tale* of miscegenation, of families separated by slavery, and

    of chaotic loves torn by jealous intrigue.   _____

12. The tragic *mulatto,* caught between the hatred of blacks and the

    scorn of whites, is a prominent theme.   _____

13. Characters give lengthy *discourses* on womanhood, on prejudice,

    on lynchings, and on the uplifting of the African American race.   _____

14. The 402-page novel *sold* for one dollar and fifty cents.   _____

15. The novel *established* Hopkins as a voice for her people.   _____

Subordinate Clauses   In **1d(1)** you studied one kind of subordinate clause—the noun clause, which can function as a subject or object. (As you may remember, a subordinate clause contains both a subject and a verb, but, unlike a main clause, cannot stand by itself as a sentence because of the subordinator that introduces it.) Other kinds of subordinate clauses—the adjective clause and the adverb clause—act as modifiers.

Adjective Clauses   Adjective clauses are introduced by a subordinator such as *who, whom, that, which,* or *whose*—often referred to as *relative pronouns*. A relative pronoun relates the rest of the words in its clause to a word in the main clause, and, as a pronoun, also serves some noun function in its own clause, often as the subject. (Remember that a clause, unlike a phrase, has both a subject and a verb.)

Zora Neale Hurston, *who* was born to sharecropper parents in an all-black town in Florida,

became one of the least reserved of African American women writers.

[The relative pronoun, *who*, relates the subordinate clause to the subject of the main clause, *Zora Neale Hurston,* and also serves as subject of the verb, *was born,* in the adjective clause.]

An adjective clause follows the noun or pronoun that it modifies. It cannot be moved elsewhere without confusing either the meaning or the structure of the sentence.

CORRECT PLACEMENT   Hurston's interests *which engrossed her in folklore expeditions* contrasted with those of other women writers.

INCORRECT PLACEMENT   Hurston's interests contrasted with those of other women writers *which engrossed her in folklore expeditions.*

Sometimes the relative pronoun is omitted when the clause is short and no misreading could result.

WITH SUBORDINATOR   Hurston is one writer *whom* almost everyone recognizes.

WITHOUT SUBORDINATOR   Hurston is one writer almost everyone recognizes.

Adverb Clauses   An adverb clause is introduced by a subordinator such as *since, when, if, because, although,* or *so that* (see the Appendix for a list of the most commonly used subordinators). Like the adjective clause, the adverb clause adds another subject and verb (and sometimes other elements) to the sentence. But unlike the relative pronoun that introduces the adjective clause, the subordinator of an adverb clause does not function as a main part of its own clause. The adverb clause usually modifies the verb of the main clause, but it may also modify an adjective or adverb in the main clause.

CRISIS was the official magazine of the NAACP *when* Jessie Fauset became literary editor

in 1919, and *because* she proved to be a brilliant editor, it soon became an important

outlet for young writers.

[The subordinator *when* introduces the first adverb clause which modifies the verb *was*. The subordinator *because* introduces the second adverb clause which modifies the verb *became*.]

Fauset is not as famous today *as* is Zora Neale Hurston.

[The subordinator *as* introduces the adverb clause, which modifies the adjective *famous*.]

Unlike an adjective clause, an adverb clause can often move around freely in the sentence without changing the meaning or confusing the structure of the sentence. (See also chapter **25**.)

After she left CRISIS *in 1923,* Fauset returned to teaching.

Fauset, *after she left* CRISIS *in 1923,* returned to teaching.

Fauset returned to teaching *after she left* CRISIS *in 1923.*

Subordinate Clause Modifiers:
Adjectives and Adverbs

Exercise 1–9

NAME _____ SCORE _____

DIRECTIONS Write *adj.* in the blank if the italicized clause is an adjective modifier and *adv.* if it is an adverb modifier. (To test your classification, try moving the italicized clause to different places in its sentence; notice whether the new arrangement affects the meaning or the structure of the sentence. If the movement of the clause affects either the meaning or the structure of the sentence, you know that it is an adjective clause.)

EXAMPLE

After she published her first novel in 1900, Pauline Hopkins became a
   leader among African American writers.   _adv._

1. THE COLORED AMERICAN was a journal *which published the work
   of African American writers.*   _____

2. *When it debuted in 1900,* THE COLORED AMERICAN contained a
   story by Pauline Hopkins.   _____

3. *While she worked to develop as a writer,* Hopkins made her living
   as a stenographer for two Republican politicians.   _____

4. She also began to lecture about African American history to groups
   who could pay her a small stipend.   _____

5. During her travels as a lecturer, Hopkins met Walter W. Wallace
   *who had the idea for THE COLORED AMERICAN, a magazine of
   creative and informative writing.*   _____

6. Wallace joined with three other men in a partnership *which they
   called the Colored Co-operative Publishing Company.*   _____

7. *Because she could see the importance of this new publishing venture,* Hopkins became a shareholder.   _____

8. She also soon became a creditor *because they could not afford to
   pay for her first story.*   _____

9. Hopkins was also reading at her lectures from the manuscript of a
   novel *that she recently had completed.*   _____

10. Hopkins was lucky to have affiliations with the Colored Co-operative Publishing Company *which soon agreed to publish the novel.* _____

11. *After new owners bought* THE COLORED AMERICAN *magazine,* Hopkins became literary editor. _____

12. She later wrote, "I was engaged as literary editor *because I was well known as a race writer [and] had gained the confidence of my people. . . ."* _____

13. As the editor she followed a racial policy *that sharply contrasted with the conciliatory policy of the followers of Booker T. Washington.* _____

14. Under her guidance the magazine became a forum for discussion of the topics *that concerned all African Americans.* _____

15. The magazine often featured articles *that were international in scope.* _____

16. A strong proponent of African American history, *which was omitted from textbooks,* Hopkins wrote a series of articles on famous men and women of the African race. _____

17. Hopkins also continued to contribute fiction *which often explored themes of interracial relationships.* _____

18. Hopkins ended her career at THE COLORED AMERICAN *after it was bought by supporters of Booker T. Washington.* _____

19. Because Hopkins had opposed Washington's policies *of conciliation between the races,* the new owners sought to muzzle or silence her. _____

20. *Although she left the magazine,* she continued to write in support of her people until her death in 1930. _____

1e Learn to use main clauses and subordinate clauses in various types of sentences.

Sometimes a writer has two or more related ideas to set forth. Depending on the relationship of the ideas and on the desired emphasis, the writer may choose to express the ideas in separate sentences or to combine them in one of several ways.

Types of Sentences   There are four types of sentences: *simple, compound, complex,* and *compound–complex.* Whichever of these types a given sentence is depends on the number of main and subordinate clauses it includes.

Simple Sentences   The simple sentence consists of only one main clause and no subordinate clauses. A simple sentence is often short but not necessarily so: one or more of the basic sentence parts—the subject, verb, or complement—may be compound and many single-word and phrase modifiers may be attached to the main clause.

SIMPLE   Rare book collectors treasure Alice Moore's first novel.

SIMPLE   **Seeking a copy of this rare book,** collectors attended the auction *of rare books* **being held in New York.**

[The main clause, or basic formula, "Collectors attended the auction," has been expanded by two verbal phrases (in boldface) and one prepositional phrase (in italics).]

SIMPLE   A **book** collector *from Duluth,* a **museum** director *from Cleveland,* and an **unidentified** woman bought two diaries and the **walking** cane *of Alice Moore.*

[The subject and the complement are compound; four single-word modifiers (in boldface) and three prepositional phrases (in italics) expand the main clause.]

Compound Sentences   A compound sentence consists of two or more main clauses (but no subordinate clauses) connected by a coordinating conjunction (*and, but, or, nor, for, so, yet*) or by a conjunctive adverb (such as *thus* or *therefore*) or other transitional expressions (such as *as a matter of fact*). (A semicolon may substitute for the coordinating conjunction; see chapter **14.**) In a compound sentence the connecting word (in boldface following) acts like the fulcrum of a seesaw, balancing grammatically equivalent structures.

43

COMPOUND   The museum director proudly added the walking cane to her museum's

collection, **and** she announced plans for future acquisitions.

[The first main clause is balanced by the grammatically equivalent second main clause. The clauses are connected by the coordinate conjunction *and*.]

COMPOUND   The desire to collect artifacts related to writers is ageless; **however,** the best

fictional treatment of that practice is a recent novel by A.S. Byatt.

[The conjunctive adverb, *however,* balances the first main clause against the grammatically equivalent second main clause.]

Complex Sentences   A complex sentence consists of one main clause and one or more subordinate clauses. The subordinate clause in a complex sentence may function as the subject, a complement, a modifier, or the object of a preposition. As is true of the compound sentence, the complex sentence has more than one subject and verb; however, at least one of the subject–verb pairs is introduced by a subordinator such as *what, whoever, who, when,* or *if* (in boldface below) which makes its clause dependent on the main clause.

COMPLEX   Alice Moore's first book was published in 1895 **when** *she was only twenty*

years old.

[The subordinate clause functions as a modifier—as an adverb clause.]

COMPLEX   Moore learned at an early age **that** her best writing would explore the rich

traditions of her native Louisiana.

[The subordinate clause functions as the complement (direct object).]

COMPLEX   A later book of fourteen stories **that** *explored themes of lost love, jealousy,*

and disappointment was the first collection of short fiction written by an

African American woman.

[The subordinate clause functions as a modifier—as an adjective clause.]

Compound–Complex Sentences   A compound–complex sentence consists of two or more main clauses and at least one subordinate clause. Thus it has three or more separate sets of subjects, verbs, and sometimes complements.

COMPOUND-COMPLEX   We <u>respect</u> <u>Moore</u> today most for **what** *she accomplished as a poet,*

and <u>we</u> often <u>find</u> her <u>poem</u>, "I Sit and Sew," in anthologies **that** *are*

used in freshman literature classes.

[The subordinate clauses (in italics), introduced by the subordinators *what* and *that* (in boldface), function as the object of a preposition and modifier (adjective) respectively.]

Compound Subjects and Verbs
and Compound Sentences

Exercise 1–10

NAME _____ SCORE _____

DIRECTIONS Underline the simple subject or subjects in each of the following main clauses once and the verb or verbs twice. If the sentence is a compound sentence, insert an inverted caret (**V**) between the two main clauses. (Notice that the main clauses are correctly joined by a comma plus a coordinating conjunction, by a semicolon, or by a semicolon plus a conjunctive adverb or transitional phrase.) In the blank write *sub* if the subject is compound, *verb* if the verb is compound, and *CS* if the sentence is compound.

EXAMPLES

Countee Cullen, Langston Hughes, and Gwendolyn Bennett were important writers of the Harlem Renaissance.   *sub*

During the 1920s Harlem became a mecca for African American artists and writers, and new African American publications helped to liberate their voices.   *CS*

1. The best remembered publication of the Harlem Renaissance is *Fire!;* it featured Gwendolyn Bennett and Zora Neale Hurston as staff members.   _____

2. *Fire!* was published in 1926, and it represented the younger writers' rebellion against conventional writing.   _____

3. The magazine elicited outrage from orthodox African American critics and survived for only one issue.   _____

4. Many unexpected benefactors assisted writers into print and created non-traditional alliances between art and other parts of the community.   _____

5. The NAACP published a biography of Norris Wright Cuney, and the National Urban League published Charles S. Johnson's *Ebony and Topaz: A Collectanea* (1927).   _____

6. The status of women writers improved during the Harlem Renaissance; however, during the height of the movement in 1928, only two women published books.   _____

7. Georgia Douglas Johnson's *An Autumn Love Cycle* and Nella Larsen's *Quicksand* were published in 1928. _____

8. Male writers and critics patronized women writers. _____

9. For example, W. E. B. DuBois wrote the foreword to Georgia Douglas Johnson's *Bronze* and used the words *simple* and *trite* to describe it. _____

10. African American women writers explored themes of race assertion, primitivism, and sex, but they clung to outdated Victorian themes and styles. _____

Subjects and Verbs in Main and Subordinate Clauses: Complex Sentences

Exercise 1–11

NAME _____ SCORE _____

DIRECTIONS   Each sentence below contains one main clause and one subordinate clause—each clause, of course, with its own subject and verb. Underline the subjects once and the verbs twice. In the blank, write the subordinator that introduces the subordinate clause. (Remember that a relative pronoun subordinator—for instance, *who, whom, that, which*—often serves as the subject or complement of its own clause. Remember also that an entire subordinate clause may serve as the subject or complement of a main clause.)

EXAMPLES

Jessie Fauset succeeded as literary editor of *Crisis* because she recognized talent in young writers.

_____*because*_____

Langston Hughes named Fauset as one of the "three people who midwifed the so-called New Negro literature into being."

_____*who*_____

1. Because she was such a versatile writer, Fauset published stories, essays, poetry, reviews, critiques, and translations in *Crisis*.

_____

2. She became literary editor of *Crisis* in 1919 after she taught in a high school for over a decade.

_____

3. Readers also recognized her style in dispatches that she sent in from her travels around the world.

_____

4. W. E. B. DuBois, whose work Fauset admired, was among her earliest supporters.

_____

5. Although Fauset and DuBois worked together for some years, they eventually quarreled over the editorial content of *Crisis*.

_____

6. DuBois objected to the more radical writers whom Fauset supported.

_____

7. Fauset's personal relationship with DuBois may have been the final reason that she left *Crisis*.

_____

8. Some historians believe that DuBois refused to repay a debt to Fauset. _____

9. Although her career at *Crisis* provided her with excellent credentials, Fauset was unable to find another position in publishing. _____

10. The double prejudices that beset African American women prevented her from working in publishing. _____

Subordinate (Dependent) Clauses:
Functions in Sentences

Exercise 1–12

NAME _____   SCORE _____

DIRECTIONS   Classify each italicized subordinate clause in the following sentences as a subject (S), a complement (C), or a modifier (M). As you do the exercise, notice the subordinator that introduces the clause.

EXAMPLE

Jessie Fauset knew *that T. S. Stribling's novel* BIRTHRIGHT *(1922) pre-sented an unrealistic picture of black America.*   _____C_____

1. At the age of forty-two she wrote THERE IS CONFUSION, *which is the first novel to depict African American middle-class life.*   _____

2. The novel, *which explores themes of middle-class values and manners, classism, racial biases, and sexism,* spans several generations of characters.   _____

3. Some white publishers rejected the novel *because the black families in it were too middle-class.*   _____

4. *That she had written an African American novel of manners in the tradition of Jane Austen* was evident to some critics.   _____

5. Fauset's second novel explores "passing," *which is a theme in recent Spike Lee movies.*   _____

6. In this novel, Fauset again presents African Americans *who are cultured and well educated.*   _____

7. Virginia and her sister Angela, *who is lighter,* are the main characters.   _____

8. *Because she easily passes for white,* Angela enters into a series of relationships with white men.   _____

9. Finally, however, Angela realizes *that she has given up too much by passing,* and returns to her race.   _____

10. *Although her first two novels were well received,* Fauset had trouble finding a publisher for her third novel.   _____

11. Of the characters in this novel Fauset wrote, "I have depicted something of the homelife of the colored American *who is not being pressed too hard by the Furies of Prejudice, Ignorance, and Injustice.*" _____

12. *That the characters of this novel are comfortably middle-class* is evident. _____

13. However, *that the novel explores serious themes of miscegenation, incest, and interracial love* is perhaps more important. _____

14. Modern readers sometimes criticize Fauset *because she did not write about lower-class African Americans.* _____

15. She realized, however, *that she had to write from her experience.* _____

16. She wrote *what she knew best*—the very human traits of an early twentieth-century African American middle class struggling with its hopes and ambitions in a racist society. _____

17. *Because her characters lack real insight and complexity,* some modern critics judge Fauset as a minor writer. _____

18. A writer such as Fauset presents special problems for the contemporary reader *who wants to learn to appreciate her.* _____

19. *That she is a minor writer* is probably undeniable. _____

20. We should also recognize *that her novels of manners explore bold interracial themes.* _____

2

In general, write complete sentences.

Once you become aware of the parts of the sentence (chapter **1**), you will sense the difference between a complete sentence and an incomplete one, a fragment. Although fragments are usually not a clear way to communicate with your reader, they may be effective, and even necessary, in a few instances, particularly in answering questions, stating exclamations, and recording dialogue.

> QUESTION AND FRAGMENT ANSWER   Did the students in your class like reading Maya Angelou's I KNOW WHY THE CAGED BIRD SINGS? *Yes, especially because she spoke to our class about writing it.*

> SENTENCE AND FRAGMENT EXCLAMATION   My teacher knew that Angelou was speaking on campus, and he asked her to set aside an hour for my class. *How lucky for you!*

> DIALOGUE   "I KNOW WHY THE CAGED BIRD SINGS tells you about Angelou's childhood," my teacher said. *"And about the end of that childhood."*

Fragments are used in dialogue simply to record people's speech patterns. The fragment used in answering a question or in stating an exclamation allows an idea to be communicated without repeating most of the preceding sentence.

Effective sentence fragments, like those used in answering questions, stating exclamations, and recording dialogue, are written intentionally. The very shortness of most fragments calls attention to them; thus they are used for emphasis. Ineffective fragments, however, are rarely written intentionally. Rather they are written because the writer could not sense the difference between a sentence part and a complete sentence.

2a Learn to sense the difference between a phrase, especially a verbal phrase, and a sentence.

Any sentence becomes a fragment when the verb is replaced by a verbal.

> SENTENCE   The importance of the written word *was* the theme of her talk.

> VERBAL PHRASE   The importance of the written word *being* the theme of her talk.
> The importance of the written word *having been* the theme of her talk.

Sometimes a prepositional phrase is incorrectly punctuated as a sentence, usually because the phrase is either very long or is introduced by words like *for example* or *such as*.

> SENTENCE   We were impressed by Angelou's successes in other professions.

> PREPOSITIONAL   For example, as a professional dancer.
> PHRASES   And in Africa as an ambassador representing the United States.

     53

An appositive is a word or word group following a noun or pronoun that defines or restates the noun or pronoun. An appositive cannot stand alone as a sentence.

SENTENCE   Angelou's appearance on campus was a high point of Black History Month.

APPOSITIVE   A month-long celebration of African American contributions to American culture.

Another common fragment is caused by the separation of the two parts of a compound predicate.

SENTENCE   Ernest Gaines was on campus the week after Angelou.

PREDICATE   And spoke to my creative writing class about his novel, *A Gathering of Old Men.*

2b Learn to sense the difference between a subordinate clause and a sentence.

Any sentence can be made a fragment by inserting a subordinator before or after the subject. (See the list of subordinators in the Appendix.)

SENTENCE   During Black History Month Ernest Gaines spoke to my creative writing class.

SUBORDINATE CLAUSE   During Black History Month *after* Ernest Gaines spoke to my creative writing class.

During Black History Month Ernest Gaines *who* spoke to my creative writing class.

2c Learn the best way to correct a fragment.

An obvious way to correct a fragment is to supply the missing part—to make the fragment into a sentence. But most fragments are best corrected by reconnecting them to the sentences to which they belong. Examine the following paragraph in which the word groups that are likely to be incorrectly written as fragments are printed in italics.

Both Maya Angelou and Ernest Gaines read from their work *and answered questions from the audience. If any theme was woven through both speakers' comments*, it was the critical importance of education, *of being able to read, to write, and to think well. During Angelou's session*, she also read several of her poems, and I felt as if I were hearing them for the first time.

Sentences and Fragments: Verbs and Verbals

Exercise 2–1

NAME _____ SCORE _____

DIRECTIONS   In the following word groups underline each subject with one straight line, each verb with two straight lines, and each verbal with a wavy line. If a word group contains no true subject and/or verb for a main clause, indicate an incomplete sentence by writing *frag.* in the blank for either subject or verb or for both. Notice that a sentence may have both a verb and one or more verbals.

	SUBJECT	VERB
EXAMPLE After studying Maya Angelou's poetry and writing a term paper on it.	frag.	frag.
1. My roommate constantly reading modern poetry.		
2. Her bedside lamp left on late into the night.		
3. I envision the poems still dancing in her head.		
4. Her counting sonnets instead of sheep.		
5. Having been born in Philadelphia she loves poetry with an urban setting.		
6. Having so little firsthand contact with nature.		
7. She doubts her reading of nature poetry.		
8. I flew home with her last month, wanting to see some of Philadelphia.		
9. Borders Bookstore featuring a different writer reading almost every week.		
10. Nikki Giovanni reading from her latest collection that week.		
11. Poems exploring the condition of a modern African American woman.		
12. Having read her earlier poetry, my roommate could understand Giovanni.		
13. My earnest attempts at listening and understanding.		

14. I remembered reading "Nikki–Rosa" in last semester's English class.   _____   _____

15. Remembering the last line of the poem about her childhood—"all the while I was quite happy."   _____   _____

16. Giovanni, being sure of African American readers understanding her.   _____   _____

17. Listening to Giovanni I thought of the differences in our lives.   _____   _____

18. Of her being African American, of me not being African American.   _____   _____

19. I envied my roommate's hard-earned insight.   _____   _____

20. Giovanni the person seeming more accessible than Giovanni the poet.   _____   _____

Subordinate Clauses and Sentences

Exercise 2–2

NAME _____ SCORE _____

DIRECTIONS   In the following word groups underline each subject with one straight line, each verb with two straight lines, and each subordinator with a wavy line. (Remember that a subordinator like *who, which,* or *that* may also be the subject of its own clause.) If the word group has only a subordinate clause or clauses, write *frag.* in the blank to indicate an incomplete sentence. If the word group has no subordinate clause or has a subordinate clause plus a main, or independent clause, write *C* in the blank to indicate a complete sentence.

EXAMPLES

After Langston Hughes studied a year at Columbia.   *frag.*

He left school to see more of the world, an ambition that he pursued all of his life.   *C*

1. Because he visited some thirty African ports.   _____

2. However, by 1925 he had returned to New York which remained his home for the rest of his life.   _____

3. Although he wanted to be a writer, he soon took a job as a hotel busboy.   _____

4. While he was working in the dining room.   _____

5. He met the poet Vachel Lindsay who graciously accepted the manuscripts of three poems from Hughes.   _____

6. In a newspaper interview the next day, Lindsay revealed that he had discovered a busboy poet.   _____

7. As reporters began clamoring for interviews with Hughes.   _____

8. They took pictures of Hughes as he held a tray of dishes above his head.   _____

9. Lindsay wrote Hughes a note that read, "Do not let lionizers stampede you. Hide and write and study and think."   _____

10. Because the press coverage made Hughes famous.   _____

11. He soon found publishers for two books that increased his fame.   _____

12. Some reviewers who attacked the books for their reliance on lower-class characters.   _____

13. Hughes, however, as he tried to follow Lindsay's advice.   _____

14. He tried to create a lifestyle which gave him time to write, to study, and to think.   _____

15. However, his wanderlust which soon took him to the South, the West, Haiti, and Cuba.   _____

Sentences and Fragments

Exercise 2–3

NAME _____ SCORE _____

DIRECTIONS   In the following paragraphs are ten fragments of various types—prepositional and verbal phrases, subordinate clauses, appositives, and parts of compound predicates. First, circle the numbers that stand in front of fragments, then revise the fragments by attaching them to the sentences to which they belong. (See **12b** and **12d** if you need help with punctuation.)

[1]If we were to pick a focal point of the Harlem Renaissance. [2]It would be 1925. [3]When the African American scholar Alan Locke published an anthology called *The New Negro: An Interpretation.* [4]He stated that the new generation was vibrant with a new psychology. [5]That a "new spirit" was awake in the "masses." [6]With, in general, "renewed self-respect and self-dependence."

[7]Black migration to the city was a social factor contributing to the Renaissance. [8]Before World War I, most of the African American population lived in the country. [9]Most of them in the South. [10]Economic motivation caused urban migration. [11]First to cities like Birmingham and Atlanta. [12]Labor demands of the First World War provided incentives and opportunities. [13]And shifted northward the goal of general migration. [14]As for the African American man's new northward migration. [15]Underlying it was the old desire to escape from the social restrictions in the South. [16]Now, in the African American community of a great city. [17]The migrant was living. [18]For the first time, in what seemed to be almost a totally black world.

Fragments: Effective and Ineffective   Exercise 2–4

NAME _____   SCORE _____

DIRECTIONS   The following paragraphs include six effective fragments (see page 53) and seventeen ineffective fragments, incomplete sentences that the writer did not plan. Circle the number that stands in front of each fragment. Then revise the ineffective fragments either by rewriting them as complete sentences or by connecting them to the sentences to which they belong. (See **12b** and **12d** if you need help with punctuation.) Place an X by the number of each effective fragment.

[1]The first African American man to make a literary career.

[2]An innovative poet.

[3]A true artist.

[4]The creator of Jess B. Simple, a timeless literary character in the tradition of Huck Finn and George Babbitt.

[5]These accolades describe Langston Hughes. [6]Who more than any other figure represents the heritage of African American writers.

[7]Hughes was born of a mother and father of mixed ancestry. [8]He was abandoned at an early age by his father, and he was raised in part by a grandmother who read to him from *Crisis* and the works of W. E. B. DuBois. [9]During those early years. [10]Hughes lived an itinerant life. [11]Before he graduated from high school, he had lived in several states and in Mexico. [12]Where he visited his father, an embittered man. [13]Who thought of nothing but money. [14]And who directed all of his old resentments and his contempt at Native Americans. [15]Hughes later wrote about this visit with his father. [16]That it had caused him much anguish because he had realized that he hated his father for being mean-spirited and a bigot.

[17]Early in his life Hughes turned to writing. [18]Expressing himself in lyrics that owed much to Carl Sandburg. [19]At the age of nineteen he published his first poem in *Crisis*. [20]A poem entitled "The Negro Speaks of Rivers." [21]In the same year Hughes entered Columbia. [22]And became acquainted with Harlem and Broadway. [23]Wanderlust, however, prompted him to abandon Columbia after a year and embark on a world tour.

[24]In 1925, back in New York and working as a busboy. [25]He was discovered by Vachel Lindsay. [26]By 1927 he had published two books and was being aided by a wealthy white patroness, Mrs. Rufus Osgood Mason. [27]In time, Mrs. Mason tried too much to control Hughes's career. [28]He broke away from her and turned his attention totally to the lives of African Americans. [29]Although he was penniless. [30]This period of association with other African Americans was very important to Hughes. [31]He moved in the world of common life. [32]Of common black life, to find a deeper identification with his people in their deprivation and suffering during the Depression.

[33]His wandering continued. [34]First, back to the South. [35]Then visits to Negro colleges. [36]Then west and to Mexico again. [37]He traveled to the then Soviet Union and later worked as a correspondent covering the Civil War in Spain. [38]He was back in Harlem by 1938.

[39]Over the next thirty years he published poems, stories, novels, plays, movie scripts, and countless pieces of non-fiction. [40]Establishing a reputation as one of the most eloquent of American writers. [41]Perhaps the most memorable character that he created being Jess B. Simple. [42]Simple is the archetypal underdog. [43]He is beaten, downtrodden, ignorant, and blundering, but, somehow, he is gallant, ironic,

clear-sighted, generous-spirited, and indestructible. [44]The stories of Simple have been around for over fifty years, but they still feel contemporary in spirit.

[45]What should we think of Langston Hughes today? [46]That he was a writer who told the story of his part of America with honesty, with wisdom, and with good humor. [47]And that he was, as he said, "a writer who wrote mostly because when I felt bad, writing kept me from feeling worse."

3

Learn the standard ways to link two closely related main clauses.

In chapter **1** you studied the two main ways to expand a sentence—subordination and coordination. Subordination often requires the use of a comma or commas for the subordinated addition to the main clause. (See also **12b** and **12d**.)

Coordination, too, requires a comma when two main clauses are connected by a coordinating conjunction—*and, but, or, nor, for, so,* and *yet.*

> Miguel Torres entered the United States as an illegal immigrant, *so* the Immigration Service deported him shortly after his arrival.

If the coordinating conjunction is removed, the two main clauses may still be connected; however, the standard mark of punctuation between the two clauses then becomes the semicolon.

> Miguel Torres entered the United States as an illegal immigrant; the Immigration Service deported him shortly after his arrival.

Even if another type of connective—a conjunctive adverb like *then, therefore,* or *however*—is inserted between the main clauses, a semicolon is still the standard mark of punctuation to be used after the first main clause.

> Miguel Torres entered the United States as an illegal immigrant; *however,* the Immigration Service deported him shortly after his arrival.

If a comma is used between two main clauses not connected by a coordinating conjunction, the sentence contains a *comma splice.* In other words, the comma has been made to perform a function that standard usage has not given it.

> COMMA SPLICE   Miguel Torres entered the United States as an illegal immigrant, the Immigration Service deported him shortly after his arrival.
>
> COMMA SPLICE   Miguel Torres entered the United States as an illegal immigrant, however, the Immigration Service deported him shortly after his arrival.

Some students feel they can avoid comma splices by omitting all commas from their writing. And they are right. But in so doing they violate standard practices of punctuation even further. Instead of writing comma splice sentences, they write *fused* (or run-on) sentences. And fused sentences are even more ineffective than comma splice sentences because they are more difficult to understand at first reading.

> FUSED SENTENCE   A guide named Coyote lead Torres across the border he charged $300 for the trip.

3a The standard punctuation of two main clauses not connected by a coordinating conjunction is the semicolon.

> Torres told his story to an interpreter; he had just returned from being deported to Mexico for the third time. [The semicolon acts like the fulcrum of a seesaw with the idea in one main clause balanced by the idea in the other.]

There are two other ways to avoid a comma splice or fused sentence.

TWO SENTENCES	Torres told his story to an interpreter. He had just returned from being deported to Mexico for the third time. [Placing the two ideas in separate sentences emphasizes them equally.]
SUBORDINATION	After Torres returned from being deported to Mexico for the third time, he told his story to an interpreter. [Subordinating one of the ideas establishes a cause and effect relationship.]

3b The standard punctuation of two main clauses connected by a conjunctive adverb or a transitional phrase is the semicolon.

> Agents patrol the border with Mexico; *however,* Torres describes their job as impossible.

> Deported aliens often return very quickly; *in fact,* Torres was back at his California job three days after being deported.

Notice that a conjunctive adverb or a transitional phrase may also be placed in the middle of a main clause and that the standard marks of punctuation are then commas.

> Torres's desire to improve himself, *however,* reminds me of myself.

> He is, *in fact,* as determined to succeed as I am.

You may need to consult or even memorize the list of commonly used conjunctive adverbs and transitional phrases in the Appendix.

3c The standard mark of punctuation for a divided quotation made up of two main clauses is the semicolon or an end mark (a period, question mark, or exclamation point).

> "A man I know was hitchhiking along the road near San Diego, and someone picked him up," said Torres; "it was the Immigration man who had just brought him back to Mexico."

> "A man I know was hitchhiking along the road near San Diego, and someone picked him up," said Torres. "It was the Immigration man who had just brought him back to Mexico."

Comma Splices and Fused Sentences

Exercise 3–1

NAME _____ SCORE _____

DIRECTIONS   In each of the following sentences insert an inverted caret (**V**) between main clauses. Then indicate in the first blank at the right whether the sentence is correctly punctuated according to standard practice (*C*), contains a comma splice (*CS*), or is fused (*F*). Correct each error by the method you consider best, showing in the second blank whether you have used subordination (*sub.*), a period (*.*), a semicolon (*;*), or a comma plus a coordinating conjunction (*conj.*).

EXAMPLE

I wanted to come to the United States to work $\overset{\text{V}}{}$ $\overset{\text{, so}}{}$ I could
earn more money there.   ___F___   ___conj.___

1. Coyote rounded up five other guys and me, then he
    hired a guide to take us across the river.   _____   _____

2. I was here for two months before I got my first job,
    first I picked celery and later prunes.   _____   _____

3. One day the immigration showed up I ran and hid
    in the river next to the orchard.   _____   _____

4. They caught me and took me and some more aliens
    to Mexicali, near the border, then they let us go. _____   _____

5. We caught a bus to Tijuana, that night we found
    Coyote again and paid him to get us back over the
    border.   _____   _____

6. I had to pay $250, however, because he knew me,
    he let me pay $30 a week.   _____   _____

7. It's the money when you get into the U.S., you can
    make more money.   _____   _____

8. In Mexico I could make 25 or 30 pesos a day, that's maybe two or three dollars. _____ _____

9. Sometimes here I can make $30 a day although living here is expensive, I can live off that much. _____ _____

10. I'd like to learn English; if I could say to the Immigration, "What's the matter with you?" they wouldn't recognize me as an alien. _____ _____

Comma Splices and Fused Sentences Exercise 3–2

NAME _____ SCORE _____

DIRECTIONS In each of the following sentences insert an inverted caret (V) between main clauses. Then indicate in the blank whether the sentence contains a comma splice (CS) or is fused (F). Rewrite each comma splice or fused sentence using two of the four possible methods: subordination, an end mark (two sentences), a semicolon, or a comma plus a coordinating conjunction. (You may want to discuss the effect each of the methods has on the ideas in the two clauses: to emphasize one or both ideas, to balance one idea with another, or to establish a relationship betwen the ideas.)

EXAMPLE

Vo Thi Tam was one of the Vietnamese "boat people,"ᵛ she fled South Vietnam in 1979 after the communist takeover.   *CS*

Vo Thi Tam was one of the Vietnamese "boat people" who fled South Vietnam in 1979 after the communist takeover.

1. Vo Thi Tam, her husband, and several other villagers plotted to escape, they pooled their money to buy a boat and supplies which they hid on the Mekong Delta.   _____

2. She and her husband were separated, however, at the final rendezvous, in fact, she was forced to leave without him.   _____

3. Once on the high seas, the emigrants discovered a leak in their water container, then they had to ration water.   _____

4. After seven days they were out of water, they had only raw rice and lemon juice to eat. _____

5. Near death they were raided by a succession of pirate boats the first pirates robbed them, and the later pirates beat them and tore the boat apart looking for gold. _____

6. "That night at about 9:00 P.M. we arrived on the shore [of Malaysia]," she said, "we knelt down on the beach and prayed…to thank God." _____

7. The story of Vo Thi Tam's journey is printed in *American Mosaic,* it is a collection of immigrants' accounts of their experiences coming to and adjusting to America. _____

**Comma Splices, Fused Sentences,
and Fragments: A Review**

Exercise 3–3

NAME _____ SCORE _____

DIRECTIONS   Classify each of the following word groups as a fragment (*frag.*), a comma splice (*CS*), a fused sentence (*F*), or a correct sentence (*C*). Revise each faulty word group.

EXAMPLE

writes

Irving Howe ~~writing~~ about Ellis Island in his book, *World of Our Fathers.*   __frag.__

1. European immigrants who entered the United States between 1892 and 1943 and who had to be processed through bureaucratic red tape at Ellis Island.   _____

2. Howe vividly evokes the anxiety that immigrants experienced, as their ships neared Ellis Island, each of them wondered if he or she would be sent back.   _____

3. "On Ellis Island they pile into the massive hall that occupies the entire width of the building," writes Howe, "they break into dozens of lines, divided by metal railings, where they file past the first doctor."   _____

4. Men or women who show signs of physical infirmity are marked with chalk for later inspection one out of five or six needs further checking.   _____

5. A second doctor inspects for contagious diseases, leprosy, venereal disease, and parasitic infestations are common.   _____

6. Then to the third doctor, often feared the most.   _____

7. His examination of their eyes is over quickly, however, by this time the immigrants are bewildered by this first encounter with America.   _____

8. The questions that follow further confusing them, questions about family, money, work, crime, insanity, and character.   _____

9. "Especially bewildering is the idea that if you say you have a job waiting for you in the United States, you are liable to deportation," explains Howe, "because an 1885 law prohibits the importation of contract labor."   _____

10. During the year 1907 five thousand was fixed as the maximum number of immigrants who would be examined at Ellis Island in one day yet during the spring of that year more than fifteen thousand immigrants arrived at the port of New York in a single day.   _____

ADJECTIVES AND ADVERBS

ad 4

4

Master the uses and forms of adjectives and adverbs.

Both adjectives and adverbs function as modifiers; that is, they make the meaning of the words they refer to more exact. In the examples below, notice that the meaning becomes clearer and more detailed as modifiers are added (adjectives are in boldface, adverbs in italics).

> An interview with her grandmother provided the plot for her play.

> An **extended** interview with her **Jewish immigrant** grandmother provided the **touching** plot for her **successful one-act** play.

> An **extended** interview with her **Jewish immigrant** grandmother *recently* provided the plot for her *surprisingly* **successful one-act** play.

The adjective *extended* modifies the noun subject *interview;* the adjectives *Jewish* and *immigrant* modify *grandmother,* the object of a preposition; the adjectives *successful* and *one-act* modify *play,* the object of a preposition. Typically, adjectives modify nouns and sometimes pronouns. The adverbs—*recently* and *surprisingly*—modify the verb *provided* and the adjective *successful.* Typically, adverbs modify verbs and modifiers (both adjectives and adverbs).

A modern dictionary will show you the current usage of adjective and adverb modifiers. But here are a few guidelines.

4a Use adverbs to modify verbs, adjectives, and other adverbs.

> She *always* has drawn from her family the ideas for her plays. [*Always* modifies the verb *has drawn.*]

> She *often* uses the relationships between generations to develop *extremely* interesting themes. [*Often* modifies the verb *uses; extremely* modifies the adjective *interesting.*]

> She *increasingly often* portrays the older women characters as being challenged to preserve tradition. [*Often* modifies the verb *portrays; increasingly* modifies the adverb *often.*]

4b Distinguish between adjectives used as complements and adverbs used to modify verbs.

Adjectives, like nouns, are used as complements after linking verbs such as *be, appear, become, feel, look, seem, smell,* and *taste.* Such adjective complements refer to the subjects of their clauses.

In the first scene the old woman's voice is *forceful* and *commanding,* but by the play's end it is *feeble* and almost *inaudible.*

[*Forceful* and *commanding* refer to *voice,* the subject of the first main clause; *feeble* and *inaudible* refer to *it,* the subject of the second main clause.]

The daughter believes that her mother is *indestructible.*

[*Indestructible* refers to *mother,* the subject of the subordinate clause.]

Heart-wrenching are those early scenes.

[For emphasis, the complement, *heart-wrenching,* comes before but still refers to the subject, *scenes.*]

A sensory verb like *feel, taste,* or *look* is followed by an adverb instead of an adjective when the modifier refers to the verb.

> The author looked *perceptively* at her relationship with her mother. [Compare "The author looked *perceptive,*" in which *perceptive,* an adjective complement, modifies the subject, *author.*]

A linking verb followed by an adjective complement may also be modified by one or more adverbs, coming either before or after.

> The author *suddenly* looked happy *yesterday.* [Both adverbs modify *looked.*]

4c Use the appropriate forms of adjectives and adverbs for the comparative and the superlative.

Many adjectives and adverbs change form to indicate degree. The comparative degree (a comparison of two things) is usually formed by adding *-er* to the modifier or by putting *more* or *less* before the modifier. The superlative degree (a comparison of three or more things) is formed by adding *-est* to the modifier or by putting the word *most* or *least* before the modifier. Some desk dictionaries show the *-er* and *-est* endings for these adjectives and adverbs that form their comparative and superlative degrees in this way (for example, old, old*er,* old*est*). Most dictionaries show the changes for highly irregular modifiers (for example, good, *better, best*). As a rule of thumb, most one-syllable adjectives and most two-syllable adjectives ending in a vowel sound (*tidy, narrow*) form the comparative with *-er* and the superlative with *-est.* Most adjectives of two or more syllables and most adverbs form the comparative by adding the word *more* (*less*) and the superlative by adding the word *most* (*least*).

NONSTANDARD	The dialog seemed more better written.
	[The *-er* shows the comparative degree; *more* is superfluous.]
STANDARD	The dialog seemed better written.

NONSTANDARD	She was the better prepared of all the actors.
	[*Better* is used to compare only two things.]
STANDARD	She was the best prepared of all the actors.

Note: Current usage, however illogical it may seem, accepts comparisons of many adjectives or adverbs with absolute meanings, such as "*a more perfect* society," "*the deadest* campus," and "*less completely* exhausted." But many writers make an exception of unique—using "*more nearly* unique" rather than "*more* unique." They consider *unique* an absolute adjective—one without degrees of comparison.

4d Avoid the awkward substitution of a noun form for an adjective.

We correctly use many nouns as modifiers of other nouns—*soap* opera, *book* club, *moon* beam—because there are no suitable adjective forms available. But when adjective forms are available, you should avoid awkward noun substitutes.

AWKWARD	Education television presented a special on Alex Haley.
BETTER	*Educational* television presented a special on Alex Haley.

4e Avoid the double negative.

The term *double negative* refers to the use of two negatives to express a single negation.

NONSTANDARD	He did not have no time to see the play. [double negative: *not* and *no*]
STANDARD	He did not have time to see the play. [single negative: *not*]
	OR
	He had no time to see the play. [single negative: *no*]

Another redundant construction occurs when a negative such as *not, nothing,* or *without* is combined with *hardly, barely,* or *scarcely.*

NONSTANDARD	She couldn't hardly stop talking about the Lincoln Theatre.
STANDARD	She could hardly stop talking about the Lincoln Theatre.
NONSTANDARD	The stage was bare, without scarcely any props.
STANDARD	The stage was bare, with scarcely any props.

Adjectives and Adverbs

Exercise 4–1

NAME _____ SCORE _____

DIRECTIONS   In each of the following sentences cross out the incorrect modifier within the parentheses and write in the blank the choice that represents standard usage. In the sentence, underline the word or words being modified by the modifier you chose. (Consult your dictionary if you are in doubt about the proper form of the comparative or superlative degree of an adjective or adverb.)

EXAMPLE

Phillip K. Chiu writes (~~sensitive~~, sensitively) about Chinese American life.

sensitively

1. About sixty years ago, he explains, movies gave us the insidious Fu Manchu and the ever (inscrutable, ~~inscrutably~~) Charlie Chan.

inscrutable

2. In World War II the Chinese were our allies, and we read of the clean, (amiable, amiably), upright, and industrious Chinese who helped us win the American West.

amiable

3. The Korean War brought a picture of (ferocious, ~~ferociously~~) Chinese hordes marching to conquer Asia.

ferocious

4. After the war China was (~~relative~~, relatively) isolated from the rest of the world for several decades.

relatively

5. In 1972 President Nixon visited China, and the world suddenly had access to this (more, ~~most~~) populous country.

more

6. Interest in anything Chinese leads Americans to investigate Chinese Americans more (~~close~~, closely).

closely

7. (Hopeful, ~~Hopefully~~) of a good story, investigators began close examination of Chinese Americans.

hopeful

8. Chiu believes that only in recent years has there been (accurate, ~~accurately~~) reporting about Chinese Americans.

accurate

9. The (stereotypical, stereotypically) Chinese American is an overachieving bookworm.

stereotypical

10. Chiu welcomes stories about Chinese Americans who steal when they are (desperately, desperate) or who sell drugs to make easy money.

desperate

11. He wants us to read about some Chinese Americans who are (more, most) interested in money than in family.

more

12. The truth is (more, most) important, he says.

most

13. If we do not see Chinese Americans as being like us, we can dismiss them with (relative, relatively) ease.

relative

DIRECTIONS   Below, make the choices that avoid double negatives.

14. I did not know (anything, nothing) about Chinese Americans until I read Phillip Chiu, Maxine Hong Kingston, and Amy Tan.

anything

15. After I moved to San Francisco, I (could, could not) hardly ignore China Town.

could

16. I began going for lunchtime walks in China Town, and I could find scarcely (any, no) food that I did not like.

any

17. My first friend in China Town was an old man who did not speak (any, no) English.

any

18. He spoke to me with elegant gestures and kind eyes that left hardly (anything, nothing) unsaid.

anything

Adjectives and Adverbs   Exercise 4–2

NAME _____ SCORE _____

DIRECTIONS   While preserving the meaning, rewrite each of the following sentences, changing the italicized adjective to an adverb and the italicized noun to a verb or an adjective, as in the example below. (You will have to make a few other changes in the sentence in addition to changing the italicized words.)

   EXAMPLE
   During English class our teacher demonstrated an *unexpected enthusiasm* for rap music.

   During English class our teacher's unexpectedly
   enthusiastic response to rap music surprised us.

1.   Ms. Cortner devised an *ingenious plan* for teaching Langston Hughes.

2.   The musical qualities of Hughes' poem, "Harlem," were a *great delight* to Ms. Cortner.

3.   She extended an *excited invitation* to the class to sing the poetry as rap songs.

4.   We felt *great relief* that she was not giving us a written test.

5.   My group's rap rendition of "Harlem" made a *strong impression* on Ms. Cortner.

5

Master the case forms of pronouns to show their functions in sentences.

The form that a noun or pronoun has in a sentence indicates its function, or *case: subjective, objective,* or *possessive.* Nouns usually change their form for only one case—the possessive. (In chapter **15** you will study the ways the apostrophe indicates that change.) Certain pronouns, however, change their form for each case, and you must be aware of the various forms if you want to use these pronouns correctly.

SUBJECTIVE	OBJECTIVE	POSSESSIVE
I	me	mine
we	us	our OR ours
he, she	him, her	his, her, OR hers
they	them	their OR theirs
who OR whoever	whom OR whomever	whose

5a A pronoun has the same case form in a compound or an appositive construction as it would have if it were used alone.

When you are using a single pronoun, you may have no difficulty choosing the right case.

> *I* attended the play with *her.*

But when other pronouns or nouns are added, you may become confused about case and write, "Him and me attended the play with Ted and she." If you tend to make such errors in case, think of the function each pronoun would have if it were used in a separate sentence.

> *He* sat in the balcony.   [NOT *Him* sat in the balcony.]
> *I* sat in the balcony.   [NOT *Me* sat in the balcony.]
> I sat in the balcony with *her.*   [NOT I sat in the balcony with *she.*]

Then you will be more likely to write the correct case forms:

> *He* and *I* attended the play with Ted and *her.*

5b The case of a pronoun depends on its use in its own clause.

When a sentence has only one clause, the function of a pronoun may seem clear to you.

> *Who* is sponsoring the performance?   [*Who* is the subject of the verb *is sponsoring.*]

But when another clause is added, you must be careful to determine the pronoun's use in its own clause.

> I know *who* is sponsoring the performance. [Although *who* introduces a clause that acts as the direct object of the verb *know*, in its own clause *who* is the subject of the verb *is sponsoring*.]

An implied rather than a stated clause often follows the subordinating conjunctions *than* or *as*.

> She enjoyed the performance as much as *I*. [The implied meaning is "as I did."]
> Janice knows you better than *me*. [The implied meaning is "than Janice knows me."]

5c In formal writing use *whom* for all pronouns as objects. (See also 5b.)

> The actress *whom* they named in the lead role has resigned. [object of the verb *named*]
> The actress to *whom* they gave the lead role has resigned. [object of the preposition *to*]
> *Whom* did they choose to replace her? [object of the verb *choose*]

5d In general, use the possessive case before a verbal used as a noun.

A gerund is a verbal that ends in *-ing* and is used as a noun (see 1d[1]). The possessive case is used before a gerund, which acts as a noun, but not before a participle, which also sometimes has an *-ing* ending but acts as an adjective.

> Jason's parents grew weary of *his* complaining that he had nothing new to wear. [*Complaining* is a gerund and functions as the object of the preposition *of*.]
> That afternoon they found *him* admiring his new tatoo. [*Admiring* is a participle, an adjective modifying *him*.]

5e Use the objective case for direct and indirect objects, for objects of prepositions, and for both subjects and objects of infinitives (*to* plus the verb).

> The director gave *me* instructions for playing the scene.
> Between *you* and *me*, I was too excited to remember *them*.
> As a result it was easy for *him* to visualize the scene, but impossible for *me*. ["To do it" is implied after *for me*.]

5f Use the subjective case for subjects and for subject complements.

> *She* and *I* played the scene well.
> The director is *he*. [You may find it more comfortable to avoid using the pronoun as a complement. If so, write "He is the director."]

5g Add *-self* to a pronoun (*himself, herself, itself, ourselves, themselves*) when a reflexive or an intensive pronoun is needed.

A reflexive pronoun follows the verb and refers to the subject; an intensive pronoun emphasizes the noun or pronoun it refers to.

> I blamed *myself* for forgetting the lines. [*Myself* refers back to *I*.]
> I *myself* take the blame for forgetting the lines. [*Myself* intensifies *I*.]

The pronoun ending in *-self* is not used as a subject or an object unless it refers to the same person as the subject.

> The other actors asked *me* to represent *them*.   [NOT *myself* and *themselves*]
>
> *He* persuaded *himself* to try out for the play.   [*Himself*, the object, refers to the same person as *He*, the subject.]

Case of Pronouns

NAME _____ SCORE _____

DIRECTIONS   In the following sentences cross out the incorrect case form or forms in parentheses and write the correct form in the blank.

EXAMPLE

As I grew up in Hawaii, I learned two versions of history, the book version in school and the version taught (me, ~~myself~~) by my family.

me

1. My family told me of the old ones (who, whom) fished and planted and shared the fruits of their labors.

who

2. The old ones had sailed thousands of miles to these islands. And (they, them) had flourished until the coming of the whites, the *haole.*

they

3. At school I read about "pagan Hawaiians" (who, whom) could neither read nor write.

whom

4. For (them, they) Captain Cook's arrival was another opportunity to practice cannibalism.

them

5. The teachers told (us, we) students about the disease and death that the Christian god visited on the pagans after they killed Cook.

us

6. (Me, My) going to college affected how I thought about these contrasting versions of island history.

My

7. In college I learned about Haunani-Kay Trask, an islander (who, whom) also had been troubled by the two versions of her people's past.

who

8. She and (me, I) had similar childhoods.

I

9. Like (me, myself) she trusted her family's account, but at first she could not explain why the history books were wrong.

myself

10. Trask remembered what the elders said about the whites: did these historians know the language? How long had (they, them) lived among our people?   *they*

11. If our language was not important to (they, them), how could they know how we feel and think?   *them*

12. Trask discovered that the history books simply repeated what other Europeans and Americans had said and never reflected the thinking of people (who, whom) knew the culture intimately.   *who*

13. By (them, their) not learning our language, these people revealed something essential about (theirselves, themselves).   *their*   *themselves*

14. Neither you nor (me, I) could miss the point. They thought that "there is no value in things Hawaiian; all value comes from things *haole*."   *I*

Case of Pronouns   Exercise 5–2

NAME _____ SCORE _____

DIRECTIONS   In the following sentences cross out the incorrect case form or forms in parentheses and write the correct form in the blank.

EXAMPLE

Haunani-Kay Trask believes that historians should recon-
sider the conventional interpretations of Hawaiian history.
She is someone (~~who~~, whom) we admire for her impas-
sioned defense of her heritage.   ___whom___

1. By studying Trask's scholarship we can learn much
   about how a colonialized people viewed (theirselves,
   themselves).   ___themselves___

2. She describes a colonial point of view that judged
   Western culture as much preferable to Hawaiian
   culture. To you and (I, me) this may seem a logical
   conclusion.   ___I___

3. But to one (who, whom) is Hawaiian, such a conclusion may be suspect because it seems to benefit
   Westerners even as it harms those being colonized.   ___who___

4. Trask has been influenced by the work of Franz Fanon
   who was (hisself, himself) a leading advocate of the
   victims of colonialization.   ___himself___

5. Fanon pointed out that one of the first steps of coloniz-
   ing is deculturation. What better way to deculture,
   Trask asks, than to remake the image of a people so
   that they do not even recognize (theirselves,
   themselves)?   ___themselves___

6. If colonized people come to believe the Western view
   of their culture, they are likely to submit more meekly
   to their colonizers. (Them, Their) being colonized will
   come to seem an act of a benevolent god.   ___their___

87

7. Trask gives several examples of how the Western historians imposed Western values on a culture that (they, them) did not fully understand or appreciate.   _they_

8. For example, historians describe pre-*haole* (pre-white) Hawaii as feudal; but, Trask says, Hawaiians believed that no one owned the land. The land and sea were there for all of the people (who, whom) wished to use them.   _who_

9. If, however, the Hawaiian chiefs are seen as feudal lords and their people as serfs, Western colonization liberates a people (who, whom) traditional culture has abused.   _whom_

10. Trask also describes the horrible effects of contact with Western culture on her ancestors (who, whom) were decimated by Western diseases.   _who_

11. She reports that within half a century of first contact, eighty percent of the native islanders were dead. Westerners had appropriated much of the land for (them, themselves) and had stripped forests bare for export.   _themselves_

12. Missionaries had insinuated (theirselves, themselves) everywhere.   _theirselves_

13. To (we, us) today, this is an obvious injustice.   _us_

14. However, Trask says, historians continue to use the argument that Hawaiians were liberated from a feudal past. Historians to (who, whom) this argument now seems hollow are turning to the oral history of Hawaii for corrections.   _whom_

15. Trask wants the truth told so that Hawaiians can find themselves in the written accounts of their past. She is a brave and persistent voice (who, whom) we should listen to carefully.   _who_

6

Make a verb agree in number with its subject; make a pronoun agree in number with its antecedent.

Subjects and verbs must have the same number: a singular subject requires a singular verb, and a plural subject requires a plural verb. (Remember that an -*s* ending shows plural number for the subject but singular number for the verb.)

SINGULAR   A *reader* at the poetry slam often *reads* contemporary poetry.

PLURAL   *Readers* at the poetry slam often *read* contemporary poetry.

Similarly, a pronoun must agree in number with its antecedent, the noun or pronoun it refers to.

SINGULAR   The first *reader* at the poetry slam would not read from *his* own poetry because *he* was too nervous.

PLURAL   The first *readers* at the poetry slam would not read from *their* own poetry because *they* were too nervous.

6a The verb agrees in number with its subject.

(1) The verb must be matched with its subject, not with the object of a preposition or with some other word that comes between the subject and verb.

The *participation* of so many students *makes* the poetry slam a success.   [*Participation,* not *students,* is the subject.]

A video *camera,* together with lights and extra microphones, *is* in place to record all of the readings.   [Most writers agree that nouns following expressions like "together with," "in addition to," and "along with" do not affect the number of the subject. Notice that the whole phrase is set off by commas.]

Subjects and verbs that end in -*sk* or -*st* must be carefully matched. Because of our tendency to leave out certain difficult sounds when speaking, many of us also fail in our writing to add a needed -*s* to a verb or to a subject ending in -*sk* or -*st*.

Artists should try to paint the poetry slam.

An *artist* tries to paint each poetry slam.

(2) Subjects joined by *and* usually take a plural verb.

The president of the Honor Society and her roommate *have* not *attended* the last two poetry slams.

Exception: If the two subjects refer to the same person or thing, or if *each* or *every* comes before the subject, the verb is singular.

89

The well-known poet and director of the honors program *begins* the poetry slam.

Every poetry slam and every presentation of the senior play *begins* the same way.

(3) Singular subjects joined by *or, nor, either…or*, and *neither…nor* usually take a singular verb.

Either a poem by Marge Piercy or one by Denise Levertov *is* my choice.

Exception: If one subject is singular and one plural, the verb is matched with the nearer subject, or the sentence is revised to avoid the agreement difficulty.

Neither the Dean nor his guests *were prepared* to read.

OR

The Dean *was* not *prepared* to read, and neither *were* his guests.

(4) When the subject follows the verb (as in sentences beginning with *there is* or *there are*), special care is needed to match up subject and verb.

There *is* a large *audience* at tonight's reading.

There *are* no *plans* to meet after the reading.

Included among tonight's readers *are two songwriters* from Nashville.

(5) A relative pronoun (*who, whom, which, that*) used as the subject of a clause is singular or plural depending on its antecedent.

There are poetry slams that *offer* cash prizes to the winners. [*Slams*, the antecedent, is plural; therefore, *that* is considered plural.]

Every poet who *attends* tonight will be photographed with Dr. Montgomery. [*Poet*, the antecedent, is singular; therefore, *who* is considered singular.]

(6) Pronoun subjects like *each, one, anybody, everybody, either*, and *neither* usually take singular verbs.

Each of us *plans* to read his or her original poem at the slam.

Everybody with a seat on the front row *gets* a whistle to blow.

Pronoun subjects like *all, any, half, most, none*, and *some* may take either a singular or plural verb—the context determines the verb form.

All of my poems *are* sonnets.

All of the poetry *is* to be printed in the university journal of modern poetry.

(7) In general, use a singular verb with collective nouns regarded as a unit and with nouns that are plural in form but singular in meaning.

The number of readers *influences* the success of the slam. [*The number* is usually regarded as a unit.]

A *number* of readers *plan* to read poetry by Native Americans. [*A number* usually refers to individuals or items.]

(8) The verb agrees with the subject, not the subject complement, but it is usually best to avoid disagreement of verb and subject complement by revising the sentence to eliminate the linking verb.

AWKWARD   My usual *snack* at a poetry slam *is* a *Butterfinger* and a *Jolt.* [The verb *is* correctly agrees with the subject *snack,* but the disagreement of verb and subject complement seems awkward to many writers.]

REVISED   At poetry slams I usually snack on a *Butterfinger* and a *Jolt.* [Replacing the linking verb with an active verb eliminates the problem of disagreement of verb and subject complement.]

(9) Even though they have the -s ending, nouns like *news, civics,* and *measles* take singular verbs. The dictionary is the best guide for determining which nouns with plural endings take singular verbs.

Tonight *politics determines* the choice of poems read at the slam. [The dictionary describes *politics* as singular.]

(10) Single titles, even if plural in form, are considered singular in number, as are words referred to as words.

"Fay Wray to the King" *was* the first poem by Judith Rechter that I read.
Persiflage is often misspelled. Do you know what it means?

6b A pronoun agrees in number with its antecedent. (See also **27b.**)

(1) Use a singular pronoun to refer to such antecedents as *each, everyone, nobody, one, a person, a woman, a man.*

Each of the women takes *her* turn reading.

Today writers make every effort to avoid sexism in the use of personal pronouns. Whereas writers once wrote, "Each of us should do his best," they now try to avoid using the masculine pronoun to refer to both men and women. To avoid sexism, some writers give both masculine and feminine pronoun references.

Each of us took *his* or *her* turn.
Each of us took *his/her* turn.

Other writers prefer to use *one's* in place of *his* or *her.*

One should take *one's* turn.

Perhaps the easiest way to avoid sexism is to use plural pronouns and antecedents—unless a feminine or masculine pronoun is clearly called for as *her* would be in reference to Whoopi Goldberg.

All of them took *their* turns.
All of us took *our* turns.

(2) Use a plural pronoun to refer to two or more antecedents joined by *and*; use a singular pronoun to refer to two or more antecedents joined by *or* or *nor*.

> Kim *and* Ruby have taken *their* turns reading from Marge Piercy's poetry.
> Neither Kim *nor* Ruby wants *her* turn to be over.

If it is necessary to have one singular and one plural antecedent, make the pronoun agree with the closer antecedent.

> Neither Morgan nor her *friends* know when *they* will have a turn.

Again, as with the verb (see **6a[6]**), it is sometimes best to rephrase to avoid the pronoun difficulty.

> Morgan and her friends do not know when *they* will have *their* turns.

(3) Use either a singular or a plural pronoun to refer to a collective noun like *team, staff*, or *group*, depending on whether the noun is considered a unit or a group of individuals.

> The newspaper *staff* is planning *its* next edition.   [Here *staff* acts as a unit. Notice that
> both the pronoun and the verb must agree with the subject.]
> The *staff* are disagreeing about what *their* responsibilities will be for the next edition.
> [The individuals on the staff are being referred to; thus both the pronoun and the verb
> are plural.]

When the collective noun is considered plural, as *staff* is in the preceding example, many writers prefer to use *staff members* rather than a noun that looks singular in number.

> The staff *members* are disagreeing about what *their* responsibilities will be for the next
> edition.

(4) The pronoun that refers to such antecedents as *all, most, half, none,* and *some* is usually plural, but in a few contexts it can be singular.

> *All* of them took *their* turns.
> *Most* of the audience heard more poetry than *they* ever had before.
> *Most* of our preparation proved *itself* worthwhile.

Agreement of Subject and Verb

NAME _____ SCORE _85%_ (B)

DIRECTIONS   In each of the following sentences underline the subject of the verb in parentheses with one line; then match it mentally with the correct verb. Cross out the verb that does not agree with the subject, and write the verb that does agree in the blank.

EXAMPLE

The students in the honors program (present, ~~presents~~) a
poetry slam every fall semester.   _present_

1. A poetry slam (is, are) a competitive event.   _is_

2. Contestants (read, reads) to an audience their own
poetry or poetry by other writers.   _read_

3. Some of the poetry (is, are) very good.   _is_

4. Each of the poems (is, are) rated by the audience.   _are_

5. If the poetry is bad, the audience (snap, snaps) their   _its_
fingers.   _snaps_

6. If the poetry gets worse, they (stamp, stamps) their
feet.   _stamp_

7. If it is just terrible, everyone (groan, groans).   _groans_

8. If it is so bad that it is good, we all (yell, yells)
"Beowulf."   _yell_

9. Mediocre poems never (receive, receives) applause.   _receive_

10. Instead we stare at the poet until he or she (get, gets)
the idea.   _gets_

11. Not everyone (believe, believes) poetry slams are a
good idea.   _believes_

12. Our university poet (call, calls) it the "gong show" of
poetry.   _calls_

13. Most slammers, however, (advise, advises) him not to take himself so seriously.

advise

14. One purpose of the slams (is, are) to have fun with poetry.

is

15. If people (has, have) fun with poetry, they are likely to connect with it permanently.

fun

16. More than twenty cities in this country now (has, have) an active competitive poetry scene.

have

17. Either Marc Smith of Chicago or three poets from Wilkes–Barre (is, are) the inspiration for the slam.

is

18. Neither Wallace Stegner nor Marge Piercy (help, helps) with the slams.

help

19. A number of poems in tonight's reading (is, are) by Native American writers.

are

20. The number of minority writers that are represented (increase, increases) each year.

increases

plural or | sing.
plural nor | sing
sing. or | sing.
sing nor | sing.
or | plural
nor | plural

Verb is Singular

The men or the dog marches on.

Agreement of Subject and Verb

β Exercise 6-2

NAME _____ SCORE __65/0__

DIRECTIONS   In the following sentences the subjects and verbs are in agreement. Rewrite the sentences, making all italicized singular subjects and verbs plural and all italicized plural subjects and verbs singular. (You will need to drop or add an article—*a, an, the*—before the subject and sometimes change another word or two to make the sentence sound right.) When your answers have been checked, you may want to read the sentences aloud to accustom your ear to the forms that agree with each other.

EXAMPLE

A poetry *slam,* like rap, *makes* poetry "cool."

Poetry slams, like rap, make poetry "cool."

1. These *audiences want* an evening of listening to performance poetry.

    The audience wants an evening of listening to performance poetry.

2. Such *events are* becoming "cool" enough to be commercialized.

    Such an event is becoming "cool" enough to be commercialized.

3. Some public television *stations* now *carry* slams.

    Some public television station now carries slams.

4. The raucous *atmosphere* of a slam *obscures* the seriousness of the performers.

    The raucous atmospheres of a slam obscure the seriousness of the performers.

C 5. One *poet* *delivers* her lines from memory, never referring to a manuscript.

Some Poets deliver their lines from memory, never referring to a manuscript.

C 6. *Performance* for her *means* a delivery straight from the heart.

Performances for her mean a delivery straight from the heart.

C 7. *Critics* of slams *point* to the intellectually simple language.

A critic of slams points to the intellectually simple language.

C 8. *People* *need* a lot of image meat.

A person needs a lot of image meat.

9. *All* of us *need* to be able to sink our teeth into metaphors and similes.

One of us needs to be able to sink our teeth into metaphors and similes.

C 10. But a slam *poem* *has* to be understood on the first reading, not on the fifth reading.

But slam poems have to be understood on the first reading, not on the fifth reading.

7

Use the appropriate forms of verbs.

You will remember from chapter **1** that the verb is the most essential part of the basic formula for a sentence. Sentences may be written without subjects—though few are, of course. And sentences are frequently written without complements. But without a verb, there is no sentence. To use this essential part of the sentence correctly, you must know not only how to make the present tense of the verb agree with its subject in number (see chapter **6**) but also how to choose the right tense of the verb to express the time of the verb you intend: present, past, future, present perfect, past perfect, or future perfect.

Verbs have three main tenses—present, past, and future—and three secondary tenses—present perfect, past perfect, and future perfect. A verb's ending (called its *inflection*) and/or the helping verb or verbs used with it determine the verb's tense.

PRESENT	write
PAST	wrote
FUTURE	will write
PRESENT PERFECT	has or have written
PAST PERFECT	had written
FUTURE PERFECT	will [OR shall] have written

Actually there are several ways to form a given tense in English. For the past tense, for example, you could write any of these forms:

He *wrote* operas.

He *was writing* operas. [continuing past time]

He *did write* operas.   [Emphatic. Notice that this form of the past tenses uses *did* plus the present form of the main verb, *write.*]

He *used to write* operas.   [*Used to* (NOT *use to*) suggests an action that no longer occurs.]

Native speakers of English use most forms of a verb correctly without even thinking. But there are a few forms and a few verbs that give many of us difficulty; this section concentrates on these forms and these verbs.

7a Avoid misusing the principal parts of verbs and confusing similar verbs.
(See the Appendix for a list of the principal parts of some of the most common troublesome verbs.)

Most verbs are *regular* verbs; that is, they form their tenses in a predictable way. The *-ed* ending is used for the past tense and all the perfect tenses, including the past participle form of a verbal. The *-ing* ending is used to form the progressive and the present participle.

PAST	She *entered* the dance competition.
PRESENT PERFECT	She *has entered* the dance competition. They *have entered* the dance competition.
PAST PERFECT	She *had entered* the dance competition before she strained a muscle.
FUTURE PERFECT	After only two years of training she *will have entered* three major competitions.
PAST PARTICIPLE	*Having entered* the competition, she nervously watched the other competitors.
PROGRESSIVE	She *is entering* the competition. [also *was entering, has been entering, had been entering, will have been entering*]
PRESENT PARTICIPLE	*Entering* the competition, she begins the next phase of her career.

Most dictionaries do not list the principal parts of a regular verb like *enter: enter* (present), *entered* (past and past participle), and *entering* (present participle).

But if a verb is irregular—that is, if it forms its past tense in some other way than by adding an *-ed*—the dictionary will usually list three or four principal parts.

race, raced, racing [Notice that only a *-d* is added to form the past and past participle; therefore the principal parts may be listed in the dictionary.]

drive, drove, driven, driving [This verb has four listings in the dictionary because it changes form for the past and the past participle as well as the present participle.]

If a verb undergoes no change except for the *-ing* ending of the present participle, the dictionary still lists three principal parts because the verb is not a regular verb.

burst, burst, bursting

Be careful to distinguish between verbs with similar spellings like *sit/set, lie/lay,* and *rise/raise.* Remember that *sit, lie,* and *rise* cannot take objects, but *set, lay,* and *raise* can.

object

While Diana *sat* in her favorite chair, Rucker *laid out* several books on the table for her to

object

read and *raised* the television to a comfortable viewing level.

The books *were set* on a nearby table.

Notice in the second example above that the word you expect to be the object of *set*—that is, *books*—is made the subject of the sentence. Thus the subject of the sentence is not acting but is being acted upon. In such a case, the verb is said to be *passive.*

The verbs *set, lay,* and *raise* can be made passive, but the verbs *sit, lie,* and *rise* cannot because they cannot take objects.

The books were *set* down.   [NOT *sat* down]
The books were *laid* down.   [NOT *lain* down]
The television was *raised*.   [NOT was *risen*]

Of these six difficult verbs, the most troublesome combination is *lie/lay* because the past tense form of *lie* is *lay*.

He *lays* out the books and then *lies* down to rest.
After he had *laid* out the books, he *lay* down to rest.

Be careful to add the *-d* or *-ed* ending to the past and perfect tenses of verbs like *use* and to verbs that end in *-k* or *-t*.

He has us*ed* only ten minutes of his nap time.
She ask*ed* for her copy of Kate Chopin's *The Awakening*.

Be careful to spell correctly the principal parts of verbs like *occur, pay,* and *die* that double or change letters.

occur, occur*r*ed, occur*r*ing

pay, pa*i*d, pay*i*ng

die, died, d*y*ing

7b Make the tense forms of verbs and/or verbals relate logically between subordinate clauses and the main clause and in compound constructions.

Verbs in Main and Subordinate Clauses   When both the main-clause verb and the subordinate-clause verb refer to action occurring now or to action that could occur at any time, use the present tense for both verbs.

When Rucker *studies* art history, he usually *is looking* for inspiration.   [*Is looking*, the progressive form, denotes action that takes place in the past, present, and (probably) future.]

When both the main and the subordinate verbs refer to action that occurred at a definite time in the past, use the past tense for both verbs.

While he *was studying* Impressionist painters, he *discovered* the work of Mary Cassatt. [*Was studying*, the past progressive form, suggests an action that took place in the past but on a continuing basis.]

When both the main and the subordinate verbs refer to action that continued for some time but was completed before now, use the present perfect tense for both verbs.

He *has stopped* painting landscapes because he *has discovered* the portraits of Cassatt.

Notice that the present tense can be used with the present perfect tense without causing a shift.

Some painters *have stopped* studying the old masters because they *cannot find* inspiration in them.

Some painters *do* not *study* the old masters because they *have found* no inspiration in them.

Main Verbs and Verbals   When the main verb's action occurs at the same time as the verbal's, use the present-tense form of the verbal.

> Rucker *continues* to practice his portraits.
> Rucker *continued* to practice his portraits.
> *Continuing* to practice his portraits, Rucker *asks* two of his friends to serve as models.
> *Continuing* to practice his portraits, Rucker *asked* two of his friends to serve as models.

On the few occasions when the action of the verbal occurs before the action of the main verb, use the present-perfect tense form of the verbal.

> Rucker *would like to have painted* landscapes of his family's Mississippi farm.   [Compare "Rucker *wishes he had painted* landscapes."]
> *Having failed* to paint the farm in his youth, he now makes annual pilgrimages south to paint the scenes of his childhood.   [The failure to paint occurred before the annual pilgrimages.]

Compound Constructions   Be sure that verb tenses in compound predicates are consistent.

> He first *photographs* various scenes on the old farm and later *paints* the scenes using the photographs as models.

7c In writing, use the subjunctive mood in the few expressions in which it is still appropriate.

> If Rucker *were asked,* he would fly to the old farm today.   [a hypothetical condition]
> He wishes that he *were* free to return.   [a wish or idea contrary to fact]
> I move that the report *be* approved.   [*that* clause after a verb that makes a suggestion]

Verbs

NAME _____ SCORE _____

DIRECTIONS Use your dictionary to look up the principal parts of the verbs listed below. If the verb is a regular verb—that is, adds an -ed for the past and past participle and an -ing for the present participle—write *regular* in the blank. But if the verb is not predictable in its tense forms, write *irregular* in the blank and fill in the two or three other parts that your dictionary lists after the present tense form.

EXAMPLE

think   irregular—thought, thinking

look   regular

1. talk   regular

2. see   regular

3. last   regular

4. grow _____

5. write _____

6. drown _____

7. send _____

8. fly _____

9. attack _____

10. break _____

11. choose _____

12. lead _____

13. kiss _____

14. prepare _____

15. occur _____

VERBS

16. take   _____

17. fill   _____

18. pass   _____

19. add   _____

20. carry   _____

21. start   _____

22. surpass _____

23. hit   _____

24. sail   _____

25. fail   _____

Troublesome Verbs

Exercise 7–2

NAME _____ SCORE _____

DIRECTIONS   In the following sentences cross out the incorrect form or forms of the verb in parentheses and write the correct form in the blank.

EXAMPLE

I (use, used) to go to market with my mom every Sunday morning in Hong Kong.

___**used**___

1. In the market there (is, was) a fish market owner named Mr. Fish.

_____

2. I named him Mr. Fish since I (think, thought) he was president of Fish.

_____

3. One Sunday morning mom and I (go, went) to the market to buy some food.

_____

4. We went to Mr. Fish's shop and (buy, bought) two fish.

_____

5. Mr. Fish (invites, invited) my mom and me to go on his boat the next day to help catch the fish.

_____

6. The next morning (arrives, arrived) and we met Mr. Fish at his boat.

_____

7. I learned that morning that Mr. Fish's wife and three children (help, helped) with the fishing.

_____

8. Mr. Fish had (begin, began, begun) taking the children fishing shortly after they were born.

_____

9. Soon we (are, were) ready to leave the harbor.

_____

10. A little motor on the back of the boat (helps, helped) us to maneuver through the boat traffic in the harbor.

_____

11. Soon we (are, was, were) out of the harbor and in the open sea.

_____

12. Mr. Fish smiled, took deep breaths of the salty air, and said, "I (love, loved, have loved) getting away from the smells of the city."   _____

13. As we (leave, left, have left) the harbor, Mr. Fish shut off the motor and raised the sails.   _____

14. I (remember, remembered) the snap and pop as the sails caught the wind.   _____

15. Mr. Fish must have (known, knew) my excitement because he let me stand with him at the tiller.   _____

16. Somehow Mr. Fish (knows, knew) when we needed to begin fishing.   _____

17. He and his children (begin, began, begun) putting out the nets.   _____

18. We used the boat to pull the nets in a big circle and (start, started) to haul the nets on board.   _____

19. Soon the deck (was, were) slippery with silver fish.   _____

20. We (laughed, laugh) as we caught the fish and put them into baskets.   _____

Verbs Exercise 7–3

NAME _____ SCORE _____

DIRECTIONS   In the following sentences cross out the incorrect form or forms of the verb in parentheses and write the correct form in the blank.

EXAMPLE

I would like (~~to be~~, to have been) a witness to many of my
friend Gina's adventures in Hong Kong.   *to have been*

1. Gina wants to be a writer, and she (~~learned~~, has learned) to use her childhood memories as the basis for her stories.   *has learned*

2. In 1980 Gina and her family moved here to southern California, and she and I soon (became, ~~have become~~) best friends.   *became*

3. She (learned, ~~had learned~~) English in school in Hong Kong.   *learned*

4. In our first year of friendship Gina (~~tells~~, told) me that she wanted to write books for children.   *told*

5. Although her parents (speak, ~~spoke~~, ~~have spoken~~) limited English, I could understand the stories that they told.   *speak*

6. They were glad to be in America, but they missed the many friends in Hong Kong who (continue, ~~continued~~) to write to them.   *continue*

7. As I listened intently (to understand, ~~to have understood~~) those stories, I realized that Gina should write them down.   *to understand*

8. While we were in college together, she (~~publishes~~, published) her first story.   *published*

9. It was the story of Mr. Fish, a man who (owns, ~~owned~~) a fish market in Hong Kong.   *owns*

10. Gina and her mother often shared memories of Mr. Fish and his kind attempts (to teach, ~~to have taught~~) them to fish.

to teach

11. I (~~hear, heard~~, have heard) the story so often that I can tell all of its details.

have heard

12. I see the sails as they catch the wind and the silvery fish as they (gleam, ~~gleamed~~) in the sunlight.

gleam

13. Because Gina (~~writes, wrote~~, has written) for children, she retains some of the simplicity of those family stories.

has written

14. She also tries (to convey, ~~to have conveyed~~) some of the moral lessons that the stories often have.

to convey

15. Mr. Fish, for example, teaches us a lesson of friendship and (reminds, ~~reminded~~) me of the simple beauties of the sea.

reminds

MANUSCRIPT FORM   ms 8

8

Follow acceptable form in writing your paper.

Your instructor may indicate the exact form needed for preparing your papers. Usually an instructor's guidelines include the points discussed in this section.

8a Use proper materials.

If you handwrite your papers, use wide-lined, 8½ x 11-inch theme paper (not torn from a spiral notebook). Write in blue or black ink on one side of the paper only.

If you type your papers, use regular white 8½ x 11-inch paper (not onionskin or erasable bond). Use a black ribbon, double-space between lines, and type on one side of the paper only.

If you use a word processor to prepare your papers, make sure the typeface and size and the paper you plan to use will be acceptable to your instructor. Ask your instructor to examine a sample from your printer to see if it is acceptable quality.

8b Arrange the writing on the page in an orderly way.

Margins and Indention   Theme paper has the margins marked for you. But with unlined paper, leave about one inch of margin on all sides. Indent the first line of each paragraph about one inch if you handwrite and five spaces if you type, but leave no long gap at the end of any line except the last one in a paragraph.

Paging   Use Arabic numbers (2, 3, and so on) in the upper right-hand corner to mark all pages.

Title   On the first page, center your title about 1½ inches from the top or on the first ruled line. Do not use either quotation marks or underlining with your title. Capitalize the first word of the title and all other words except articles, prepositions, coordinating conjunctions, and the *to* in infinitives; then begin the first paragraph of your paper on the third line. Leave one blank line between your title and the first paragraph. (Your instructor may ask you to make a title page. If so, you may or may not rewrite the title on the first page of the paper.)

Identification   Instructors vary in what information they require and where they want this information placed. The identification will probably include your name, your course title and number, the instructor's name, and the date.

Punctuation   Never begin a line of your paper with a comma, a colon, a semicolon, or an end mark of punctuation; never end a line with the first of a pair of brackets, parentheses, or quotations.

107

Poetry   If you quote four or more lines of poetry, indent the lines about one inch from the left margin and arrange them as in the original. Long prose quotations (more than four lines) should also be indented. (See also **16a**.)

8c Write clearly and neatly.

Write so that your instructor can read your paper easily. Most instructors will accept a composition that has a few words crossed out with substitutions written neatly above, but if your changes are so plentiful that your paper looks messy or is difficult to read, you should recopy the page.

8d Divide words at the ends of lines according to standard practice.

The best way to determine where to divide a word that comes at the end of a line is to check a dictionary for the syllable markings (usually indicated by dots). In general, though, remember these guidelines: never divide a single-syllable word; do not carry over to the next line a syllable like *ed* or one letter of a word; divide a hyphenated word only at the hyphen. Keep in mind that an uneven right margin is expected and that too many divisions at the ends of lines make a paper difficult to read.

8e Proofread your papers carefully.

Always leave a few minutes at the end of an in-class writing assignment for proofreading. Few people write good papers without revising their first drafts. When you need to make a change, draw a straight horizontal line through the part to be deleted, insert a caret (Λ) at the point where the addition is to be made, and write the new material above the line. When writing out-of-class papers, try to set your first draft aside for several hours or even for a day so that you can proofread it with a fresh mind.

9/10

Use capitals and italics in accordance with current practices.

A recently published dictionary is the best guide to current standards for capitals, italics, abbreviations, and numbers. There are a few general rules to follow for these problems in mechanics (chapters **9, 10,** and **11**), but whenever you are in doubt about how to handle a particular word, you should consult an up-to-date dictionary.

9a Capitalize words referring to specific persons, personifications, places, things, times, organizations, peoples and their languages, religions and their adherents, holy books, holy days, and words denoting the Supreme Being. Capitalize words derived from proper names and words used as essential parts of proper names.

PERSONS	Shakespeare, Buddha, Mr. Salazar
PERSONIFICATIONS	Mother Nature, Uncle Sam, John Doe
PLACES	Key West; LaGrange, Georgia; Byron Avenue; the South (referred to as an area)
THINGS	the Liberty Bell, the Bible, History 201, the Second World War
TIMES	Wednesday, April 14; Easter; The Age of Enlightenment
ORGANIZATIONS	the Peace Corps, the Exchange Club, Phi Beta Kappa
RACES AND LANGUAGES	Thai, English, Latin
RELIGIONS AND THEIR ADHERENTS	Islam, Christianity, Judaism, Moslem, Christian, Jew
HOLY BOOKS AND HOLY DAYS	Koran, the Bible, Torah, Ramadan, Advent, Passover
WORDS DENOTING THE SUPREME BEING	Allah, God, Jehovah
WORDS DERIVED FROM PROPER NAMES	Swedish, New Yorker, Anglican
ESSENTIAL PARTS OF PROPER NAMES	the Bill of Rights, the Battle of Little Big Horn, the New River

9b In general, capitalize a person's title if it immediately precedes the person's name but not a title that follows the name.

In the last election, **R**epresentative Andrew Nunnery faced Angel Gleason, former governor, in the race for senator.

Note that usage varies with regard to capitalization of titles of high rank when not followed by a proper name (Senator OR senator). Titles of family members are capitalized only when they are written in combination with a name (Uncle Ben) or when they are used in place of a name (I asked Father for a loan).

9c Capitalize the first and last words of a title or subtitle and all other key words within it.

> A writer friend of mine suggested that I read two articles: "What's a **F**loppy **D**isk **F**or?" and "**M**aking **F**riends with **Y**our **W**ord **P**rocessor."

Caution: Articles—*a, an, the*—prepositions, coordinating conjunctions, and the *to* in infinitives are not capitalized unless they are the first or last words.

9d Capitalize the pronoun *I* and the interjection *Oh*.

9e Capitalize the first word of each sentence, including a quoted sentence.

> **W**riters agree that many good novels were rejected by publishers last year.
>
> OR
>
> "**W**riters agree that many good novels were rejected by publishers last year," Ms. Chiu explained.
> "**O**h, really!" exclaimed a student.

9f Avoid capitals for words that name classes rather than specific persons, places, and things.

> The **d**octors held a **c**onference at a **c**onvention **c**enter in the **d**owntown section of our town.

Also avoid the common tendency to capitalize seasons, directions, and general courses of study.

> This **s**pring I am going to study **c**hemistry at a **w**estern university.

10 To show italics, underline the titles of books, films, plays, works of art, magazines, newspapers, and long poems; the names of ships and airplanes; foreign words; and words, letters, and figures spoken of as such.

> The word <u>modern</u> becomes important when you consider these works of art: Proust's novel <u>Remembrance of Things Past</u>; Modigliani's inspiring sculpture <u>Flight</u>; Matisse's masterpiece painted in 1906, <u>Le Bonheur de Vivre</u>; and even a work of engineering such as the <u>Golden Gate Bridge</u>.

Caution: Do not underline the title of your own essay or overuse italics for emphasis.

Capitals and Italics   Exercise 9/10–1

NAME _____ SCORE _____

DIRECTIONS   Words in one of each of the following groups should be capitalized and/or italicized (underlined). Identify the group that needs capitalization and/or italics by writing either *a* or *b* in the blank at right.   Then make the necessary revision for the appropriate group of words.

   EXAMPLE

   (a)   a class at our college

   (b)   *G*eology 203 at *G*allaudet *C*ollege   *b*

1. (a)   responded, "*Y*ou will see me again."

   (b)   responded that you will see me again   *a*

2. (a)   a course in history

   (b)   a course in *R*ussian   *b*

3. (a)   visited another country during the holiday

   (b)   visited my family in *M*exico during the *c*hristmas holiday   *b*

4. (a)   reading the *L*ast of the *M*ohicans by *J*ames *F*enimore *C*ooper

   (b)   reading a novel about colonial times   *a*

5. (a)   boarded the *S*tella *G*enari for its crossing to *E*llis *I*sland

   (b)   boarded a cargo ship for its transoceanic voyage   *a*

6. (a)   a story in a weekly magazine about the death of a popular rock

   singer

   (b)   "*T*he *t*ragedy of the *k*ing's *l*ast *y*ears," a story in *N*ewsweek

   about the death of *E*lvis   *b*

CAPITALS/ITALICS

7. (a) senator inouye visiting tennessee
   (corrections: S over senator, I over inouye, T over tennessee)

   (b) the senator visiting our state   _a_

8. (a) admired the painting by the artist

   (b) admired les demoiselles by picasso   _b_
   (corrections: L, D over les demoiselles, P over picasso)

9. (a) the pronunciation of the word party as "pah-ty" in the south
   (correction: S over south)

   (b) the pronunciation of words in a southern state   _a_

10. (a) a famous war in history

    (b) the war of 1812   _b_
    (correction: W over war)

11. (a) went to see a well-known play during our annual trip to a neighboring city

    (b) went to see man of la mancha during our annual trip to new york   _b_
    (corrections: M, L, M over man of la mancha; N over new; Y over york)

12. (a) the president of our country will be inaugurated on tuesday, january 20
    (corrections: T over tuesday, J over january)

    (b) the president of the debate club at our college   _a_

13. (a) keats's courting of death in la belle dame sans merci
    (corrections: K over keats's; L-B, D, S, M over la belle dame sans merci)

    (b) the many poems that personify human qualities   _a_

14. (a) economics 211 to be offered in the spring
    (correction: E over economics)

    (b) a course in economics to be offered in the spring   _a_

15. (a) the grandmother who joined a charitable organization

    (b) my chinese grandmother who is a red cross volunteer   _b_
    (corrections: C over chinese; R, C over red cross)

11

Learn when to use abbreviations, acronyms, and numbers.

In specialized kinds of writing—such as tables, indexes, and footnotes—abbreviations, acronyms, and figures are appropriate, but in ordinary writing abbreviations are used sparingly, figures are used only for numbers that would require three or more words to write out, and acronyms should be spelled out the first time they are used.

11a Before proper names, use the abbreviations *Mr., Mrs., Ms., Dr.,* and *St.* (for *Saint*) as appropriate. Use such designations as *Jr., Sr., II,* and *Ph.D.* after a proper name.

> *Ms.* Gunter asked *Dr.* Cantrell to tell the story of *St.* Jude.

11b Spell out names of states, countries, continents, months, days of the week, and units of measurement.

> When Marta was born on *July* 8 at the hospital in Barcelona, *Spain,* she weighed six *pounds,* eleven *ounces;* but seven days later, at home in San Francisco, *California,* she weighed nine *pounds.*

11c Spell out Street, Road, Park, River, Company, and similar words when used as part of proper names.

> From London *Avenue* in Riverview *Park* you can see the Stones *River* and the Tennessee *State* Agriculture Center.

11d Spell out the words *volume, chapter,* and *page* and the names of courses of study.

> The notes on *chemistry* are taken from *chapter* 7, *page* 63.   [*Ch.* 7, *p.* 63 would be acceptable in a footnote.]

11e Spell out the meaning of any acronym that may not be familiar to your reader when you use it for the first time.

> At this year's South Atlantic Modern Language Association (*SAMLA*) meeting in Knoxville I heard Galway Kinnell read his poetry. At next year's meeting of *SAMLA* in Atlanta another poet will give a reading.
>
> OR
>
> At this year's meeting of *SAMLA* (South Atlantic Modern Language Association) in Knoxville I heard Galway Kinnell read his poetry.

11f Spell out numbers that require only one or two words, but use figures for other numbers.

> During the last *twenty-five* years, I have gone from a *twenty-nine* inch waist to a *thirty-four* inch waist.
>
> Our home covers *2,500* square feet.

Note the ways figures are used in the following instances:

(1) the hour of the day: *4:00* P.M. (p.m.) OR four o'clock in the afternoon

(2) dates: April *14, 1992*

(3) addresses: *1310* West Main

(4) identification numbers: Channel *27*, Interstate *81*

(5) pages or divisions of a book: page *87*, chapter *9*

(6) decimals and percentages: *.87* inches, *10* percent

(7) a series of numbers: a room *20* feet long, *12* feet wide, and *8* feet high; The vote was *19* to *4* in favor with *7* abstentions.

(8) large round numbers: *two million* light years

(9) at the beginning of the sentence: *One hundred fifty* people applied for the position.

11g Recognize the meanings of several common Latin expressions, which are usually spelled out in English in formal writing.

> i.e. [that is], e.g. [for example], viz. [formerly], cf. [compare], etc. [and so forth], vs. OR v. [versus]

Caution: Never write *and etc.*, and use the word *etc.* itself sparingly. In general, naming another item is more effective.

> This course covers Japanese literature, history, geography, demographics, and food. [Naming another item, *food,* is more effective than writing *etc.*]

Abbreviations and Numbers Exercise 11–1

NAME _____ SCORE _____

DIRECTIONS   Rewrite each of the following items using an abbreviation or a figure if the abbreviation or the figure would be appropriate in ordinary writing. If not, simply rewrite the item as it stands.

EXAMPLES

three o'clock in the afternoon

3:00 P.M. OR 3:00 p.m.

on Tuesday afternoon

on Tuesday afternoon

1. on page fifteen of chapter three

   On page 15 of chapter 3

2. fourteen thousand dollars

   14000 dollars

3. Rose Gonzales, the doctor on our street

   Rose Gonzales is the Doctor on our street

4. the Braves versus the Giants

   the Braves versus the Giants

5. Eighty percent of those registered voted.

   8 percent of those registered voted

6. debate about the Equal Rights Amendment

   debate about the Equal Rights Amendment (ERA)

7. life in California in nineteen ninety-two

   life in California in 1992

8. the economics class in Peck Hall

the Economics class in Peck Hall

9. one hundred pounds

100 pounds

10. on the twenty-first of January

On January 21

11. Riverview Park off Thompson Lane

Riverview Park off Thompson Lane

12. Susan Collier, our senator

Our Senator Susan Collier

13. André Freneau, a certified public accountant

André Freneau, a Certified Public Accountant (CPA)

14. between the United States and Canada

between the United States and Canada

15. a lot that is one hundred feet long and ninety-five feet wide with seventy-five feet of road frontage

a lot that is 100 feet long and 75 feet wide with 75 feet of road frontage

THE COMMA ,/ 12

12

Let your sentence sense guide you in the use of the comma.

In speaking, you make the meaning of a sentence clearer or easier to follow by pauses and by changes in voice pitch. When you read the following sentence aloud, notice that you pause twice (and that your voice also drops in pitch) to make the sentence easier for a listener to follow:

> The following essay, written for the July 1988 issue of *Ms.* magazine, narrates a series of stories from Grace Ming-Yee Wai's childhood.

In writing, of course, you use punctuation marks, not voice pitch, to make your sentences easier to follow. And you decide where to put the punctuation marks on the basis of your sentence sense (chapter **1**).

> SUBJECT–VERB–COMPLEMENT.
> The essay is inspiring.

Often when you write a sentence that varies in some way from this pattern, you will use a comma or commas. If you add something before the subject, you often follow the introductory addition with a comma.

> Addition, S–V–C.
> However, the essay is inspiring.

Note: A dash may sometimes be used in the same way as a comma (chapter **17**).

If you interrupt the sentence pattern, you often use two commas:

> S, addition, V–C
> The essay, however, is inspiring.
> S-V, addition, C.
> The essay is, however, inspiring.

If you add a word or group of words to the end of the sentence pattern, you often use a comma:

> S-V-C, addition.
> The essay is inspiring, however.

Of all the marks of punctuation, the most frequently used is the comma. Commas have four main uses:

a to follow a main clause that is linked to another main clause by a coordinate conjunction (*and, but, or, nor, for, so,* or *yet*);

b to follow certain introductory elements;

c to separate items in a series, including coordinate (equal in rank) adjectives;

d to set off nonrestrictive, parenthetical, and miscellaneous elements.

12a A comma follows a main clause that is linked to another main clause by a coordinating conjunction: *and, but, or, nor, for, so,* or *yet.*

> Grace Wai's family owned a small grocery store in Tennessee. And they developed a strong work ethic in Grace.

When the two main clauses are linked by a coordinating conjunction, a compound sentence results.

> PATTERN **MAIN CLAUSE,** coordinating conjunction **MAIN CLAUSE.**

> Grace Wai's family owned a small grocery store in Tennessee, and they developed a strong work ethic in Grace.

The semicolon may also be used when the two main clauses that are linked by a coordinating conjunction contain other commas.

> Although neither of Grace's parents had a college education, they planned for their children to go to college; and they worked long hours in the grocery to fulfill that dream. [Remember that the addition of another main clause, rather than the presence of the coordinating conjunction, is the reason for the punctuation mark.]

Notice in the following examples that a comma is used before a coordinating conjunction only when the conjunction links two main clauses.

> TWO VERB PHRASES Grace's parents immigrated from Hong Kong and settled in a city with a small Asian population.

> TWO SUBORDINATE CLAUSES Because they came to America with few resources and because they wished to build a better life for their children, Grace's parents worked long hours in the grocery.

> TWO MAIN CLAUSES We can appreciate the immigrant spirit, and we can recognize it as one of the strengths of this country.

Commas between Main Clauses   Exercise 12–1

NAME _____ SCORE _____

DIRECTIONS   In the following sentences, insert an inverted caret (**V**) wherever two main elements are joined. Then insert either a comma or a semicolon after the first main clause. Write the mark that you added in the blank at the right as well. If a sentence does not have two main clauses, write *C* in the blank to show that the sentence is correct and needs no punctuation mark.

EXAMPLES

Black Elk was an Oglala chief and medicine man who watched the destruction of his people at the hands of the invading whites.   *C*

In his account of his life Black Elk explains the belief system of his people, and he records many of their chants and songs.   **,**

1. When he met Neihardt, Black Elk was living near Wounded Knee. _____

2. There he and his people built little gray houses of logs because the houses were square, Black Elk believed they were a bad place to live. _____

3. Everything a Native American does is in a circle because the power of the world works in a circle and everything tries to be in a circle. _____

4. When the Oglala were a happy people, all of their power came from the sacred hoop of the nation the people flourished. _____

5. The flowering tree was the living center of the hoop and the circle of the four quarters nourished it. _____

6. The east gave peace and light and the south gave warmth. _____

7. The west gave rain the north, with its cold and mighty wind, gave strength and endurance. _____

8. The sky is round and the earth is a round ball. _____

9. The wind, in its greatest power, whirls. _____

10. Birds make their nests in circles the sun comes forth and goes down again in a circle. _____

11. The moon does the same and both are round. _____

12. The life of a man is a circle from childhood to childhood so it is in everything where power moves. _____

13. Our tepees, which are set in a circle, are also round like the nests of birds. _____

14. Now the Wasichus have put the Oglala in square houses because our power is gone, we are dying. _____

15. When we were living by the power of the circle, boys were men at twelve or thirteen years of age but now it takes them very much longer to mature. _____

12b A comma usually follows adverb clauses that precede main clauses. A comma often follows introductory phrases (especially adverb phrases) and transitional expressions. A comma follows an introductory interjection or an introductory *yes* or *no*.

The introductory element, which offers a variation from subject-first word order (see also **30b**), is usually followed by a comma.

> PATTERN   Introductory element**,** **MAIN CLAUSE.**

> *When Grace Ming-Yee Wai was ten years old***,** her father was killed by a robber.

(1) When an adverb clause precedes the main clause, it is usually followed by a comma.

> *Although her father was a struggling immigrant***,** he still found resources to help his family.

There is usually no comma before the adverb clause when it follows the main clause.

> He supported a niece *while she studied nursing.*

But if the adverb clause at the end begins with *although,* a comma is normally used.

> Grace viewed her father as the strongest person in her world**,** *although she also recognized his frail health.*

Some writers omit the comma after the introductory adverb clause when the clause is very short or when it has the same subject as the main clause, but there is nothing wrong with including the comma.

> *Because he worked long hours* he neglected his health.
>
> OR
>
> *Because he worked long hours***,** he neglected his health.

(2) A comma usually follows an introductory verbal phrase and may follow an introductory prepositional phrase.

> *Working long hours and neglecting his health***,** he often had to be hospitalized. [introductory verbal phrase]
>
> *In this story and in earlier accounts***,** Grace records her responses to seeing her father in the hospital.   [introductory prepositional phrase]

The comma is often omitted after prepositional phrases if no misreading could result.

> *In 1988* Grace published an essay about her father in *Ms.* magazine.
>
> *Before reading***,** the students discussed other Chinese American writers.

(3) A comma follows an introductory transitional expression, an interjection, and sometimes a single-word modifier.

To be thorough, we looked up Grace Wai in the on-line catalog.

Yes, we also looked up Maxine Hong Kingston.

Unfocused, the on-line search could have taken too much time.

Certainly we meant to include all Chinese American writers in the search.   [Writers may or may not use a comma after an introductory word like *yet, thus,* and *certainly,* depending on how closely they feel the word is related to the rest of the sentence. If they see the word as functioning primarily for transition, they use a comma; if they see it primarily as an adverb, closely related to the verb, they do not use a comma.]

Commas after Introductory Elements   Exercise 12–2

NAME _____   SCORE _____

DIRECTIONS   After each introductory element, either write a zero (0) to indicate that no comma is needed or add a comma. Also write the zero or the comma in the blank.

EXAMPLES

Speaking slowly and eloquently ͮ Black Elk told his story.   ____,____

In 1932 ᴼ John G. Neihardt published *Black Elk Speaks: Being the Life Story of a Holy Man of the Oglala Sioux.*   ____0____

1. One day in June I [Black Elk] asked One Side to come over to eat.   _____

2. Recently I had been thinking about the four-rayed herb that I needed as medicine.   _____

3. Although I had seen the place of its growing in a vision I had been unable to find the place.   _____

4. After One Side and I had eaten I asked him to help me find the herb.   _____

5. Eager to help he got on his horse, and we rode off in search of the herb.   _____

6. As we rode I remembered my vision.   _____

7. In fact I decided to sing again the song I had heard in my vision.   _____

8. After I had sung the song I looked toward the west.   _____

9. At a certain spot beside the creek were crows and magpies, chicken hawks and spotted eagles circling around and around.   _____

10. Then I said to One Side, "Friend, right there is where the herb is growing."   _____

11. Quickly we remounted our horses and rode toward the creek.   _____

12. As we neared the creek the birds all flew away.   _____

13. As in my vision the herb was growing there on the bank of the creek.   _____

14. Although I had only seen the herb in a vision I recognized it
    immediately.   _____

15. With a root about eighteen inches long the herb grew deep into
    the soil.   _____

16. After we got off our horses I made an offering to the Six Powers. _____

17. Next I offered a prayer to the herb.   _____

18. Because the herb grew in sandy soil it was easy to harvest.   _____

19. After a few minutes of digging the herb we started back.   _____

20. After we forded the creek we stopped to wrap the herb in some
    sage growing there.   _____

12c Commas are used between items in a series and between coordinate adjectives. A series is a succession of three or more parallel elements.

(1) Use commas between three or more items in a series.

PATTERN   1, 2, and 3

OR   1, 2, 3

                                           1   2   3

For the first ten minutes we discussed the test, the grades, and the next assignment.

                                                                                                          1

Tanya decided to do her senior thesis on Maxine Hong Kingston because she wanted to

                                                                2

study a contemporary writer, because she already had read *Woman Warrior,* and

                                          3

because she had seen a PBS special on Kingston.

Tanya also decided to take her oral exam over three writers who champion minorities:

                  1   2   3

Leslie Silko, Zora Neale Hurston, and Richard Wright.

The comma before the *and* may be omitted only if there is no difficulty reading the series or if the two items should be regarded as one unit.

                                      1 2   3

Dr. Perez marked pages 4, 7, and 9 of Tanya's thesis as needing revision.   [Without the

last comma the series remains clear: Dr. Perez marked pages 4, 7 and 9 of Tanya's the-

sis as needing revision.]

                                           1   2   3

Tanya had marked the text with numbers, letters, and blue and white Post-it notes.   [*Blue*

and white refers as a unit to notes; thus there is no comma before the last *and.*]

All the commas are normally omitted when a coordinating conjunction is used between each item in the series.

                                        1   2   3

Some students ignore or misread or even refuse to believe the remarks that their teachers

put on their papers.

Semicolons may be used between the items in the series if the items themselves contain commas or if the items are main clauses. (See also **12a.**)

1

Tanya's revision process involves three steps: first, she sets a draft aside for a few days;

2

second, she reads the draft carefully for unclear language, underdeveloped passages,

3

and errors; third, she passes the corrected draft to Dr. Perez for her approval or

corrections.

Caution: Remember that no comma is used when only two items are linked by a conjunction.

> *Putting the draft aside* and *working on something else* enables her to become objective about the draft.

(2) Use commas between coordinate adjectives that are not linked by a coordinating conjunction.

If the adjectives are coordinate, you can reverse their order or insert *and* or *or* between them without loss of sense.

a   b   a   b

Tanya's *longest, most successful* chapter discusses the *difficult,* extremely *intricate*

symbolism in T\ :sub:`RIPMASTER` M\ :sub:`ONKEY`.

> a b a b

Tanya's *most successful* and *longest* chapter discusses the extremely *intricate* and *difficult*

symbolism in T\ :sub:`RIPMASTER` M\ :sub:`ONKEY`.

Caution: Adjectives that are not coordinate take no commas between them.

> The *brief concluding* chapter suggests other approaches to Kingston's work that Tanya hopes to explore.   [You would not say *"brief* and *concluding* chapter."]

> COORDINATE ADJECTIVES   *recurring, insightful* allusions   [You may say *"insightful, recurring* allusions" or *"recurring* and *insightful* allusions."]

> ADJECTIVES THAT ARE NOT COORDINATE   *famous lyric* poem and *longest first* sentence [You would not say *"famous* and *lyric* poem" or *"first longest* sentence."]

**Commas between Items in a Series
and between Coordinate Adjectives**

Exercise 12–3

NAME _____ SCORE _____

DIRECTIONS   In each sentence identify each series that needs commas by writing *1, 2, 3* and so on above the items and in the blank on the right; identify coordinate adjectives by writing *a, b* above the adjectives and in the blank. Insert commas where they belong in the sentence and also in the blank to show the punctuation of the pattern. Write *C* in the blank if a sentence has no items in a series or no coordinate adjectives that need punctuation.

EXAMPLES

1 2 3
A man named Cuts to Pieces began yelling "Hey, hey, hey!" for he was in

trouble.   <u>1, 2, 3</u>

a   b
He was worried about his small, sickly boy.   <u>a, b</u>

1. "You have great mystical powers of healing," he said to me.   _____

2. I was afraid because I had never cured anyone before because I
   was unsure what ceremony to use for the boy and because I was
   not sure I had the proper herbs.   _____

3. "Go home," I said to Cuts to Pieces, "and bring me a clay smoking
   pipe with an eagle feather on it."   _____

4. He returned with the pipe, and I said, "Take it to the left of me
   leave it there and pass out to the right of me."   _____

5. I sent for One Side, and together we went to the sick little boy. _____

6. I made a low rumbling sound on the drum as an offering to the
   Spirit of the World.   _____

7. We entered the tepee on the south walked inside from right to left
   and stopped on the west side after we had made a circle.   _____

8. I had brought much to help me: the pipe the drum the four-rayed

   herb a wooden cup for water and an eagle bone whistle.   _____

9. In the distance I heard the warm westerly winds begin to stir.   _____

10. I filled the pipe with red willow bark gave it to the daughter of

   Cuts to Pieces told her to hold it and began to sing.   _____

12d Commas are used to set off (1) nonrestrictive clauses and phrases, (2) paren-thetical elements such as transitional expressions, and (3) items in dates and addresses.

A parenthetical or nonrestrictive addition that comes before the basic sentence pattern is followed by a comma.

> *One of the best books in recent years by an American writer,* LEGACIES: A CHINESE MOSAIC, traces the author's Chinese heritage.

If the parenthetical or nonrestrictive addition comes after the basic sentence, a comma precedes it.

> LEGACIES: A CHINESE MOSAIC tells the story of Bette Bao Lord, *a best-selling American author.*

The most common position for the parenthetical or nonrestrictive addition is in the middle of the sentence, where one comma precedes it and another comma follows it.

> In the second chapter, *"Black Armbands, Red Armbands,"* Lord begins to tell the stories of many who resisted communist rule.
> Many of the people closest to her, *including members of her family,* had been members of the Red Guard.

(1) Nonrestrictive clauses and phrases are set off by commas. Restrictive clauses and phrases are not set off. (See also 13d.)

A restrictive clause or phrase limits the meaning of the word it refers to.

> The magazine *that published a brief biography of Bette Bao Lord* is called Ms. [The *that* clause limits the meaning of the word *magazine.* Note that the relative pronoun *that* always introduces a relative clause.]
> Anyone *reading this magazine* is impressed with the informative articles. [The verbal phrase *reading this magazine* limits the meaning of the word *anyone.*]

A nonrestrictive clause or phrase does not limit the meaning of the word it refers to; rather, it adds information about a word that is already clearly limited in meaning. The nonrestrictive clause or phrase is set off with commas.

> *"An American in China," taken from Ms. magazine,* explores Bette Bao Lord's experiences in China as the spouse of a diplomat. [The verbal phrase *taken from Ms. magazine* adds further information about the subject "An American in China."]
> Adam Matzger, *who is a free-lance writer living in Beijing,* is familiar with Lord and with her contacts in China. [The *who* clause adds information about *Adam Matzger.*]

Of course, not all adjective clauses and phrases are as obviously restrictive or non-restrictive as the ones used in the above examples. Many times you can determine whether a clause or phrase is restrictive or nonrestrictive only by referring to the preceding sentence or sentences.

> Prior to moving to Beijing in 1989, Matzger had briefly studied Oriental languages at Berkeley. But when he arrived in China, he discovered that the academic training had

not prepared him to understand what he heard in daily conversation. Conversation with natives of Beijing, *which he compared to his experiences in the Berkeley language lab,* quickly taught him that he knew too little Chinese. [Without the first two sentences, the *which* clause would be restrictive, or necessary to limit the meaning of *conversation.*]

Sometimes, depending on the writer's intended meaning, a clause or phrase may be either restrictive or nonrestrictive. Notice the differences in meaning between the two sentences below, which differ only in punctuation.

Matzger learned that Beijing citizens *who spoke a dialect unique to Beijing* were especially difficult to understand. [Without commas around the *who* clause, the sentence suggests that some Beijing citizens speak the Beijing dialect and are difficult to understand; other citizens do not speak the dialect and are less difficult to understand.]

Matzger learned that Beijing citizens, *who spoke a dialect unique to Beijing,* were especially difficult to understand. [Set off by commas, the *who* clause suggests that all Beijing citizens speak the Beijing dialect and are difficult to understand.]

(2) Parenthetical elements, nonrestrictive appositives, absolute and contrasted elements, and words in direct address are set off by commas.

Parenthetical elements include a variety of constructions that introduce supplementary information to a sentence or that make up transitions between sentences.

We read several articles, *such as "Holes in the Great Wall" and "Astigmatism Among Pandas,"* about China. [In this sentence *such as* introduces a nonrestrictive phrase. In the sentence "An essay *such as 'Holes in the Great Wall'* explains that the wall constantly needs repair," *such as* introduces a restrictive phrase. Note also that when a comma is used with *such as,* the comma comes before *such,* with no comma after *as.*]

"If you visit China," *Adam Matzger says,* "you must visit the wall." [An expression such as *Adam Matzger says (claims, replies,* and so on) is considered parenthetical. See **16a(2)** for further information on the placement of commas in dialogue.]

Matzger, *as well as some other recent writers,* is not optimistic about the plight of the panda. [Expressions like *as well as, in addition to,* and *along with* usually introduce parenthetical matter.]

In fact, Matzger believes that the panda will become extinct in the wild. [A transitional expression such as *in fact* is always considered parenthetical.]

A Chinese naturalist, *who also has been helping Matzger improve his language skills,* is the source of information about the panda population. [A subordinate clause may introduce parenthetical matter.]

Appositives are usually set off by commas, though on a few occasions they are restrictive.

The essay *"The Language of Pandas"* combines Matzger's interests in language and in pandas. [The title of the essay is a restrictive appositive needed to identify which essay is being referred to; thus it is not set off with commas.]

"The Language of Pandas," *a recent article in Smithsonian magazine,* examines the rhetorical importance of pandas in China's foreign relations. [The appositive is nonrestrictive; thus it is set off with commas.]

Absolute phrases are verbal phrases that are preceded by their subjects. They affect the meaning of the entire sentence in which they appear (not just a single word, phrase, or clause). Absolute phrases are always set off by commas.

> According to Matzger, the Chinese authorities are trying to protect panda habitat, *the pandas' needs effectively countering the human desire to create more arable land.* [The verbal *countering* has its own subject, *needs.*]

Contrasted elements are always set off by commas.

> Matzger believes that the survival of the pandas, *not China's concerns for its exploding population,* should decide land use.

Words in direct address do just what you would expect them to do: they address someone or something directly. They are always set off by commas.

> "Do not lose this unique symbol of your country, *China,* by bowing to short-term concerns," Matzger seems to be saying.

(3) Geographical names and items in dates and addresses (except for zip codes) are set off by commas.

> Send your application by April 14, 1994, to Box 289, Murfreesboro, Tennessee 37130.

Dates are sometimes written and punctuated differently in official documents and reports.

> On Friday, 21 March 1995, the finalists checked into the hotel.

When only the month and year are given, no comma is necessary.

> May 1993.

12e A comma is occasionally used to prevent misreading even when it is not called for by any of the principles already discussed.

> CONFUSING   Those of you who wish to write for further details.

> CLEAR   Those of you who wish to, write for further details.

Commas to Set Off Nonrestrictive Clauses and Phrases and Parenthetical Elements

Exercise 12–4

NAME _____ SCORE _____

DIRECTIONS   In the following sentences, set off each nonrestrictive or parenthetical addition with a comma or commas. Then in the blank write (1) a dash followed by a comma (—,) if the nonrestrictive or parenthetical addition begins the sentence, (2) a comma followed by a dash (,—) if the nonrestrictive or parenthetical addition ends the sentence, (3) a dash enclosed with commas (,—,) if the nonrestrictive or parenthetical addition comes within the sentence, or (4) *C* if there is no nonrestrictive or parenthetical addition to set off.

EXAMPLE

"Great Spirit, you are the only one who can heal this boy," Black Elk chanted.   _,—,_

1. Because I had never healed anyone before I called on every spirit to help me. _____

2. Today I understand however that one power would have healed the boy. _____

3. I had been facing the west the direction to send words. _____

4. Now I walked to the north and to the east and to the south stopping there where the source of all life is. _____

5. While I sang I felt something strange something that made me want to cry for all unhappy things. _____

6. Now I walked to the quarter of the west where I lit the pipe. _____

7. After I had taken a whiff of smoke I passed the pipe around. _____

8. I could feel that the boy who turned and smiled at me was getting stronger. _____

9. Standing before the boy I stamped the ground four times. _____

10. Then putting my mouth to the pit of his stomach I drew through him the cleansing wind of the north. _____

11. I chewed some herb and put it in water afterward blowing some of it on the boy and to the four quarters.   _____

12. The cup with the rest of the water I gave to the virgin who gave it to the boy to drink.   _____

13. "Rise up" I said "and walk around in a circle."   _____

14. With the virgin's help he began to walk.   _____

15. Then I went away.   _____

16. I knew because I could feel the powers grow within him that the boy would be well.   _____

17. On the next day his father reported his improvement.   _____

18. The boy he said was sitting up and taking food.   _____

19. In later years working on similar cases I knew to simplify the healing ritual.   _____

20. And as you can see I have lived to be an old man.   _____

All Uses of the Comma

NAME _____ SCORE _____

DIRECTIONS   Decide whether each comma used in the following sentences (a) separates main clauses, (b) sets off an introductory addition, (c) separates items in a series or coordinate adjectives, or (d) sets off a parenthetical or nonrestrictive addition. Write *a, b, c,* or *d* above each comma and in the blank to the right of the sentence.

EXAMPLE

Let us consider, for a moment, the writings of Thomas S. Whitecloud.   *d d*

(commas marked with d and d above)

1. Whitecloud graduated from the medical school of Tulane University in New Orleans, Louisiana.   _____

2. In an essay, which was published in 1938, he discusses memories of his home in Wisconsin.   _____

3. Whitecloud misses the dramatically changing seasons, the smell of wild rice and venison cooking, the call of the loon, and the tracks left by animals in the snow.   _____

4. This beautiful, calm land calls to him to return and to be with his people.   _____

5. He is weary, he says, of having to pretend to be civilized.   _____

6. He longs for his people who know how to share, how to tear a piece of meat in two and give a portion to one's brother.   _____

7. They know how to make songs for each person in the tribe, and they have no need for a radio.   _____

8. Because they can work with their hands, they can make beads from wood and a thing of beauty from birch bark.   _____

9. "I am tired," he says, "and I want to walk again among the ghost birches."   _____

10. I want to see the leaves in autumn, the clusters of gold and red that trail in the west wind.   _____

11. Smoke will rise from the lodge-houses, and the blue winds will blow.   _____

12. Lying in my bed, I will close my eyes and listen to the drums.   _____

13. Civilized people are driving Whitecloud away by saying that his people worship sticks of wood, by saying that his race is not intelligent, and by saying that the Bible was not written for his people.   _____

14. He hears a train whistle in the night, calling him home.   _____

All Uses of the Comma

NAME _____ SCORE _____

DIRECTIONS   In the following sentences insert all necessary commas. Then write *a, b, c,* or *d* above each comma and in the blank to the right of each sentence to indicate that the comma (a) separates main clauses, (b) sets off an introductory addition, (c) separates items in a series or coordinate adjectives, or (d) sets off a parenthetical or nonrestrictive addition.

EXAMPLE

As Whitecloud hears the train,*b* he imagines it carrying him home.   *b*

1. When he arrives home he encounters people from his tribe.   _____

2. Laughing he walks into the woods.   _____

3. He hears the drums the soft music of the night.   _____

4. The village a collection of simple box houses beckons.   _____

5. It is Christmas and no one knows he is home.   _____

6. He peers into his house and sees his family seated about the table preparing to eat Christmas dinner.   _____

7. After the meal he and his father go to the lodge and they meet there many old friends.   _____

8. The sound of the snow creaking beneath his feet the soft night wind and the sounds of sleepy birds seem to be calling welcome to him.   _____

9. "Inside the lodge" he says "many Indians dance to the drum beat."   _____

10. There are women with long dark hair women with children on their hips women whose eyes glint fire.   _____

11. Gentle wise old men line the wall.   _____

12. They are dressed in their fine clothes beaded moccasins and vests of leather.   _____

13. He looks in their eyes and he hopes to see himself.   _____

14. He has come home longing to know once again where he belongs.   _____

All Uses of the Comma   Exercise 12–7

NAME _____ SCORE _____

DIRECTIONS   Write a sentence to illustrate each of the items listed.

EXAMPLE

an absolute element

According to my roommate we need to vote next week,
our vote potentially helping John to win a close race.

1. a complete date

2. a nonrestrictive clause

3. a contrasted element

4. a restrictive phrase

5. a transitional expression

6. items in a series

7. a parenthetical element introduced by *such as*

8. two main clauses linked by a coordinating conjunction

9. an introductory verbal phrase

10. a complete address, including zip code

13

Superfluous or misplaced commas make sentences difficult to read.

The comma is the most frequently used punctuation mark. It is also the most frequently *misused* punctuation mark. While trying to master the correct use of the
comma, many people tend to overuse it and to misplace it in sentence patterns, especially if they rely too much on the pause test for placement. Some short-winded writers, who pause after every third or fourth word, fill their sentences with commas that
make the writing difficult to follow. In the example below, the circled commas should
not be included.

> CONFUSING   Students ⊙ who are interested in Native American literature ⊙ should take
> Professor Strawman's seminar ⊙ in the summer term.

Actually, this sentence requires no internal punctuation at all, for the clauses and
phrases that have been added to the basic sentence pattern are all restrictive; they are
necessary to define or to limit the meaning of the words they modify.

> CORRECT   Students who are interested in Native American literature should take
> Professor Strawman's seminar in the summer term.

Chapter **13** is included as a caution against overuse and misplacement of commas.
The circled commas throughout the examples in this section should be omitted.

13a Do not use a comma to separate the subject from its verb or the verb from its complement.

Remember that commas are used to set off nonrestrictive or parenthetical additions. Do
not use them to separate the parts of the basic (Subject–Verb–Complement) sentence.

> Studying Native American literature ⊙ will occupy my whole summer.   [The subject,
> *studying,* should not be separated by a comma from its verb *will occupy.*]
> Most of my friends agree ⊙ that we have much to learn from this literature.   [The verb,
> *agree,* should not be separated by a comma from its complement, the *that* clause.]

13b Do not use a comma after a coordinating conjunction; do not use a comma before a coordinating conjunction when only a word, phrase, or subordinate clause (rather than a main clause) follows the conjunction. (See also 12a.)

> The first story by Black Elk tells of his life as a medicine man, and ⊙ it contains the songs
> he used to sing.   [The comma comes **before, not after,** the coordinating conjunction.]
> Black Elk used herbs in his healing ⊙ but never used white man's medicines.   [compound
> predicate—no comma before *but*]

13c Do not use commas to set off words or short phrases (especially introductory ones) that are not parenthetical or that are very slightly so.

Before class ⊙ we should listen to the audio tape that came with the text.

The circle ⊙ to Black Elk ⊙ represents harmony and perfection.

13d Do not use commas to set off restrictive clauses, phrases, or appositives. (See also **12d**.)

The book ⊙ *Eagles and Ospreys* ⊙ discusses the Sioux nation in the last chapter. [No commas are needed because the title *Eagles and Ospreys* is a restrictive appositive needed to define or limit *book*.]

The end of the story was so moving ⊙ that all of us in the class were close to tears. [No comma is needed because the *that* clause is necessary to define or limit *moving*.]

Readers ⊙ trying to understand the writing style ⊙ must remember it comes from an oral tradition. [No commas are needed because the verbal phrase is a restrictive addition needed to define or limit *readers*.]

13e Do not use a comma before the first or after the last item in a series.

Journals such as ⊙ *American Literature, College English,* and *CCC* ⊙ have reviewed his book.

13f In general, do not use a comma before an adverb clause at the end of a sentence. (See also **12b**.)

Most of us head for the computer lab ⊙ when we have to write a paper. [If the *when* clause came at the beginning of the sentence as an introductory addition, it would be followed by a comma.]

13g Do not use a comma between adjectives that are not coordinate. (See also **12c**.)

Serious ⊙ older students often make many ⊙ difficult sacrifices in order to stay in school.

Superfluous Commas   Exercise 13–1

NAME _____   SCORE _____

DIRECTIONS   Each of the following sentences is correctly punctuated. Explain why a comma is not added to each sentence at the place or places indicated in the question by listing the rule of caution (see **13a–13g**) that applies.

EXAMPLE

Reading these essays for class has been time consuming.

Why is *essays* not followed by a comma?   ___13c___

1. A writer like Black Elk can change the way we look at our heritage.

   Why is *like Black Elk* not set off by commas?   _____

2. I began to read Native American literature when I met Professor Strawman.

   Why is there no comma before *when*?   _____

3. He was the teacher in my freshman English class and introduced me to some Native American writers.

   Why is there not a comma before *and*?   _____

4. I wanted to take a course in modern poetry this semester, but I learned of the seminar in Native American writers.

   Why is there no comma after *but*?   _____

5. Until this year my favorite works by American writers had been *Walden, The Scarlet Letter,* and *Little Women.*

   Why is *had been* not followed by a comma?   _____

6. Studying with Professor Strawman and Professor Ware I have learned that I need also to appreciate the non-canonical writers.

   Why is there no comma after *learned*?   _____

7. The canonical writers are writers who have been labeled as important.

   Why is there no comma after the second *writers*?   _____

8. The work produced by canonical writers is still important.

Why is *produced by canonical writers* not set off by commas? _____

9. The term "canon" has several definitions.

Why is *canon* not set off by commas? _____

10. The definition that fits this context is "an authoritative list."

Why is *an* not followed by a comma? _____

11. Kate Chopin is another non-canonical writer, but she has reached near-canonical status in recent years.

Why is there no comma after *but*? _____

12. It is her novel *The Awakening* that has brought her fame and acceptance.

Why is there not a comma after *Awakening*? _____

13. Professor Strawman says the writers have achieved near-canonical status when they begin to appear in literature anthologies.

Why is there no comma after *status*? _____

14. Most of these Native American writers will never become part of the canon, but we still should read them.

Why is there no comma after *but*? _____

15. Professor Strawman believes that we are responsible for keeping these writers alive by reading them.

Why is there no comma after *believes*? _____

THE SEMICOLON   ;/14

14

Use the semicolon between parts of equal grammatical rank: (a) between two main clauses not joined by a coordinating conjunction and (b) between coordinate elements that already contain commas.

A semicolon indicates that one part of a coordinate construction is finished. The semi-colon acts like the fulcrum of a seesaw, balancing parts of equal grammatical rank.

> We divided the class into four groups, each with five students; my group is reading the work of Mourning Dove. [two main clauses with no coordinating conjunction]
>
> Fred's group is studying three writers: Maxine Hong Kingston, particularly *Woman Warrior*; Amy Tan; and Black Elk, focusing on his narratives. [items in a series, some of which contain commas]

14a Use the semicolon to separate two main clauses not joined by a coordinating conjunction or two main clauses that contain commas and are also joined by a coordinating conjunction.

PATTERN   **MAIN CLAUSE; MAIN CLAUSE.**

> I wanted to interview William Least Heat Moon; Alice found an interview of him in the learning resources center. [two main clauses with no coordinating conjunction]
>
> The center also had interviews with Louise Erdich, Maxine Hong Kingston, and Amy Tan; *so* we used those in our report. [The first clause already contains commas, so a semi-colon must be used before the coordinating conjunction *so*.]

Caution: In a divided quotation, be especially careful to use a semicolon between the two main clauses of a sentence when they are not connected by a coordinating conjunction.

> "We need a video of one of the writers," Fred said; "we need to think about a mixed media presentation."

Remember that a conjunctive adverb, like *however,* or a transitional expression, like *for example* (see chapter **1**), is not the same as a coordinating conjunction—*and, but, or, nor, for, so,* or *yet.* Thus when a conjunctive adverb or a transitional expression is used to link two main clauses, a semicolon must come before it.

> Alice wrote the text for our presentation; *however,* Teresa made all of the slides.

14b Use the semicolon to separate a series of equal elements which themselves contain commas.

> We concluded our presentation with a series of questions: what Native American writers have you read; what can you say now about the unique perspectives of these writers; with our next presentation in mind, what writers do you suggest that we include?

2ght © 1994 by Harcourt Brace & Company. All rights reserved.

145

I knew that the group would work well together—that Alice would be a quiet, determined leader; that Jennifer would be eager and bright; and that Andy would seem too quiet, but would surprise with his insights.

14c Use the semicolon between parts of equal rank only, not between a clause and a phrase or a subordinate clause and a main clause.

The report on Mourning Dove will be perfect for the March deadline, because March is National Women's History month and because that week the English department is featuring Native American Women.   [The subordinate clauses, introduced by *because,* are not equal in rank to the main clause; thus a semicolon would be inappropriate.]

Semicolons

Exercise 14–1

NAME _____*Gelian*_____ SCORE _____

DIRECTIONS   In the following sentences insert an inverted caret (**V**) between main clauses and add semicolons as needed. In the blank, copy the semicolon and the word or transitional expression immediately following, along with the comma if there is one. Write *C* in the blank if the sentence is correctly punctuated. (Not all sentences have two main clauses.)

EXAMPLE

Lame Deer believes that most Americans are doing everything
    V
wrong;indeed, according to Lame Deer, we have "declawed and

malformed" ourselves and forgotten how to live.   ___; indeed,___

1. Let's sit down here, all of us on the open prairie, where we

   can't see a highway or a fence;let's have no blankets to sit on,

   but feel the ground with our bodies, the earth, the yielding

   shrubs.   ___; let's___

2. Let's have the grass for a mattress, experiencing its sharpness

   and its softness let us become like stones, plants, and trees.   ___; let___

3. Listen to the air you can feel it, smell it, taste it.   ___; you___

4. You have made it hard for us to experience nature in the

   good way by being part of it even here we are conscious that

   somewhere out in those hills there are missile silos and radar

   stations.   ___; even___

5. White men always pick unspoiled sites for such abominations

   therefore, you leave behind raped and violated lands.   ___; therefore___

6. Our reservation is beautiful land, however, and now you

   even speak of making it a national park.   ___; and___

7. You have even changed the animals; in fact, you have even

   changed the buffalo.   ___; in___

8. There is power in a buffalo;there is no power in an Angus.   ___; there___

9. There is power in an antelope, but not in a goat or sheep

   they will hold still while you butcher them.   ___; they___

10. There was great power in a wolf, in a coyote; in contrast, there is no power in a poodle or Pekingese. _____ C ✓ _____

11. You can't do much with a cat, which is like an Indian, unchangeable; however, you alter it, declaw it, even experiment on it in laboratories. _____ ; however _____

12. You have even changed the birds of the field, the partridge, quail, and pheasant; as a result, they are now chickens, tame birds that peck each other's eyes out. _____ ; as _____

13. On some farms you breed chickens for breast meat by confining them to low cages so that they have to stoop over. _____ C ✓ _____

14. Forcing them to hunch over makes the breast bigger; soothing music, Muzak, is played all day to keep them calm. _____ ; soothing _____

15. Having to spend all their lives stooped over makes an unnatural, crazy, no-good bird; it also makes unnatural, no-good human beings. _____ ; it _____

Commas and Semicolons

Exercise 14–2

NAME _____ *Uzelian* _____ SCORE _____

DIRECTIONS   In the following sentences insert either a semicolon or a comma as needed within the sentences and also in the blank.

EXAMPLE

"You have not only altered, declawed, and malformed your winged and four-legged cousins," said Lame Deer; "you have done it to yourselves."   **;**

1. You have changed men into chairmen of boards, into office workers, and into time-clock punchers.   **,**

2. You have changed women into housewives, truly fearful creatures.   **;**

3. You live in prisons which you have built for yourselves, calling them homes, offices, factories.   **,**

4. Sometimes I think that even our pitiful tarpaper shacks are better; walking a hundred feet in snow to the outhouse on a clear wintry night reminds us of our ties to nature.   **;**

5. I think white people are so afraid of the world they created that they do not want to see, feel, smell, or hear it.   **,**

6. The feeling of rain on your face, being numbed by an icy wind; coming out of a hot sweat bath and plunging into a cold stream— these things make you alive.   **;**

7. "You treat your food as you do your bodies," he said, "taking out the nature part and replacing it with the artificial."   **,**

8. We full-bloods like to sink our teeth into raw liver, raw kidney in fact; we used to eat buffalo intestines raw.   **;**

9. That was food; it had power.   **;**

10. You do not have the courage to kill honestly to cut off the chicken's head pluck it and gut it.   **;**

THE SEMICOLON

11. It all comes in a neat plastic bag cut up and ready to eat.

12. When we killed a buffalo we knew what we were doing.

13. We apologized to his spirit and tried to make him understand why we did it therefore, we honored him for his sacrifice.

14. To us life all life is sacred.

15. The animals which the Great Spirit put here are sacred they are fellow creatures in this great world.

150

Copyright © 1994 by Harcourt Brace & Company. All rights reserved.

15

Use the apostrophe (a) to indicate the possessive case—except for personal pronouns, (b) to mark omissions in contracted words and numerals, and (c) to form certain plurals.

The apostrophe, in most of its uses, indicates that something has been omitted.

> don't [do *not*]
> they're [they *are*]
> children's books [books *of, for,* or *by* children]
> the artist's paintings [paintings *of* or *by* the artist]

15a Use the apostrophe to indicate the possessive case.

In general, a noun or a pronoun does not come immediately before another noun or pronoun: we do not write "children books" or "artist painting." When we do need to use a noun or pronoun before another noun or pronoun, we make the first one possessive by using an apostrophe. In a sense, we say that the first noun or pronoun owns the second one.

> parent's duty [duty of one parent]
> parents' duty [duty of two or more parents]
> everyone's duty [duty of everyone]
> crater's edge [edge of the crater]
> craters' edges [edges of the craters]

(1) Add the apostrophe and an *s* (*'s*) to a noun or indefinite pronoun to indicate the singular possessive case. (See the list of indefinite pronouns in the Appendix.)

> The poet's picture hung on the president's wall.
> One's questions often go unanswered.

Option: To form the possessive case of a singular noun that ends in *s*, add either the apostrophe and *s* or only the apostrophe.

> James' essay   OR   James's essay

(2) Add the apostrophe (') to all plural nouns that end in *s* to indicate the plural possessive case. Add the apostrophe and an *s* (*'s*) to all plural nouns not ending in *s* to indicate the plural possessive case.

Always form the plural of the noun first. Then, if the plural noun ends in *s*, add only the apostrophe to show the possessive case.

> photographer [singular]   photographers [plural]
> dignitary [singular]   dignitaries [plural]
> The photographers' pictures hung in several dignitaries' offices.

If the plural noun does not end in *s*, add the apostrophe and an *s* to show the possessive case.

man [singular]   men [plural]
woman [singular]   women [plural]
Men*'s* and women*'s* art work will be exhibited next week in the Art Barn.

(3) Add the apostrophe and an *s* to the last word of compounds or word groups.

my father-in-law*'s* car
someone else*'s* turn
the secretary of state*'s* position

(4) Add the apostrophe and an *s* to each name to indicate individual ownership, but to only the final name to indicate joint ownership.

Anita*'s* and Alejandro*'s* classes are studying the Black Fox wetlands.   [Anita and Alejandro are in different classes.].
Anita and Alejandro*'s* class is studying the Black Fox wetlands.   [Anita and Alejandro are in the same class.]

15b Use the apostrophe to indicate omissions in contracted words and numerals.

Be careful to place the apostrophe exactly where the omission occurs.

The class of *'94* [1994] *can't* [can not] decide what to include in the time capsule *that's* [that is] to be buried on the town square.

15c Use the apostrophe and an *s* to form the plural of lowercase letters. If needed to prevent confusion, the apostrophe and an *s* can be used to form the plural of figures, symbols, abbreviations, and words referred to as words, but frequently only an *s* is added.

final *k's*
the 1970*'s*   OR   the 1970s
V.F.W.*'s*   OR   V.F.W.s
and's   OR   *ands*

15d The apostrophe is not needed for possessive pronouns—*his, hers, its, ours, yours, theirs,* and *whose*—or for plural pronouns not in the possessive case.

Whose messages are these—*yours* or *theirs*?
Her department regularly held *its* reception at the *Kims*.   [*Kims* is plural but not possessive.]

Apostrophes

NAME _____ SCORE _____

DIRECTIONS   Add all apostrophes needed in the following sentences. In the blank enter each word, number, or letter to which you have added an apostrophe. Be careful not to add needless apostrophes. If a sentence is correct, write C in the blank.

EXAMPLE

There's no apostrophe after the *s* in the word group "ethics rules." _____there's_____

1. James Tiptree, Jr.s biography is a story of multiple successes. _____Jr.'s_____

2. The Science Fiction Writers of America annually award their highest honor, The Nebula Award, to writers in a variety of genres. _____writers'_____

3. Tiptrees work has earned several Nebulas. _____Tiptree's_____

4. Nebula Awards for best short story (1973), best novella (1976), and best novelette (1977) confirmed fans high regard for Tiptree. _____

5. The writers biography includes an exotic childhood. _____writer's_____

6. She spent her childhood in Africa and India on her parents typically adventurous expeditions. _____C_____

7. As an adult she has lead an adventurous life equal to her parents. _____C_____

8. Her fictions success often derives from her ability to involve readers in foreign cultures. _____

9. This ability to engage readers sympathies in foreign cultures has caught the attention of critics. _____readers'_____

10. Tiptree, whose real name is Alice Sheldon, chose a male *nom de plume* as writers camouflage. _____C_____

11. A mans writing, she believes, is more easily accepted, is even considered as normative. — *man's*

12. Readers, however, believe that a woman cannot naturally write like a man. — *C*

13. A mans fiction may be concerned with universal motives. — *man's*

14. If a woman writes of universal motives, she is accused of imitating a male writer. — *C*

15. Sheldons decision to adopt a male name enabled her to avoid the issue of gender. — *Sheldon's*

16. She wanted readers to judge her stories worth and not to concern themselves with her gender. — *C*

17. Tiptree also is well known for her assumptions about her readers experiences and sensibilities. — *readers'*

18. The writers travels enable her to fill her stories with geographical and cultural details which she expects her readers to come to understand and to share. —

19. A woman writer who presumes so much about her audiences experiences often is labeled an elitist. — *C*

20. A man who makes similar assumptions will earn the critics applause as being erudite and sophisticated. — *C*

Apostrophes

NAME _____ SCORE _____

DIRECTIONS   Rewrite the following word groups as a noun or a pronoun preceded by another noun or pronoun in the possessive case.

EXAMPLES

a responsibility of everybody

everybody's responsibility

the responsibilities of the United Nations

the United Nations' responsibilities

OR

the United Nations's responsibilities

1. the records of NOW

   the NOW's records

2. a poem by Sharon Olds

   Sharon Olds's poems

3. the green card of the musician

4. the representative of the United States

5. the burial mounds of the Iroquois

6. an invitation sent by Mr. and Mrs. Gonzales

7. the sari of the Hindu

8. an address by the governor of Massachusetts

9. the interests of the activists

10. a telescope shared by Martin and Chandra

11. the example of the women

12. a reunion at the Burtons

13. opinions held by one

14. the dome of the mosque

15. the computers of Zeos

16. the riddle of the Sphinx

17. the visits of Anna and Adam to Berkeley

18. the lawn mower of the son-in-law

19. the hood of the Toyota

20. the word processor of Nguyen

16

Learn to use quotation marks to set off all direct quotations, titles of short works, and words used in a special sense, and to place other marks of punctuation in proper relation to quotation marks.

When you use quotation marks, you let your reader know that you are quoting directly (that is, you are stating in the exact words) what someone has written, said, or thought.

> "Will you return this book to the library for me?" Gabrielle asked.
> "I'll be glad to," I told her. But I thought to myself, "I think I will check it out in my name and read it this weekend."

16a Use quotation marks for direct quotations and in all dialogue. Set off long quotations by indention.

(1) Use double quotation marks (" ") before and after all direct quotations; use a single quotation mark (' ') before and after a quotation within a quotation.

INDIRECT QUOTATION	She asked me if I wanted to visit Nashville.
INDIRECT QUOTATION	I told her that we could drive there this afternoon. [*That* frequently introduces an indirect quotation.]
DIRECT QUOTATION	She asked me, "Do you want to visit Nashville?"
DIRECT QUOTATION	The tour guide booklet recommends a visit to the Grand Ole Opry, "the longest running radio broadcast in America." [A phrase from the booklet is quoted.]
QUOTATION WITHIN A QUOTATION	David asked, "Did you see the exhibit 'Mississippi Plains Indians' in the Cumberland Museum?"

(2) In quoting dialogue (conversation), a new paragraph begins each time the speaker changes.

> Eleven-year-old Juan proudly announced to his brother, "I scored 9,700 points today on the new computer game."
> "That's great. You even beat Julio's best score," replied nine-year-old Andrew.
> "When we get home from school today, I'll show you how to play," promised Juan.
> "Okay, but I will have to do my homework first," said Andrew, "and then you can show me."

Note: Commas set off expressions such as *he said* that introduce, interrupt, or follow direct quotations.

> Their mother reminded, "Boys, be sure to turn off the computer before you go to bed."
> "Boys," their mother reminded, "be sure to turn off the computer before you go to bed."
> "Boys, be sure to turn off the computer before you go to bed," reminded their mother.

If the quoted speech is a question or an exclamation, a question mark or exclamation point—instead of a comma—follows the quoted passage.

> "John, do not lay that magnet on the computer!" cautioned Vinh. "It could ruin your hard disk."

Caution: Remember that a divided quotation made up of two main clauses or two complete sentences must be punctuated with a semicolon or an end mark.

> "A magnet can ruin a hard drive or floppy disk," Andrew added; "it also can affect the monitor."

OR

> "A magnet can ruin a hard drive or floppy disk," Andrew added. "It can also affect the monitor."

(3) Prose quotations that would require four or more lines of typing and poetry that would require four or more lines are indented from the rest of the text.

Prose When you quote one paragraph or less, all lines of a long quotation (more than four lines) are indented ten spaces from the left margin and are double-spaced. When you quote two or more paragraphs, indent the first line of each complete paragraph thirteen spaces rather than the usual ten. Use quotation marks only if they appear in the original. (If the quotation is run in with the text, remember that it should begin and end with a double quotation mark.)

In <u>The Creators</u>, Daniel Boorstin devotes chapters to important individuals in the creative history of Western civilization. He begins his discussion of Charles Dickens by alluding to G. K. Chesterton's estimate of Dickens.

> Even if Dickens had not been a great event in English literature, he would be a great event in English history. For, as G. K. Chesterton reminds us, "the man lead a mob. He did what no English statesman, perhaps, has really done: he called out the people." Dickens' career was a grand literary love affair with the English public, not just the reading public but the whole listening public (364).

Poetry Fewer than four lines of poetry may be run into the text. If run in, the quoted material should begin and end with a double quotation mark. Use quotation marks only if they appear in the original.

The classical poet Sappho often wrote brief poems whose effect depended on metaphorical contrast. In this poem she describes love in terms of a serpent's venom which she describes as "irresistible / and bittersweet / that loosener / of limbs." [Use a slash to mark the end of a line when poetry is run into the text.]

OR

```
The classical poet Sappho was particularly skilled at extending a
metaphor as the central structure for an entire poem. Here she
compares love to a serpent's venom:
```

> With his venom
> Irresistible
> and bittersweet
> that loosener
> of limbs, Love
> reptile-like
> strikes me down

16b Use quotation marks for minor titles—of short works such as television shows, short stories, essays, short poems, one-act plays, songs, articles from periodiocals—and for subdivisions of books.

For her senior thesis Shana examined the poems in Sharon Olds's collection *The Dead and the Living* and concentrated on "New Mother" and "Ecstasy."

Beth Nielsen Chapman writes and sings beautiful songs about sometimes surprising subjects. In "Child Again" she sings of an elderly woman in a nursing home, in "Emily" she sings of visiting a sick friend, and somehow both songs are hauntingly beautiful.

16c Use quotation marks to enclose words used in a special sense.

The term "research paper" is broadly applied to anything from a three-source, five-page paper to a one-hundred-source, book-length doctoral dissertation. [*Research paper* may be either italicized or enclosed in quotation marks: see chapter **10**.]

Avoid the tendency some writers have of using quotation marks freely throughout a paper to call attention to what they consider clever phrasings. Often what they think are clever phrases are really only trite expressions, slang, or colloquialisms that could be better phrased. (See also **20c**.)

INEFFECTIVE   The computer was "up to" more of its "strange" ways: it "wasted" crew members one by one.

BETTER   The computer demonstrated a terrifying intelligence: it killed the crew methodically and mercilessly.

16d Do not overuse quotation marks.

Quotation marks are not used for titles that head compositions. Quotation marks also are not used to enclose a cliché or to mark a *yes* or *no* in indirect discourse.

Yes, he did accuse her of beating around the bush.

NOT

"Yes," he did accuse her of "beating around the bush."

16e Follow the conventions of American printers in deciding whether various marks of punctuation belong inside or outside the quotation marks.

(1) The period and the comma are usually placed inside the quotation marks.

"Well," he said, "I am ready to hear Jill McCorkle read from her new novel."

Exception: If you are citing a page reference for a quotation, place the comma or the period after the page citation—and thus after the quotation marks.

McCorkle's *Ferris Beach* begins, "Our neighborhood was never the same after Misty Rhodes and her family moved in across the street" (1).

(2) The semicolon and the colon are placed outside the quotation marks.

He read the instructions on the VHS cassette labeled "Jill McCorkle": "Return by Wednesday, 3:00 P.M."

Another cassette was labeled "Lee Smith"; it contained a tape of her recent reading at the Southern Festival of Books.

(3) The dash, the question mark, and the exclamation point are placed inside the quotation marks when they apply to the quoted matter and outside the quotation marks when they apply to the whole sentence.

"Where is my saddle?" asked Nadia.   [The question mark applies to the quoted material.]

Did you notice the bill marked "Pay today"?   [The question mark applies to the whole sentence.]

At what point did he say, "Why are you telling me this?"   [a question within a question—one question mark inside the quotation marks]

Quotation Marks   Exercise 16–1

NAME _____   SCORE _____

DIRECTIONS   In the sentences below, insert all needed quotation marks. Then enter the quotation marks and the first and last word of each quoted part in the blanks. Be sure to include the other marks of punctuation used with the quotation marks in their proper position—either inside or outside the quotation marks. Do not enclose an indirect quotation. Write *C* in the blank if a sentence is correct without quotation marks.

EXAMPLE

My father-in-law always said, "That was mighty good Mrs.
Pearson," as he rose to leave the table after the noon meal.   *"That-Pearson,"*

1. For a story in her creative writing class, Vicki tried to capture the dialect and regional language that she had heard as a child. For example, one of her characters sprayed two fighting dogs with a hose-pipe, a term used for garden hose.   *C*

2. The main character is an old woman who greets her husband after a long day with the question, Well, have ye et yet?   *"Well – yet?"*

3. There is much talk of food. Mrs. Burton refers to a mixture of turnip greens, collards, and mustard greens as simply greens.   *"greens,"*

4. Be sure to put some fatback in them greens, Mr. Burton reminds her. I can't rightly do without my fatback.   *"Bo – greens,"*

5. Although Mr. Burton seems perfectly healthy, Mrs. Burton seems convinced his end is imminent. She often prefaces her sentences with the remark, When something happens to John. . . .   *"When – John"*

6. Now Lavinia, he will say, ain't nothing going to happen to me anytime soon.   *"Now – Lavinia"*
     "ain't – soon"

7. Mr. Burton is also fond of naming machinery that he uses. The most memorable names include: "Fred" for his tiller, "Roy" for his car, and "Metamucil" for his band saw.

C ✓

_____

8. This tendency toward the bizarre in naming applies to the names for their children. The daughter is Lourlene Lavinia Burton II referred to by the term Precious; the son is George Washington Burton, referred to as Big Man.

"Precious", "Big Man"

9. Mrs. Burton loves to meet acquaintances in Kroger and hold up the checkout line while she recounts the latest exploits of Precious and Big Man. You know I don't like to brag, she'll say, but have I told you about Precious's latest little accomplishment?

"You – brag"
"but – accomplishment?"

10. The Burtons are composites of many people that I knew growing up, Vicki has told me.

C

17

Learn to use the period, the question mark, the exclamation point, the colon, the dash, parentheses, brackets, the slash, and ellipsis points in accordance with conventional practices.

The end marks of punctuation give most writers little difficulty except when they are used with direct quotations.

17a The period follows declarative and mildly imperative (command) sentences, indirect questions, and many abbreviations.

DECLARATIVE SENTENCE	Shane Cleaveland, director of the Stones River Creative Writing Program, explains that this semester his students will focus on poetry by women writers.
MILDLY IMPERATIVE SENTENCE	Read about Cleaveland's plans for the poetry reading next week.
INDIRECT QUESTION	He was asked if Marge Piercy will attend.
ABBREVIATION	Dr. Montgomery also will give a reading of her poetry at 7:00 P.M. under the tent on the green.

17b The question mark follows direct (but not indirect) questions.

DIRECT QUESTION	Would you like to attend the readings?
QUOTED QUESTION	"Will there be an autograph session after Nikki Giovanni reads?" I wondered. [No comma or period follows the question mark used at the end of a quoted passage.]

Sometimes a declarative or imperative sentence can be made into a question by simply changing the period to a question mark.

The Women's Caucus helped plan the semester? [Compare "Did the Women's Caucus help plan the semester?" in which the verb must change to form a question.]

17c The exclamation point follows emphatic interjections and statements of strong emotion.

Sharon Olds's first collection of poetry received the Lamont Poetry Selection award. Amazing!

"Bravo!" cried the audience after a performance of the dance group Blue Moves. [No comma or period follows the exclamation point used at the end of a quoted passage.]

Avoid using an exclamation point just to make your writing sound exciting or important.

Galway Kinnell is one of Carla's favorite poets, and she got a letter from him yesterday. [The content of the sentence, not an exclamation point at the end, communicates the writer's belief in the importance of the facts.]

OTHER MARKS

Of the internal marks of punctuation (those that do not mark the end of a sentence), the semicolon (see chapter **14**), the colon, and the dash are most closely related to the period because they bring the reader to a full stop—rather than to a pause as the comma does. Notice the difference between the way you read aloud a sentence that has a comma and one that has a colon, a dash, or a semicolon.

The first poet was introduced by Carolyn Dowd, a recent recipient of a Peck Research Award.   [a slight pause for the comma]

The Peck Committee named three recipients of the award: Carolyn Dowd, Robert Goodman, and William Prather. [a full stop for the colon]

The award carries a large stipend—considerably more than the teaching assistantship; therefore, the research assistants can devote full time to their scholarly work.   [a full stop for the dash and for the semicolon]

You have already studied the comma (chapter **12**) and the semicolon (chapter **14**). As you learn about the other commonly used marks of internal punctuation, you will become aware of the overlapping functions of some punctuation marks—that is, of the occasions when several different marks of punctuation are appropriate.

17d The colon, following a main clause, formally introduces a word, a phrase, a clause, or a list. It is also used to separate figures in scriptural and time references and to introduce some quoted sentences.

Following a main clause or sentence pattern, the colon and the dash often may be used interchangeably. The colon is a more formal mark of punctuation than the dash.

For one very good reason the poetry readings are being held in March: it is National Women's History month.   [The dash is not generally used when a main clause is being introduced.]

Tonight's readings under the tent will feature three poets: Rita Dove, Cathy Song, and Louise Erdich.   [A dash could also be used to introduce this list.]

Corky thought of perfect lighting for the path out to the tent: candles in paper bags lining the path.

All across campus posters advertise the readings: "Poetry Reading Tonight Under the Tent—Follow the Yellow Brick Road."   [The dash is not used to introduce quotations, but it perfectly complements the message of the poster.]

Except for this last example, in which a quotation is introduced following an expression such as *he said* (in this case, *posters advertise*), there is no reason to interrupt a sentence with a colon. Do not use a colon between a subject and verb or between a verb and its complement or object.

> Tonight's reading will present several local poets, will teach our students how to respond to a reading, and will also inspire some of them to want some day to be a reader of their own work.   [A colon after *reading* would interrupt the sentence pattern.]
>
> Tonight's reading has at least three goals: it will introduce several local poets; it will teach our students how to respond to a reading; and it will inspire our students to want some day to read their own poetry at such a gathering. [The colon introduces a list of main clauses following a main sentence pattern.]

The colon is also used between chapter and verse in scriptural passages and between hours and minutes in time references.

> John 3:16
> 2:15 P.M.

17e Like the colon, the dash may introduce a word, a phrase, a clause, or a list that follows a sentence pattern; unlike the colon, it may interrupt a sentence pattern to mark a sudden break in thought, to set off a parenthetical element for emphasis or clarity, or to set off an introductory list.

> When I read, I am not nervous—unless someone gets up and leaves noisily just as I begin—then I become a nervous wreck.   [Dashes, or sometimes parentheses, are used to set off a sudden break in thought.]
>
> The three judges—Alvarez, Gendron, and Pappas—will be in the first row.   [Colons are not used here because they would interrupt the sentence pattern. Commas are not used because the list itself contains commas. Parentheses could be used: see **17f**.]
>
> Alvarez, Gendron, and Pappas—they are the three judges, and they will be sitting in the front row.   [The colon is not used here because it would interrupt the sentence pattern. Use the dash when an introductory list precedes the sentence pattern.]
>
> Look into the tent, in the front row, and you will see the three judges—Alvarez, Gendron, and Pappas.   [The colon is also appropriate here to set off a list following the sentence pattern.]

17f Parentheses (1) set off supplementary or illustrative matter, (2) sometimes set off parenthetical matter, and (3) enclose figures or letters used for numbering, as in this rule.

The primary use of the parentheses is to set off supplementary or illustrative material that is loosely joined to the sentence.

> Claustrophobia (the fear of confined spaces) affected a woman on the elevator today. [The parentheses set off the definition; commas could also be used.]
>
> More women than men admit to having xanthelasma (see definition on preceding page). [A lowercase letter begins the information in parentheses when the material in parentheses forms a part of the sentence.]

Parenthetical matter   Three marks of punctuation are used to set off parenthetical matter. The most commonly used are commas, which cause the reader only to pause and so keep the parenthetical matter closely related to the sentence. The least frequently used are parentheses, which minimize the importance of the parenthetical matter by setting it off distinctly from the sentence. Dashes, the third mark used to enclose parenthetical matter, emphasize the parenthetical matter, since they cause the reader to stop at the beginning and the end of the matter. (Remember that dashes, or sometimes parentheses, are necessary not only for emphasis but for clarity when the parenthetical matter itself includes commas.)

> Women are more willing than men**,** as studies have shown**,** to admit their fears. [Commas would be used by most writers to set off this parenthetical matter.]
>
> Women are more willing than men **(**as studies have shown**)** to admit their fears. [Parentheses minimize the importance of the parenthetical matter.]
>
> Women are more willing than men—as studies have shown—to admit their fears. [Dashes emphasize the parenthetical matter.]
>
> Many factors—such as the size of the audience, the importance of the conference, the quality of her introduction—affect Diana when she reads her poetry.   [Dashes are needed for clarity to enclose the parenthetical matter that contains commas. Parentheses could also be used, but they would minimize the importance of the list of factors.]

17g Brackets set off editorial comments in quoted matter.

When you need to explain something about a quotation, enclose your explanation within brackets to show that it is not part of the quoted matter.

> In Jill McCorkle's story "Migration of the Love Bugs," the narrator says, "My husband and I live in a tin can **[**a mobile home**]**. He calls it the streamline model, the top of the line, the cream of the crop when it comes to moveable homes." [The writer of the sentence added *a mobile home* to explain *tin can*.]

17h The slash indicates options and shows the end of a line of poetry run in with the text. (See also 16a.)

> James Wright laments in "Small Frogs Killed on the Highway" the innumerable deaths of the small animals, but he can understand what makes them long to cross the road: "It is everything, the wet green stalk of the field **/** On the other side of the road. **/** They crouch there, too, faltering in terror **/** And take strange wing."   [Note the space before and after each slash in the poetry.]

17i Use ellipsis points (three spaced periods) to mark an omission from a quoted passage and to mark a reflective pause or hesitation.

> The old man looked away, rocking gently, resting his head against the ladderback chair. "Well, maybe I have **. . .** maybe I haven't," he said. "I disremember."
>
> —ROBERT HERRING

> Jill McCorkle's story "Comparison Shopping," like many of her stories, is filled with pop culture references. For example, the narrator says to a prospective boy friend, "You ought to be on *Jeopardy* **. . .** You know more than God."

If ellipsis points are used to indicate that the end of a quoted sentence is being omitted, and if the part that is quoted forms a complete sentence itself, use the sentence period plus ellipsis points.

> Equally good are Dickstein's chapters on reviewers and journalists. . . .
>
> —THE NEW YORK REVIEW OF BOOKS

End Marks of Punctuation

NAME _____ SCORE _____

DIRECTIONS   Write a sentence to illustrate each of the following uses of an end mark of punctuation.

EXAMPLE
a quoted direct question

Victoria asked, "Are you going to hear Galway Kinnell tonight?"

1. a mildly imperative sentence

2. a direct question

3. a sentence containing an abbreviation

4. an exclamation

5. a declarative sentence

6. an indirect quotation

7. a declarative sentence containing a quoted direct question

8. an indirect question

9. a declarative sentence containing a quoted exclamation

10. a quotation that includes the ellipsis mark

Internal Marks of Punctuation   Exercise 17–2

NAME _____ SCORE _____

DIRECTIONS   In the sentences below insert commas, semicolons, dashes, parentheses, and brackets, as needed. Then enter in the blanks the mark or marks you have added. If more than one punctuation mark is possible, choose the one you think most writers would use, but be prepared to discuss the effect of the other possible choice or choices.

EXAMPLE

Rita Dove's poems, her readers usually realize, are mysterious.   ____ , , ____

1. Although they are mysterious they also are understandable.   _____

2. She seems intent on generating wonder and enjoyment in her readers she is not interested in perplexing them.   _____

3. The first two lines of "The Secret Garden" describe the poet "I was ill, lying on my bed of old papers / when you came with white rabbits in your arms."   _____

4. The lover ministers to the ailing poet with teabags tomatoes and chalk.   _____

5. Dove's sense of the injustices committed throughout history also inspire her poetry she often brings historical figures alive for a few lines.   _____

6. One critic believes that "it history is the driving force in many of her poems."   _____

7. Benjamin Banneker 1731-1806 the first African American man to devise an almanac and predict an eclipse is the subject of one poem.   _____

8. In the poem Banneker an eccentric figure seems somewhat at odds with the world about him.   _____

9. He is rumored to be a drinker he refuses to take a wife and he goes out at night to shoot at stars.   _____

10. But Dove suggests he is imagining great works.   _____

11. In her note Dove tells us that Banneker served on the commission that surveyed what is now Washington D.C. _____

12. Washington was built on a low-lying piece of land what some people ungraciously call a swamp. _____

13. But Banneker envisions emerging from that swamp a domed citadel the capital of a nation. _____

14. Rafael Trujillo 1891-1961 inspires another poem. _____

15. Apparently looking for an excuse to murder black Dominicans in 1957 he had 20,000 of them killed because they could not pronounce the "r" in "perejil" the Spanish word for *parsley*. _____

SPELLING AND HYPHENATION   sp 18

18

Learn to spell and hyphenate in accordance with the usage shown in an up-to-date dictionary.

Everyone notices the sign that invites you to eat at the "Resturant" or the one that offers "Wood for Sell." And, right or wrong, most people tend to brand both the owner and the maker of such a sign as uneducated. There is simply no other error in composition that is so universally recognized and deplored as the misspelled word. Because of the stigma of illiteracy that it carries, misspelling should be the first and most important concern of any poor speller.

If you are a poor speller, one who regularly misspells enough words to have your classwork or professional work suffer, you should begin a definite program for improving your spelling skills. There are many excellent spelling manuals available today that make use of the latest psychological studies to present words in a logical, easy-to-learn order.

You may also find the following procedures helpful.

(1) Learn the rules of spelling presented in this section of the book.

(2) Proofread your papers carefully at least once for misspelled words only.

As you write a rough draft, it is often difficult, and always distracting, to look up a great number of words, but you can put a check or some other identifying sign above those words you have any doubts about so that you can look up their spelling when you proofread.

If you have difficulty spotting misspelled words in your own composition, try to slow down your reading of the rough draft by pointing to each word with a pencil. Or even read your writing from right to left instead of the usual left to right to be sure that you see individual words rather than groups of words. You need, whenever possible, to make more than two drafts of your paper because you will be unlikely to see your errors in a rough draft that has many words and phrases crossed through or that has barely legible handwriting.

(3) Keep a list of the words you tend to misspell.

The words that you misspell on your writing assignments should be recorded in the Individual Spelling List at the end of this *Workbook*. Because most people have a tendency to misspell certain words repeatedly, you should review your own spelling list frequently to break your bad spelling habits.

A comparison of your spelling list with someone else's will usually show—surprisingly enough—only two or three words in common. The mastery of spelling is an individual matter, differing with each person. You get some benefit from mastering lists of frequently misspelled words, but your own Individual Spelling List is the all-important one for you to work with.

(4) Write the words you misspell by syllables; then write the definitions of the words; finally, use the words in sentences.

E NIG MAT IC   puzzling or baffling   [My boss's behavior toward me was *enigmatic* until she sat down and explained what she expected of me.]

AT TRIB UTE   as a noun, an object or quality that belongs to or represents someone or something   [The *attributes* of Santa Claus have been expanded over the years.]

On the following pages are rules that will help you to avoid misspelling many commonly used words. Following the explanation of each rule is an exercise to reinforce the rule in your mind.

Misspelling Because of Mispronunciation   Exercise 18–1

NAME _____   SCORE _____

18a To avoid omitting, adding, transposing, or changing a letter in a word, pronounce the word carefully according to the way the dictionary divides it into syllables.

The places where common mistakes are made in pronunciation—and spelling—are indicated in boldface.

OMISSIONS	can**di**date, ever**y**thing, govern**m**ent
ADDITIONS	ath**l**ete, laun**d**ry, drow**n**ed
TRANSPOSITIONS	**per**form. child**ren**, trag**ed**y
CHANGES	acc**u**rate, pre**j**udice, sep**a**rate

DIRECTIONS   With the aid of your dictionary, write out each of the following words by syllables, indicate the position of the primary accent, and pronounce the word correctly and distinctly. In your pronunciation avoid any careless omission, addition, transposition, or change.

EXAMPLE
similar   sim´i•lar

1. supposedly   _____

2. prisoner   _____

3. environment   _____

4. destruction   _____

5. escape   _____

6. circumstance   _____

7. surprise   _____

8. further   _____

9. candidate   _____

10. recognize   _____

11. temperament   _____

12. asked   _____

13. interpret   _____

14. perhaps   _____

15. prepare   _____

16. partner   _____

17. describe   _____

18. especially   _____

19. mischievous   _____

20. family   _____

21. prescription   _____

22. used   _____

23. hindrance   _____

24. interest   _____

25. athletic   _____

26. hungry   _____

27. library   _____

28. represent   _____

29. sophomore   _____

30. accidentally   _____

Confusion of Words Similar in Sound and/or Spelling   Exercise 18–2

NAME _____   SCORE _____

18b Distinguish between words that have a similar sound and/or spelling, such as *lose-loose* and *to-too-two.*

DIRECTIONS   In the following sentences, cross out the spelling or spellings in parentheses that do not fit the meaning, and write the correct spelling in the blank. Consult your dictionary freely.

EXAMPLE

In April the city council announced that it was (~~holey~~, wholly, ~~holy~~) committed to building a senior citizens' center.   _____wholly_____

1. As we (herd, heard) the news we applauded.   _____

2. From a few pessimists there immediately came the (prophesy, prophecy) that it would never be built.   _____

3. But the general (affect, effect) of the announcement was positive.   _____

4. Those of us who had lived (through, threw) the previous mayor's administration felt vindicated.   _____

5. He had managed to (loose, lose) federal matching funds for the center.   _____

6. There were other (instances, instants) of mismanagement of funds that made us all despair.   _____

7. Now we already are thinking about the logo that will adorn the new center's (stationary, stationery).   _____

8. All the printers in town (except, accept) one have offered free services to design the logo.   _____

9. And two lawyers have offered, temporarily, to provide free services as legal (counsel, council).   _____

10. Of more immediate concern is (advise, advice) about the building's location.   _____

11. We need to choose the (site, cite, sight) carefully. _____

12. Anyone with good (ideals, ideas) should contact us by
    next Friday. _____

13. Our (principal, principle) concern is accessibility for
    the entire town. _____

14. We believe this center will raise the (moral, morale) of
    everyone. _____

15. All of us are (conscience, conscious) of our obligation
    to the public. _____

Adding Prefixes   Exercise 18–3

NAME _____ SCORE _____

18c Add the prefix to the root word without doubling or adding letters. (The root is the base word to which the prefix or suffix is added.)

un-	+	necessary	=	unnecessary
mis-	+	spell	=	misspell
dis-	+	agree	=	disagree

DIRECTIONS   In the blank at the right enter the correct spelling of each word with the prefix added. Consult your dictionary freely. Some dictionaries hyphenate some of the following words (see also **18f**).

EXAMPLES

mis- + quote _____ misquote _____

pre- + eminent _____ preeminent _____

1. dis- + satisfied _____

2. dis- + appear _____

3. mis- + pronounce _____

4. mis- + understand _____

5. mis- + step _____

6. un- + noticed _____

7. un- + usual _____

8. dis- + approve _____

9. dis- + similar _____

10. mis- + spent _____

11. mis- + behave   _____

12. dis- + able   _____

13. mis- + interpret   _____

14. re- + take   _____

15. re- + evaluate   _____

Adding Suffixes—Final *e*

Exercise 18–4

NAME _____ SCORE _____

18d(1) Drop the final *e* before a suffix beginning with a vowel but not before a suffix beginning with a consonant.

bride	+	-al	=	bridal	fame	+	-ous	=	famous
care	+	-ful	=	careful	entire	+	-ly	=	entirely

Exceptions: *due, duly; awe, awful; hoe, hoeing; singe, singeing.* After *c* or *g* the final *e* is retained before suffixes beginning with *a* or *o*: *notice, noticeable; courage, courageous.*

DIRECTIONS   With the aid of your dictionary, write the correct spelling of each word with the suffix added. Write *(ex)* after each answer that is an exception to rule **18d(1)**.

EXAMPLES

argue + -ing _____ arguing _____

dye + -ing _____ dyeing (ex) _____

1. become + -ing _____

2. use + -age _____

3. hope + -ing _____

4. excite + -able _____

5. drive + -ing _____

6. outrage + -ous _____

7. like + -ly _____

8. write + -ing _____

9. advise + -able _____

10. arrange + -ment _____

SPELLING AND HYPHENATION

11. value   + -able   _____

12. manage   + -ment   _____

13. advantage + -ous   _____

14. judge   + -ment   _____

15. extreme   + -ly   _____

Adding Suffixes—Doubling the Consonant

Exercise 18–5

NAME _____ SCORE _____

18d(2) When the suffix begins with a vowel (*ing, ed, ence, ance, able*), double a final single consonant if it is preceded by a single vowel and is in an accented syllable. (A word of one syllable, of course, is always accented.)

mop, mo**pp**ed   [compare with *mope, moped*]
mop, mo**pp**ing   [compare with *mope, moping*]
con•fer´, con•fer´red   [final consonant in the accented syllable]
ben´e•fit; ben´e•fited   [final consonant not in the accented syllable]
need, needed   [final consonant not preceded by a single vowel]

DIRECTIONS   In the blank at the right enter the correct spelling of each word with the suffix added. Consult your dictionary freely.

EXAMPLE

control   + -ed   _____ controlled _____

1. stop   + -ing   _____

2. occur   + -ing   _____

3. pour   + -ing   _____

4. proceed   + -ed   _____

5. unforget   + -able   _____

6. begin   + -ing   _____

7. control   + -able   _____

8. transmit   + -ing   _____

9. equip   + -ed   _____

10. meet   + -ing   _____

11. prefer   + -ed   _____

12. big   + -est   _____

13. push   + -ed   _____

14. fat   + -er   _____

15. attach   + -ed   _____

Adding Suffixes—Final *y*

NAME _____ SCORE _____

18d(3) Except before *ing*, final *y* preceded by a consonant is changed to *i* before a suffix.

defy + -ance = defiance	happy + -ness = happiness
modify + -er = modifier	modify + -ing = modifying

To make a noun plural or a verb singular, final *y* preceded by a consonant is changed to *i* and *es* is added (see also **18d[4]**).

duty + -es = duties	deny + -es = denies
ally + -es = allies	copy + -es = copies

Final *y* preceded by a vowel is usually not changed before a suffix.

annoy + -ed = annoyed   turkey + -s = turkeys

Exceptions: *pay, paid; lay, laid; say, said; day, daily.*

DIRECTIONS   With the aid of your dictionary, enter the correct spelling of each word with the suffix added. Write (*ex*) after each word that is an exception to rule **18d(3)**.

EXAMPLES

boundary   + -es   _boundaries_

pay   + -d   _paid (ex)_

1. monkey   + -s   _____

2. try   + -es   _____

3. accompany + -es   _____

4. chimney   + -s   _____

5. bury   + -ed   _____

6. lay   + -ed   _____

7. fallacy   + -es   _____

8. hungry   + -ly   _____

9. lonely   + -ness   _____

10. donkey   + -s   _____

Forming the Plural

NAME _____ SCORE _____

18d(4) Form the plural of most nouns by (1) adding *s* to the singular form of the noun, (2) adding *es* to singular nouns ending in *s, ch, sh,* or *x,* or (3) changing the *y* to *i* and adding *es* if the noun ends in a *y* preceded by a consonant.

boy→boys	fox→foxes	mystery→mysteries
cupful→cupfuls	Harris→Harrises	beauty→beauties
Drehmel→Drehmels	genius→geniuses	reply→replies

A few nouns change their form for the plural: *woman→women; child→children.* And a few nouns ending in *o* take the *es* plural: *potato→potatoes; hero→heroes.* And a few nouns change an *f* to a *v* and add *s* or *es: calf→calves; knife→knives.*

DIRECTIONS   In the blank enter the plural form of each word. Consult your dictionary freely.

EXAMPLES

day   _____*days*_____

scratch   ___*scratches*___

1. speech	_____	11. question	_____
2. box	_____	12. ghetto	_____
3. industry	_____	13. article	_____
4. veto	_____	14. leaf	_____
5. wolf	_____	15. watch	_____
6. Long	_____	16. man	_____
7. witch	_____	17. professor	_____
8. scientist	_____	18. business	_____
9. address	_____	19. Jones	_____
10. city	_____	20. army	_____

Confusion of *ei* and *ie*   Exercise 18–8

NAME _____ SCORE _____

18e When the sound is *ee* (as in *see*), write *ei* after *c* (*receipt, ceiling*), and *ie* after any other letter (*relieve, priest*); when the sound is other than *ee*, usually write *ei* (*eight, their, reign*).

Exceptions: *either, neither, financier, leisure, seize, species, weird.*

Note: This rule does not apply when *ei* or *ie* is not pronounced as one simple sound (*alien, audience, fiery*) or when *cie* stands for *shə* (*ancient, conscience, efficient*).

DIRECTIONS   With the aid of your dictionary, fill in the blanks in the following words by writing *ei* or *ie*. Write (*ex*) after any word that is an exception to rule **18e**.

EXAMPLES

dec _____*ei*_____ ve

_____*ei*_____ ther (*ex*)

1. rec __*ie*_____ ve   11. th ____*ei*_____ f

2. bel _____ s   12. gr ___*ie*_____ ve

3. ch __*ie*____ f   13. spec ___*ie*_____ s

4. s _*ei*_____ ge   14. w __*ei*_____ ght

5. conc __*ei*____ ted   15. c __*ei*_____ ling

6. y __*ei*_____ ld   16. rel __*ie*_____ ve

7. gr __*ie*____ f   17. h __*ei*_____ ght

8. l _*ei*_____ sure   18. f __*ie*_____ nd

9. misch __*ie*____ f   19. n __*ei*_____ ther

10. sl __*ei*_____ gh   20. f __*ie*_____ ld

Hyphenated Words

NAME _____ SCORE _____

18f In general, use the hyphen (1) between two or more words serving as a single adjective before a noun, (2) with compound numbers from twenty-one to ninety-nine and with spelled out fractions, (3) with prefixes or suffixes for clarity, (4) with the prefixes *ex-*, *self-*, *all-*, and *great-* and the suffix *elect*, and (5) between a prefix and a proper name.

    (1) a *know-it-all* expression
    (2) *sixty-six, one-half*
    (3) *re-collect* the supplies (to distinguish from recollect an event)
    (4) *ex-wife, self-help, all-important, great-grandmother, mayor-elect*
    (5) *mid-July, un-American*

DIRECTIONS   Supply hyphens where they are needed in the following list. Not all items require hyphens.

    EXAMPLES

    a well-spent childhood

    a childhood well spent

1. a long-distance call   (*long - distance*)
2. a four foot barricade   (*four-foot*)
3. a twenty five year old coach   (*twenty - five*)
4. ex President Carter   (*ex - President*)
5. President elect Walker   (*President - elect*)
6. a high rise apartment   (*high - rise*)
7. a commonly used adjective
8. chocolate covered cherries   (*chocolate - covered*)
9. students who are career minded
10. the all seeing eye of the camera   (*all - seeing*)
11. a two thirds vote of the senate   (*two - thirds*)
12. Two thirds of the senate approved.   (*Two - thirds*)
13. western style jeans
14. the clumsily executed dance
15. He is forty five.   (*forty - five*)
16. She is my great aunt.   (*great - aunt*)

17. an all inclusive study   (all-inclusive)
18. results that are long lasting   (long-lasting)
19. long lasting results   (long-lasting)
20. My small daughter is amazingly self sufficient.   (self-sufficient)
21. The officer re searched the suspect.   (re-searched)
22. a two part answer   (two-part)
23. The answer had two parts.
24. The up and down motion of the roller coaster made her ill.   (up-and-down)
25. The shop specializes in young people's fashions.
26. I feel all right today.
27. We are all ready to go.
28. a win at any cost attitude
29. in mid December   (mid-December)
30. a walk in closet   (walk-in)

GOOD USAGE

19

Learn the ways that an up-to-date dictionary can guide you in the choice of words appropriate to your writing needs.

An up-to-date desk dictionary is a necessary reference tool for today's student and professional person. (A desk dictionary is based on one of the unabridged dictionaries, such as *Webster's Third New International,* usually found on a lectern in the library.) You have already seen how essential a current dictionary is for checking the spelling and hyphenation of words and for finding out when to abbreviate, capitalize, and italicize words. But an up-to-date dictionary serves still other purposes. For example, (1) it shows you how to pronounce a word like *harass;* (2) it lists the forms and possible uses of a verb like *sing;* (3) it explains what a given word means and gives example phrases and sentences which clarify the definition; (4) it gives the synonyms and antonyms of a word like *oppose;* (5) it gives information about a word's origin; and (6) it may provide usage labels for words like *poke, nowheres,* and *irregardless.* A desk dictionary may also supply you with miscellaneous information such as a brief history of the English language, the dates and identities of famous people, geographical facts, and lists of colleges and universities in the United States and Canada. A current desk dictionary, then, is one of the best investments you can make.

19a Learn to use an up-to-date dictionary intelligently.

Study the introductory matter to find out what your dictionary's guides to abbreviations and pronunciation are; to know what plural and tense forms your dictionary lists; to learn what attitude your dictionary takes toward usage labels (dictionaries vary in the kinds of labels they use, and some dictionaries label more words than others do); and to understand the order in which the meanings of words are listed—that is, in order of common usage or of historical development.

19b Use words that have no usage labels unless the occasion demands otherwise.

Most words (and most meanings of words) in dictionaries are unlabeled; that is, they are appropriate on any occasion because they are in general use in the English-speaking world. But some words have labels that indicate they are used (1) by people in one section of the country (*dialectal, regional,* sometimes *colloquial*); (2) by people who are often judged uneducated (*nonstandard* and *illiterate;* sometimes words in this category are not listed at all); (3) by people who use popular expressions that often do not remain long in the language (*slang*); (4) in literature from the past (*archaic, obsolete, obsolescent, rare*); or (5) by people in a specialized field of study (technical words like *pyrexia,* which a dictionary labels *pathol.* to indicate that it is a term from pathology).

When the occasion demands the use of a word that is labeled—for example, an address to a medical convention might call for technical language or even jargon—the word may be judged appropriate because the audience will understand it. But in general speaking and writing, you should depend on the multitude of unlabeled words that most audiences or readers can be expected to understand.

LABELED WORDS   *Irregardless* of what my *screwy* friend advised, I was not *fixing to* drive my *pater's* new *set of wheels* in the demolition derby.

UNLABELED WORDS   *Regardless* of what my *crazy* friend advised, I was not *about to* drive
(STANDARD)   my *father's* new *automobile* in the demolition derby.

There is one class of words—labeled *informal,* or sometimes *colloquial*—that is commonly used and understood by most writers and speakers. These words are appropriate in speaking and in informal writing and are usually necessary in recording dialogue because most people speak less formally than they write. But, in general, you should avoid words labeled in*formal* or *colloquial* in most of your college and professional writing.

INFORMAL   The student *lifted* the passage from a critic he was studying.

STANDARD OR   The student *plagiarized* the passage from a critic he was studying.
FORMAL

Except in dialogue, contractions are usually not appropriate in formal writing.

INFORMAL   *There's* hardly anyone who *doesn't* respond to a good play.

STANDARD OR   *There is* hardly anyone who *does not* respond to a good play.
FORMAL

19c Choose words and combinations of sounds that are appropriate to clear prose writing.

A poetic style is generally not appropriate in college essays or professional reports. Usually such writing seems wordy, vague, and even ridiculous.

FLOWERY   She was a *tower of power* in our community, a *blazing meteor* in a prosperous enterprise.

PLAIN BUT   She was a *powerful* woman in our community, a *remarkably*
CLEAR   *successful* businessperson.

Using the Dictionary

NAME _____ SCORE _____

The full title, the edition, and the date of publication of my dictionary are as
follows: _____

_____

1. Abbreviations Where does the dictionary explain the abbreviations it uses?

in the very beginning

Write out the meaning of each of the abbreviations following these entries:

extend, *v.t.* *to spread or stretch forth or out*

deray, *n., Obs.* _____

nohow, *adv., Dial.* _____

coracoid, *Anat., adj.* _____

2. Spelling and Pronunciation Using your dictionary, write out by syllables each of
the words listed below, and place the accent where it belongs. With the aid of the
diacritical marks, the phonetic respelling of the word (in parentheses or slashes immediately after the word), and the key at the bottom of the page or in the introductory
matter, determine the preferred pronunciation (the first pronunciation given). Then
pronounce each word correctly several times.

exquisite \ek-'skwiz-et, 'ek-(")skwiz-\

harass _____

grimace _____

pianist _____

Write the plurals of the following words:

deer _____

index _____

criterion _____

datum _____

Rewrite each of the following words that needs a hyphen:

watercolor _____

selfconscious _____

extracurricular _____

3. Derivations   The derivation, or origin, of a word (given in brackets) often furnishes a literal meaning that helps you to remember the word. For each of the following words give (a) the source—the language from which it is derived, (b) the original word or words, and (c) the original meaning.

	Source	*Original word(s) and meaning*
nefarious	____	_____
pseudonym	____	_____
deprecate	____	_____

4. Meanings   Usually words develop several different meanings. How many meanings are listed in your dictionary for the following words?

discipline, *n.* _____   spend, *v.* _____   out, *adv.* _____

tortuous, *adj.* _____   in, *prep.* _____   magazine, *n.* _____

Does your dictionary list meanings in order of historical development or of common usage? _____

5. Special Labels   Words (or certain meanings of words) may have such precautionary or explanatory labels as *Archaic, Colloquial,* or *Nautical.* What label or special usage do you find for one meaning of each word below?

lush, *n.* _____

your'n, *pro.* _____

bust, *v.* _____

ain't, *v.* _____

hisself, *pro.* _____

yare, *adj.* _____

Using the Dictionary   Exercise 19–1 (continued)

6. Synonyms   Even among words with essentially the same meaning, one word usually fits a given context more exactly than any other. To show precise shades of meaning, some dictionaries treat in special paragraphs certain groups of closely related words. What synonyms are specially differentiated in your dictionary for the following words?

consider, *v.*   _____

sharp, *adj.*   _____

7. Capitalization   Rewrite the words that can be capitalized.

history   _____

communism   _____

spartan   _____

pisces   _____

chauvinist   _____

german   _____

8. Grammatical Information   Note that many words may serve as two or more parts of speech. List the parts of speech that each of the following words may be: *v., n., adj., adv., prep., conj., interj.*

check   _____

hold   _____

off   _____

number   _____

ring   _____

right   _____

Note the grammatical information supplied by your dictionary for verbs, adjectives, and pronouns.

List the principal parts of *lie*: _____

List the principal parts of *burst*:_____

List the principal parts of *cry*: _____

List the comparative and superlative degrees of the adjective *steady*:_____

_____

List the comparative and superlative degrees of the adjective *big*: _____

_____

Should *which* be used to refer to people?_____

What is the distinction between the relative pronouns *that* and *which*?_____

_____

9. Idiomatic Expressions   List two standard idiomatic expressions for each of the following words.

wait:_____

track: _____

die: _____

10. Miscellaneous Information   Answer the following questions by referring to your dictionary. Be prepared to tell in what part of the dictionary the information is located.

In what year was Thomas Edison born? _____

Where is Normandy located? _____

What was Valhalla?_____

Does your dictionary have a history of the English language? _____

Does your dictionary have a manual of style?_____

Appropriate Usage

NAME _____ SCORE _____

DIRECTIONS If the italicized word, with the meaning it has in its particular sentence, is labeled in your dictionary in any way, enter the label (such as *informal* or *slang*) in the blank. If the word is not labeled, write *standard* in the blank. Discuss your answers in class to compare the usage labels of various dictionaries.

EXAMPLE

We have had some *mighty* heated conversations in my

English class about television.   *informal*

1. *Most* everyone has an opinion about television. _____

2. Professor Swann has focused our class on issues *kind of*

   related to multiculturalism. _____

3. She thinks that television does not do *a lot* to promote

   multiculturalism. _____

4. My roommate Jeremy thinks of *hisself* as a TV critic, so

   he is always ready for Professor Swann's class. _____

5. Today he and Professor Swann *got into it* over *Star

   Trek: The Next Generation.* _____

6. Jeremy was *disn' Trek*, and Professor Swann wanted to

   argue. _____

7. Jeremy believes that all science fiction is *stupid.* _____

8. But Professor Swann believes *Trek* is the best series on

   TV—*sort of* a *Masterpiece Theater* in space. _____

9. She has read a paper on *Trek* at a popular culture

   meeting. In the paper she explains how to teach multi-

   culturalism using the TV series, something I *woulda*

   never thought of. _____

10. She is a wonder the way she can *come up with* these

    ideas. _____

11. I *ain't* never had a teacher as effective at getting me to

think as she is.   _____

12. Because of her class, I see themes in *Trek* that I see
    nowheres else.   _____

13. Last night the episode featured Q, an alien from the
    Q–Continuum, who tries to educate by *hisself* the mor-
    tals on the *Enterprise*.   _____

14. Captain Picard, who always manages to handle Q, gave
    him a minilecture on the importance of diversity in the
    universe. Q, a study in *wheeler-dealering*, seemed
    unfazed by Picard's lecture.   _____

Appropriate Usage

Exercise 19–3

NAME _____ SCORE _____

DIRECTIONS In each sentence, choose the proper word or words from the pairs in parentheses. Cross out the incorrect word or words and write the correct one in the blank. Rely on your dictionary to help you choose the word with the correct meaning or the word that is appropriate in a formal essay.

EXAMPLE

(~~Alot, Lots of~~, Many) of us from Professor Swann's class will

watch *Star Trek: The Next Generation* tonight.   Many

1. We are (analyzing, synthesizing) the series's recurring themes.   _____

2. We have been reading fiction and poetry by writers from (various, varied) ethnic backgrounds.   _____

3. My roommate Jeremy was only (partly, partially) serious when he suggested *Trek* as a topic for discussion.   _____

4. (Surprisedly, Surprisingly) Professor Swann agreed with Jeremy.   _____

5. She told the class about a paper she is writing on *Trek* for the (eminent, imminent) meeting of the Popular Culture Association.   _____

6. She also is (corroborating, collaborating) on a book about *Trek*.   _____

7. She writes about the (concurring, recurring) theme of multiculturalism in *Star Trek*.   _____

8. Last night's episode dealt with a planet involved in (civil, civic) war.   _____

9. The planet was divided (among, between) two warring groups.   _____

10. The two (fractions, factions) had fought for so long that they had forgotten the causes of the conflict.   _____

11. The crew of the *Enterprise* tried to (meditate, mediate) the conflict. _____

12. But at every turn they were (affronted, confronted) with the problems of stereotyping and prejudice that fed the war. _____

13. Professor Swann pointed out the similarity of this plot to the (ethic, ethnic) conflicts in Europe after the fall of communism. _____

14. The mediators from the *Enterprise* were not successful in (solving, resolving) the dispute. _____

15. The episode ended (pragmatically, enigmatically) with neither the mediators nor the viewer knowing how the conflict would end. _____

EXACTNESS

20

Choose words that are exact, idiomatic, and fresh.

Since the basic unit of communication is the word, you cannot write clearly and accurately unless you have built up a vocabulary of words to express the things you think and feel. Of the 500,000 entries in an unabridged dictionary, most college students can use no more than 15,000 in speaking and writing. Building a vocabulary, then, is a lifetime process. Usually the more people read, the more words they add to their recognition vocabularies. After they have seen the same words many times in different contexts, they add these words to their active vocabularies, the words they actually use in speaking and writing.

People who do not regularly read newspapers, magazines, and books often have few words to draw from whenever they speak or write. They may complain, "I know what I mean, but I can't put it into words." They may also say that some works by professional writers are "too hard to understand." The source of their difficulty in both writing and reading is an inadequate vocabulary.

You can begin now to increase your vocabulary by noticing the words you read in your course work and by looking up definitions of all the words of which you are uncertain. Sometimes reading a difficult paragraph aloud emphasizes the words you are not familiar with and, as a result, helps you understand why the paragraph is difficult for you.

While you are increasing your recognition vocabulary, you must take great care to make the best possible use of the words in your active vocabulary.

20a Choose words that express your ideas exactly.

To express yourself exactly, you must choose the words that have the denotations (the definitions found in dictionaries) and the connotations (the mental or emotional associations that go with the words) that you intend.

PROBLEM WITH DENOTATION	The failure of the Broadway play was *contributed* to its being under-financed.
CORRECT DENOTATION	The failure of the Broadway play was *attributed* to its being under-financed.
PROBLEM WITH CONNOTATION	I took my best friend to my *domicile* for dinner.
CORRECT CONNOTATION	I took my best friend to my *home* for dinner.

Remember that a wrong word is very noticeable when it results in a ridiculous sentence (see also **18b**).

WRONG WORD	Faust pledged his *sole* to the devil in exchange for power and knowledge.
CORRECT WORD	Faust pledged his *soul* to the devil in exchange for power and knowledge.

Whenever possible you should choose concrete rather than abstract words. Abstract words refer to ideas, whereas concrete words refer to definite objects. Abstract words are necessary to state generalizations, but it is the specific word, the specific detail, the specific example that engages the reader's attention. (See also chapter **31**.)

GENERAL	Anna Luisa described Lee Smith's story "Intensive Care" as *interesting*.
SPECIFIC	Anna Luisa described Lee Smith's story "Intensive Care" as *her favorite portrayal of a man in mid-life crisis.*
GENERAL	Nancy must write *a lot* if she is to finish her novel.
SPECIFIC	Nancy must write *at least four hours each day for the next two months* if she is to finish her novel.

20b Choose words that are idiomatic.

Idiomatic expressions are phrases that you use every day without thinking about their meaning: "I *ran across* some old biology notes today" and "Manuel *played down* the importance of not balancing his checkbook." Native English speakers use expressions like these naturally; but some idioms may seem unnatural, even ridiculous, to foreigners trying to learn our language.

Even native speakers sometimes have difficulty choosing the correct prepositions to make expressions idiomatic. For example, many would write "prior than" rather than the idiomatic "prior to." The dictionary is the best guide for helping you choose the preposition that should follow a word like *prior* to make an idiomatic expression.

UNIDIOMATIC	The citations in Su-Ling's research paper did not *comply to* MLA guidelines.
IDIOMATIC	The citations in Su-Ling's research paper did not *comply with* MLA guidelines.

20c Choose fresh expressions rather than trite ones.

Many idiomatic expressions have been used so often that they have become trite— worn out and meaningless. At one time readers would have thought the expression "tried and true" was an exact and effective choice of words. But readers today have seen and heard this expression so often that they hardly notice it, except perhaps to be bored or amused by it. Clichés of this sort are common in most people's speech and may even occur at times in the work of professional writers, but they should generally be avoided because they no longer communicate ideas exactly. Beware also of political slogans, advertising jargon, and most slang expressions: they are often so overused for a brief period of time that they quickly become meaningless.

TRITE   *Last but not least* is the dedicated student who *rises at the crack of dawn* to *hit the books.*

EXACT   *Last* is the dedicated student who *rises at 6:00* A.M. to *study.*

Vocabulary Building

NAME _____   SCORE _____

DIRECTIONS   To see how becoming aware of words in your reading can lead to a better recognition vocabulary, try this experiment. Read aloud the first paragraph below, underlining the words whose meaning you are uncertain of; then look up the definitions and write them down; finally, reread the sentences in which those words appear. When you have finished with the first paragraph, go on to the second one. Notice how the words that gave you trouble in the first paragraph seem to stand out in the second paragraph, though sometimes as a different part of speech or in a different tense. If you cannot remember the definitions of the words, look again at your notes.

PARAGRAPH 1

The lone man had been walking about Oxford, Mississippi, all day, and several residents had remarked on his presence. With his long unkempt hair, corduroy jacket, and satchel of books, he appeared to them to be the quintessential graduate student or aspiring young writer. The owner of the corner store, a resident for over forty years, said he reminded him of a young Sherwood Anderson or Sinclair Lewis. He had spoken with the young man and reported him to be polite and intense with an aseptic smile. He had asked for directions to Faulkner's grave, so that confirmed him as a writer, though not as writer manqué. As night fell the young writer made his way to Faulkner's grave and knelt beside it. He took from his satchel what they later found to be a mantilla and left it on the grave enfolding a marcescent rose.

PARAGRAPH 2

The wreath over the mantle contains marcescent roses and blue bells. It smells faintly of bay leaves and salty air. They brought it back from a trip to New Orleans, the quintessential four-day vacation after a week of intense pressure at work. They had avoided Bourbon Street; instead they had visited several old Catholic churches, he in his chinos and chambray shirts, she with a delicate lace mantilla over her head. Someone in each church had greeted them warmly and had invited them to stay for service. They had responded with compliments to the architecture and aseptic smiles. When they returned from the trip, the neighbors asked about it politely over the neatly trimmed privet hedge. They had responded with comments about the weather and aseptic smiles. Their marriage, as well they know, is a marriage manqué, a failure not of tragic proportions, just a sad and emotionless union.

Correct and Exact Words

NAME _____ SCORE _____

DIRECTIONS   In the following sentences, choose the proper word or words from the pairs in parentheses. Cross out the wrong or inexact word or words and write the correct answer in the blank. Use your dictionary freely.

EXAMPLE

The (motive, ~~motif~~) for our trip was a pilgrimage.   *motive*

1. We headed west to visit the (~~sights~~, sites, ~~cites~~) of some literary works.   *sites*

2. We thought about going to Cuba first in honor ~~(to,~~ of) Hemingway.   *of*

3. But Jana pointed out that we could not drive to Cuba; besides, she said, that would be too (~~tempestuous~~, ~~contemptuous~~, impetuous).   *impetuous*

4. You have to understand that west to us means west of Charleston, our starting place, and the home town of the (~~principle~~, principal) reason for this venture.   *principal*

5. Josephine Humphreys lives in and writes about Charleston, and she is our (~~respiration~~, inspiration).   *inspiration*

6. We heard Humphreys speak last year at the Southern Festival, and she (~~conspired~~, inspired) us.   *inspired*

7. She spoke about being young and (~~careless~~, carefree).   *carefree*

8. She seemed to miss those years without responsibility, and she urged us (~~their~~, there) in the hall to be adventurous.   *there*

9. We knew immediately that she was right—we should flee (entanglements, ~~emolumants~~) and follow our dreams.   *entanglements*

10. The first task was to name our dreams; to do that we sought (~~council~~, counsel).   *counsel*

11. Dr. Chang told us to think about Chaucer's (pilgrims, ~~pilsners~~).   *pilgrims*

12. He also ~~(eluded,~~ alluded) to the Arthurian possibilities.   *alluded*

13. We could go on a (quest, ~~quasar~~).   *quest*

14. In a way we have combined the pilgrimage with the quest in our journey as we seek the settings, the physical (locutions, ~~locations~~) for some of our favorite contemporary fiction.   *locations*

15. Charleston, of course, is (splendid, resplendent) with such settings.   *resplendent*

16. First we found the (~~statuary~~, statue) of Henry Timrod mentioned in Humphreys's *Rich in Love*.   *statue*

17. Then we looked for some of the little unfinished houses that are so important to that novel, the concrete block houses without (~~fenestrations~~, windows).   *windows*

18. Tomorrow the (destination, ~~destiny~~) is Atlanta.   *destination*

19. We are ~~(on,~~ in) quest of settings for Anne Rivers Siddons's work.   *in*

20. At the rate we are (~~preceding~~, proceeding) we may not get back to school before summer session starts.   *proceeding*

CONCISENESS: AVOIDING WORDINESS AND NEEDLESS REPETITION   w/rep 21

21

Avoid wordiness but include all words needed to make the meaning or the grammatical construction complete.

Almost every writer's first draft includes many words that are not needed and lacks some words that are. A careful revision based on close proofreading is the only way to transform a rough draft into an effective piece of writing.

ROUGH DRAFT
WITH REVISIONS

~~At this point in the semester it is the thinking~~
and our teacher Dr. Swann
~~of the class that~~ <u>we</u>∧like Barbara Kingsolver's novel *Animal Dreams* best of all the novels that we have read this semester. ~~That is also the opinion of our teacher Dr. Swann who agrees with us.~~ It ~~is a novel that~~ has a plot about the importance ~~of place,~~ of being rooted in a place and drawing an identity from those roots.

21a Use only those words or phrases that add meaning to your writing.

Most wordiness in composition results from writers' attempts to achieve what they think is a "high style"—to write sentences that sound brilliant. Too often they fill out their sentences with clichés, with roundabout phrasing, and with jargon.

WORDY

Actually *Animal Dreams* has many themes. It examines gender roles and relationships. It examines the relationship between jobs and personal identity. It also comments on parent-child relationships.

CONCISE

The many themes of *Animal Dreams* include gender roles and relationships, the connection of jobs to personal identity, and parent-child relationships.

Use one clear word instead of a long phrase whenever possible. The following is a list of some more common wordy phrases and their one-word counterparts.

Wordy	*Concise*
to be desirous of	want *or* desire
to have a preference for	prefer
to be in agreement with	agree
due to the fact that	because
in view of the fact that	because *or* since
in order to	to
at this point in time	now
in this day and age	today
with reference to	about
prior to	before
in the event of	if

Another kind of wordiness, occurring particularly in student compositions, results from the writer's lack of confidence in his/her position. Such wordiness frequently includes expressions like "I think," "it seems to me," "in my opinion," and "would be."

WORDY   In my opinion the best starting point for discussion of the novel would be Codi's relationship to her father.

CONCISE   Discussion of the novel should start with Codi's relationship to her father.

21b Restructure sentences whenever necessary to avoid wordiness.

Often you can combine sentences through subordination to avoid wordiness. (See also chapter **24**.)

WORDY   Codi's father was a physician whose approval she needed but never received. She later went to medical school to get his approval.

CONCISE   Codi went to medical school to get the approval of her father who also was a physician.   [The *who* clause subordinates one idea.]

WORDY   Codi nearly finished medical school. She had a problem delivering a baby when she could not respond to the human demands of the situation. She left school after that episode.

CONCISE   Codi learned from a baby delivery that she could not handle the human demands of being a physician, so she left medical school.   [The *that* clause subordinates one idea and helps clarify causality.]

Wordiness may also be caused by sentences that begin with *there* or *it*. To eliminate this kind of wordiness, restructure your sentences to use an active verb in place of the form of *be* that inevitably follows *there* or *is*.

WORDY   There are two novels that Kingsolver has written—*Bean Trees* and *Animal Dreams.*

CONCISE   Kingsolver has written two novels—*Bean Trees* and *Animal Dreams.*

WORDY   It is also true that both novels examine the intersection of several cultures.

CONCISE   Both novels examine the intersection of several cultures.

21c Avoid needless repetition of words and ideas.

Repetition of the same word or idea in several consecutive sentences results in monotonous writing. Using pronouns helps as much as anything to avoid this problem.

REPETITIOUS	Codi's sister Hallie has gone to the Caribbean to help the poverty-stricken farmers of the Dominican Republic. Hallie has gone south in search of a cause worthy of devoting her life to it.
CONCISE	Codi's sister Hallie, who has gone to help the poverty-stricken farmers of the Dominican Republic, is searching for a cause to which she can devote her life.

Note: Several popular expressions are always repetitious: *each and every, any and all, various and sundry, if and when, combine together, return back.* Other such expressions include *red in color, triangular in shape,* and *city of Roanoke.*

REPETITIOUS	Each and every day we have a quiz on the novel.
CONCISE	Each day we have a quiz on the novel.
REPETITIOUS	We will have a total of twenty quiz grades after next week.
CONCISE	We will have twenty quiz grades after next week.

In writing direct quotations, many students tend to overwork forms of the verb *say.* Remember that many verbs besides *said* can introduce direct quotations. *Explained, pointed out, noted, continued, described,* and *observed* are only a few.

REPETITIOUS	Dr. Swann said, "The quiz grades will count as one-fourth of your semester grade." She later said, "The three essays will count as the other three-fourths of the final grade."
CONCISE	Dr. Swann explained, "The quiz grades will count as one-fourth of your semester grade." She later added, "The three essays will count as the other three-fourths of the final grade."

Wordiness and Needless Repetition — Exercise 21–1

NAME _____ SCORE _____

DIRECTIONS Cross out needless words in each of the following sentences. For each sentence needing only that revision, write *1* in the blank; for sentences that need additional changes, even changes in punctuation, write *2* in the blank and make the needed revision. There may be more than one way to revise some sentences.

EXAMPLES

~~It can be clearly seen that~~ Shane Cleaveland's novel *Cold Trails* is autobiographical. **1**

For that reason his mother says the novel ~~it~~ is her favorite. **1**

1. The main reason why the novel has gained a wide audience is its honest portrayal of a boy's maturation. _____

2. Cleaveland explained his ideas for the novel: by saying, "It started as a simple story of a boy and his two hunting dogs. The two dogs are named Trailer and Tina. They are beagles." _____

3. As he told it in a recent interview, he said, "The story complicated itself by bringing in an old man. His name is Felix." _____

4. "In various and sundry ways Felix's relations with the boy complicate the plot." _____

5. "The complication of the plot is not a bad thing," he says. "It is a good thing," he says. _____

6. What he means to say, in my opinion, is that complication of a plot adds interest. _____

7. The relationship of Felix to the boy is interesting. It is interesting primarily because Felix becomes a guide to the boy, a mentor. _____

8. Felix has been a farmer most of his life. As a farmer he has learned much about nature. _____

9. The boy at first has one goal. His one goal is to train his dogs to hunt. _____

10. He meets Felix one day when he and the two pups are following a trail beside the creek to the river. The trail goes all the way to the river. _____

11. Felix is checking fishing poles. He has set out the poles to catch catfish and is now checking to see if he has caught a catfish. _____

12. The boy stands back a little distance and waits to be acknowledged. He will not speak until Felix speaks. _____

13. Just as Felix reaches for a pole, something big pulls it under. It goes all the way under. _____

14. "Well, boy, are you just going to stand there, or are you going to help?" he asks. He speaks this to the boy. _____

15. "Take hold of the butt of this cane pole," he says to the boy, "and don't let go." He tells the boy just what to do. _____

16. The boy who is shy and retiring and does not like to talk says nothing. _____

17. He grabs the pole. He feels the power of the fish powerfully pulling. He knows that he cannot hold on long. _____

18. Felix reaches in his bag (it is laying beside him) and brings out a small homemade gaff. _____

19. "Lay into him, boy," he says. "you got to get him to the top," he says. _____

20. The boy strains against the powerful lunges of the fish. He strains and pulls. Suddenly the water bursts open as the big blue catfish surfaces. _____

22

Do not omit a word or phrase necessary to the meaning of the sentence.

22a Be careful to include all necessary articles, pronouns, conjunctions, and prepositions. Revised omissions are indicated by a caret (∧) in the following examples.

(1) Do not omit a needed article before a noun or another adjective.

> In general, readers find Jess Kirkman to be a charming and *an* inspiring narrator.

(2) Do not omit necessary prepositions or conjunctions.

> Jess is the narrator in a type *of* story that appeals to nearly all readers.   [*Type* is not an adjective here.]

> Readers believe *in* and care for Jess.   [*Believe for* is not idiomatic phrasing.]

Do not omit *that* when it is needed as a subordinating conjunction.

> Fred Chappell realized *that* Jess should be a believable and sympathetic character if he is to be a reliable narrator.   [*That* introduces the clause that functions as the complement of the sentence.]

> Deborah Barnard, a Chappell scholar, says *that* Chappell's fiction is as accomplished as his poetry.   [Here the conjunction *that* signals the beginning of an indirect quotation.]

That may be omitted when the meaning of the sentence would be clear at first reading without it.

> Barnard believes Chappell will attend the next Southern Festival of Books.

22b Include necessary verbs and helping verbs.

> For several years now the Southern Festival has *been* and will continue to be one of the most successful book fairs.   [*Has continue to be* is an error in tense.]

22c Include all words necessary to complete a comparison.

as
The Southern Festival is as successful͜or more successful than any Nashville cultural event.

about that of
Most Americans know more about the music industry of Nashville than͜any other

American city.

22d When used as intensifiers, *so, such,* and *too* should usually be followed by a completing phrase or clause.

There is *so* much going on at the Southern Festival this year that I can hardly choose what

to attend.

Chappell's session was *too* popular so we had to move it to a larger hall.

Omission of Necessary Words

NAME _____ SCORE _____

DIRECTIONS   In the following sentences, insert the words that are needed to make the meaning or the grammatical construction complete. In the blank, write the words that you have added.

EXAMPLE

The Southern Festival of Books is a type $\overset{of}{\wedge}$ book fair.   _____ of _____

1. The Festival began Nashville several years ago.   _____

2. Thousands of avid readers have and will continue to attend the Festival.   _____

3. Festival planners knew sessions featuring women authors would be popular.   _____

4. Rita Mae Brown read from some of her earlier work and her new novel.   _____

5. Josephine Humphreys read her new novel *Ferris Beach*.   _____

6. Jill McCorkle chose short stories she had published as *Crash Diet*.   _____

7. Panels of several authors were more popular.   _____

8. One panel featured writers with Vietnam connection.   _____

9. People came to that session for a variety reasons.   _____

10. Some of the people were too intense.   _____

11. But the panelists were so understanding.   _____

12. All of the local chefs knew Julia Child would cook at the

    Festival.   _____

13. They ran into and out the main auditorium looking for her.   _____

14. Finally one of them thought look outside on the plaza.   _____

15. An enterprising Festival planner had realized that an outdoor

    demonstration kitchen would be clearly better.   _____

EFFECTIVE SENTENCES

SENTENCE UNITY   su 23

23

In a unified sentence, ideas within the sentence are clearly related; excessive detail, mixed metaphors, and mixed constructions do not obscure the ideas; and subjects and predicates fit together logically.

23a Establish a clear relationship between the clauses in a sentence; develop unrelated ideas in separate sentences.

When you write a compound sentence, you suggest that the two main clauses are closely related. Similarly, when you write a complex sentence, you make your reader expect a relationship between the ideas in the main and subordinate clauses.

UNCLEAR Richard Rodriguez only spoke Spanish, and his parents enrolled him in an English-only school.

CLEAR Although Richard Rodriguez only spoke Spanish, his parents enrolled him in an English-only school.

UNCLEAR In school he heard for the first time his name pronounced in English, and nothing could have prepared him for that first day of school.

CLEAR In school he heard for the first time his name pronounced in English. Nothing could have prepared him for that first day of school.

23b Avoid excessive or poorly ordered detail.

UNCLEAR Thirty years ago public education in America had no plan for dealing with non-native speakers who were enrolling in increasing numbers, so Hispanic American social activists who were concerned about this problem helped to establish the bilingual program which gave non-English speakers the right to use in school the language that they use at home and which Rodriguez thinks was a bad idea.

CLEAR Thirty years ago public education in America had no plan for dealing with non-native speakers who were enrolling in increasing numbers. Hispanic American social activists were concerned about this problem and helped to establish the bilingual program which gave non-English speakers the right to use in school the language that they use at home. Rodriguez thinks that this was a bad idea.

23c Be aware of mixed metaphors and mixed constructions.

UNCLEAR Richard Rodriguez, the author of *Hunger of Memory: The Education of Richard Rodriguez,* has been described as a grain of sand crying out in a forest.

CLEAR Richard Rodriguez, the author of *Hunger of Memory: The Education of Richard Rodriguez,* has been described as a voice in the wilderness.

UNCLEAR   When Rodriguez spoke out against bilingual education angered many Hispanic Americans.

CLEAR   When Rodriguez spoke out against bilingual education, he angered many Hispanic Americans.

OR

Rodriguez's objections to bilingual education angered many Hispanic Americans.

23d Avoid faulty predication.

Make the subject and predicate of a sentence fit together grammatically and logically.

ILLOGICAL Rodriguez's objections to bilingual education are a serious controversy today. [This sentence contains a mismatch between the plural subject, *objections,* and its singular complement, *controversy.* There is also a problem with logic: *objections* does not equal *controversy,* as the linking verb, *are,* suggests.]

LOGICAL   Bilingual education is often debated today.   [*Bilingual education* can be debated.]

ILLOGICAL The source of much of the controversy is because some people fear total assimilation.   [*Source* does not equal *because,* as the linking verb *is,* suggests. A *because* clause serves as a modifier, not as a basic sentence part.]

LOGICAL   Because some people fear total assimilation, they cling to bilingual education.

OR

The source of much of the controversy is some people's fear of total assimilation.

ILLOGICAL In the emotional debate over languages causes some students to lose sight of their real goal—knowledge.   [The writer has mistaken the object of a preposition, *debate,* for the subject of a sentence.]

LOGICAL   The emotional debate over languages causes some students to lose sight of their real goal—knowledge.   [Here *debate* is the subject.]

23e Define a word or an expression clearly and precisely.

The use of forms of the linking verb *be*—*is, are, was, can be,* and so on—frequently leads to faulty predication, particularly when the linking verb is followed by *when* or *where.* By substituting a nonlinking verb such as *occur* or *is found,* you can often eliminate the error in unity or logic.

ILLOGICAL An example of the continuing debate is when the Honors Program held a Lyceum on the topic of bilingual education.

LOGICAL   The debate continues when the Honors Program holds a Lyceum on bilingual education.

OR

An example of the continuing debate is the Honors Program Lyceum on bilingual education.

Unity in Sentence Structure

NAME _____ SCORE _____

DIRECTIONS   In the blanks, write *a, b, c, d,* or *e* to indicate whether the chief difficulty in each sentence is (a) an unclear relationship among ideas, (b) excessive detail and subordination, (c) mixed metaphors or mixed constructions, (d) an illogical combination of subject and predicate, or (e) unclear or imprecise definitions. Revise the sentences to make them effective.

EXAMPLE

Because Richard Rodriguez so eloquently explains his ideas on education,

~~is why~~ he has ~~such~~ a wide audience.   *d*

1. Rodriguez's parents' climb up the ladder of success was nipped in the bud. _____

2. Rodriguez's book *Hunger for Memory* believes in the liberating power of learning English. _____

3. An example of bilingual education is when schools permit non-English-speaking students to use their family language in school. _____

4. In Rodriguez's early childhood, as his parents coped very well in America and worked steadily, and because they were optimistic and ambitious, they bought a house which was many blocks from the Mexican side of town. _____

5. His parents never contemplated being unable to live where they wished, and their bright yellow house sat among the gringos' white houses. _____

6. When the Rodriguez family moved into the neighborhood angered some neighbors. _____

7. An example of the power of language is when the Rodriguez parents never felt like *los americanos* because they spoke English poorly.   _____

8. When the family had guests indicated their small circle of friends.   _____

9. The source of their problem is because their guests had to speak Spanish.   _____

10. Because relatives spoke Spanish is why they were the usual guests.   _____

11. An example of Rodriguez's desire to learn English is when he went shopping.   _____

12. Richard was desperate to belong in the world of *los americanos,* and he tried to hear and to understand every syllable of English that was spoken to him by shopkeepers.   _____

24

Use subordination to relate ideas concisely and effectively. Use coordination to give ideas equal emphasis.

Subordination is the method good writers most often use to extend their sentences and to vary the beginnings of sentences. (Subordinated additions to the sentence base are italicized in the following paragraph.)

> Let use consider some of the differences between Hispanic and Anglo American people, *exploring briefly some of the basic cultural differences that cause conflict in the Southwest, where Hispanic and Anglo American cultures meet.*

As this example shows, grammatically subordinate structures may contain very important ideas.

The following sentences demonstrate coordination, which gives equal grammatical emphasis to two or more ideas. (See also **12a**, **12c**, and chapter **26**.)

> Cultural differences are implicit in the conceptual content of the languages of these two civilizations, and their value systems stem from a long series of historical circumstances. [Here, coordination gives equal emphasis to each of the two main clauses—*differences are implicit* and *systems stem.*]

> English culture was basically insular, geographically and ideologically; was more integrated on the whole, except for some strong theological differences; and was particularly zealous of its racial purity.   [Coordination gives equal emphasis to each linking verb and its complement—*culture was insular, was integrated,* and *was zealous.* It also gives equal emphasis to each word in a pair—*geographically and ideologically.*]

24a Instead of writing a series of short, choppy sentences, choose one idea for the sentence base, or main clause, and subordinate other ideas.

Because it stands apart from other sentences in a paragraph, a short sentence is often used for emphasis (see chapter **29h**). But if the paragraph contains only short, choppy sentences, no single idea stands out, and the primary effect is monotony.

SHORT AND CHOPPY   Spanish culture included a mix of peoples. It included Mediterranean people. It also included central European and north African people.

SUBORDINATION   Spanish culture included a mix of people—Mediterranean people, north Africans, and central Europeans.   [The subordinated parts are appositives.]

SHORT AND CHOPPY   Europeans arrived in America. They isolated themselves from Native Americans. They did not want physical or cultural integration.

SUBORDINATION   When the Europeans arrived in America, they isolated themselves from the Native Americans because they did not want physical or cultural integration.   [The subordinated parts are two adverb clauses.]

227

24b Instead of linking sentences primarily with coordinating conjunctions such as *and, so,* or *but* or with conjunctive adverbs such as *however* and *therefore,* extend most sentences through subordination.

Coordination of main clauses is helpful in developing a varied style because it gives equal emphasis to separate ideas.

> The Spanish had strong notions about purity of blood, but they did not hesitate to add another strain of blood to their already mixed heritage.

But when ideas have a time, place, descriptive, or cause and effect relationship, use subordination to show the connection between clauses while emphasizing the main idea.

STRINGY	Anglo Americans initiated from an agricultural background, and they built a hugely prosperous agricultural industry in this country.
RELATED	Because Anglo Americans initiated from an agricultural background, they built a hugely successful agricultural industry in this country. [shows cause and effect]
STRINGY	Spaniards needed to discover new lands, to find a new route to India, and to find the fountain of youth, so they set out across the continent in exploration.
RELATED	To discover new lands, to find a new route to India, and to discover the fountain of youth, the Spaniards set out across the continent in exploration. [shows cause and effect]

24c Avoid faulty or excessive subordination. (See also 23a and b.)

If you overdo or overlap subordination, your reader will have difficulty deciding what the sentence base, or main clause, is.

UNCLEAR	The Spaniards, who were peripatetic by nature and who came from an equestrian background, a background that differed from the Europeans' agricultural heritage which might account for the Europeans' slowness in pushing west, were explorers, and they immediately set out to explore the continent.
CLEAR	Perhaps because the Spaniards came from an equestrian background, they were peripatetic by nature and set out to explore the continent. The Europeans, who came from an agricultural heritage, were slow in pushing west.
ILLOGICAL	Because Anglo Americans only began moving west of the Mississippi in the nineteenth century, they were more interested in developing an agricultural economy on the east coast. [Interest in developing the agricultural economy slowed exploration west of the Mississippi, not the other way around.]
LOGICAL	Because Anglo Americans were interested in developing an agricultural economy on the east coast, they only began moving west of the Mississippi in the nineteenth century.

Subordination and Coordination for Effectiveness   Exercise 24–1

NAME _____ SCORE _____

DIRECTIONS   Combine each of the following groups of short, choppy sentences into one effective sentence. Express the most important idea in the main clause and put lesser ideas in subordinate clauses, phrases, or words. Use coordination when ideas should be given equal emphasis.

EXAMPLE

Arthur Campa was born in 1905 and died in 1978. He was born in Mexico of American missionary parents. He worked as a cultural attaché at several United States embassies. He taught in the Department of Modern Languages at the University of Denver.

Arthur Campa (1905–1978) was born in Mexico of American missionary parents, worked as a cultural attaché at several United States embassies, and taught in the Department of Modern Languages at the University of Denver.

1. Campa had grown up among Hispanic and Anglo American people. He also observed the meeting of those two cultures in the Southwest. His writing about the contrasts between those two cultures is especially insightful.

2. Campa traces many conflicts to cultural differences. For example, there is the deeply ingrained individualism of Hispanics. This individualism is asserted when the ego is being fenced in.

3. Anglo Americans achieve individualism through action and self-determination. This sometimes leads to collective behavior. It can defeat the individualistic impulse.

4. The definitions of polite behavior also contrast. The Spanish have long complained about the rudeness of Anglo Americans. They first met the Anglo Americans along the Santa Fe trade trail.

5. The cultures differ in their methods for being generous. Anglo Americans donate to large organizations like the Red Cross. They establish foundations and endow them. The Hispanics simply give straight to the needy individual.

Subordination and Coordination for Effectiveness

Exercise 24–2

NAME _____   SCORE _____

DIRECTIONS   Rewrite each of the following stringy sentences to make one effective sentence. Express the most important idea in the main clause, and put lesser ideas in subordinate clauses, phrases, or words. Use coordination when ideas should be given equal emphasis.

EXAMPLE

Africans were forced into slaving ships, and invisible creatures slipped in with them, and they carried these supernatural beings in their memories, so they kept alive the stories of their homeland.

When Africans were forced into slaving ships, invisible creatures slipped in with them, and they carried these supernatural beings in their memories, thus keeping alive the stories of their homeland.

1. The supernatural beings moved into America, and they made a home for themselves in its mountains, rivers, and forests, so The Hairy Man, for example, now has the run of Georgia's woods.

2. The Hairy Man is a fat little man and an ugly man with hair all over him, and he is tricky so he can shrink or swell at will.

3. He is afraid of dogs, and he prefers to live near rivers, so he captures careless children, and that is his favorite pastime.

4. In Uruguay there is the tale of the *Lobisón,* the wolfman; he frightens peasants; according to legend every Friday night at midnight the seventh consecutive son in a family turns into an animal, and this animal has a wolf's body and a misshapen pig's head.

5. The *Lobisón* commits horrible acts, and it has great supernatural powers, so it is difficult to combat, but a wound will cause it to return to human form.

Subordination and Coordination for Effectiveness
Exercise 24–3

NAME _____ SCORE _____

DIRECTIONS   Rewrite the following paragraph, using subordination to eliminate the short, choppy sentences and the stringy compound sentences. Use coordination when ideas should be emphasized equally. (Not every sentence must be changed.) You will notice the improvement in style that proper subordination and coordination achieve if you read aloud first the original version of the paragraph and then your revision.

[1]I am afraid of growing old. [2]We all are afraid. [3]The fear of growing old is very great. [4]Every aged person is seen as an insult and a threat to society. [5]They remind us of our own death and that our body will not remain smooth and responsive and that it will some day betray us. [6]The ideal way to age would be to grow invisible. [7]We could gradually disappear. [8]Then we would cause little worry or discomfort to the young. [9]This does happen in some ways. [10]I watch people in the park. [11]Young mothers and their children gather on one side. [12]The old people from the home gather on the other. [13]Occasionally a child ventures to the old people's side. [14]The old people lean forward and smile at the child. [15]He is chasing a ball or simply exploring. [16]But no communication ever is established. [17]The young mother comes running. [18]Embarrassed she apologizes for the intrusion. [19]She escorts her child back to the correct side.

REVISION

REVISION (CONTINUED)

25

Place modifiers carefully to indicate clearly their relationships with the words they modify.

An adverb clause can usually be moved to various places in a sentence without affecting the meaning or clarity of the sentence.

> *After Renée read her essay on Western literature,* there were several questions from the audience.
>
> There were several questions from the audience *after Renée read her essay on Western literature.*
>
> There were several questions, *after Renée read her essay on Western literature,* from the audience.

The movement of the adverb clause affects the punctuation of the sentence and the part of the sentence to be emphasized (see also chapter **29**). But the sentence has the same meaning and that meaning is clear whether the adverb clause is an introductory, interrupting, or concluding addition.

Other sentence parts may not be moved around as easily, as the following discussions of various modifiers will show.

25a Avoid needless separation of related parts of a sentence.

(1) In standard written English, adverbs such as *almost, only, just, hardly, nearly,* and *merely* are usually placed immediately before the words they modify.

> MISPLACED   Renée *nearly* wrote ten pages before she identified her thesis.
>
> BETTER   Renée wrote *nearly* ten pages before she identified her thesis.
>
> MISPLACED   The first section *only* deals with two books by William Least Heat Moon.
>
> BETTER   The first section deals *only* with two books by William Least Heat Moon.

(2) Prepositional phrases are almost always placed immediately after the words they modify.

> MISPLACED   Dr. Yoshima's help enabled Renée to finish the essay *with the thesis.*
>
> CLEAR   Dr. Yoshima's help *with the thesis* enabled Renée to finish the essay.

As long as no awkwardness results, a prepositional phrase can be moved to different places in a sentence for variety. (See also **30b**.)

> Renée completely changed, *after taking the advanced writing class,* her writing style. [The *after* phrase modifies *changed.*]
>
> *After taking the advanced writing class,* Renée completely changed her writing style.
>
> Renée completely changed her writing style *after taking the advanced writing class.*

(3) Adjective clauses should be placed near the words they modify.

Unlike the adverb clause, discussed at the beginning of this chapter, an adjective clause cannot be moved around freely in a sentence without changing the meaning or causing a lack of clarity.

CLEAR Changing the structure of her essay, *which was in three parts,* involved adding a fourth section.

UNCLEAR Changing, *which was in three parts,* the structure of her essay involved adding a fourth section. [The placement of the *which* clause now suggests that *changing was in three parts.*]

UNCLEAR Changing the structure of her essay involved adding a fourth section, *which was in three parts.* [Here the *which* clause seems to modify *section.*]

For the sentence to make sense, the adjective clause must be placed immediately after the word it modifies. Other examples include:

CLEAR Jamal, *who has asked for Renée's help with an essay,* is writing on the novelist Louise Erdich.

MISPLACED Jamal is writing on the novelist Louise Erdich, *who has asked for Renée's help with an essay.*

MISPLACED A student seems likely to succeed as a writer *who is willing to ask for help.*

CLEAR A student *who is willing to ask for help* seems likely to succeed as a writer.

(4) Avoid "squinting" constructions—modifiers that may refer to either a preceding or a following word.

SQUINTING Jamal was asked *on May 21, 1993,* to read his essay before the entire class. [The adverbial phrase can modify either *was asked* or *to read.*]

CLEAR Jamal was asked to read his essay before the entire class *on May 21, 1993.*
OR
Jamal was asked to read his essay *on May 21, 1993,* before the entire class.

(5) The parts of the sentence base should not be awkwardly separated, nor should an infinitive be awkwardly split.

AWKWARD Jamal's essay, *after it was read before the class and at the Honors' Lyceum,* **generated** a great deal of interest in Louise Erdich. [The verb is awkwardly separated from its subject.]

BETTER *After it was read before the class and before the Honors' Lyceum,* Jamal's essay **generated** a great deal of interest in Louise Erdich.

AWKWARD Jamal intends **to,** *after it has been completely revised,* **submit** the paper for publication. [The prepositional phrase awkwardly splits the infinitive *to submit.*]

BETTER *After it has been completely revised,* Jamal intends **to submit** the paper for publication.

Although the awkward splitting of an infinitive should be avoided, sometimes an infinitive split by a single modifier is acceptable and sounds natural.

Jamal was able to *quickly* place two of his poems in this year's COLLAGE.

25b Avoid dangling modifiers.

Dangling modifiers are most often dangling verbal phrases that do not refer clearly and logically to a word or phrase in the sentence base. To correct a dangling modifier, either rearrange the words in the sentence base so that the modifier clearly refers to the right word, or add the missing words that will make the modifier clear and logical.

DANGLING *Written while he was in the creative writing class,* Jamal narrated his first experiences as a father. [The verbal phrase illogically modifies *Jamal.*]

CLEAR *Written while he was in the creative writing class,* Jamal's poems narrated his first experiences as a father. [The verbal phrase logically modifies *poems.*]

DANGLING *Thinking about the new life that he holds in his hands,* the poems express the awe he feels at his daughter's birth. [The verbal phrase illogically modifies *poems.*]

CLEAR *Thinking about the new life that he holds in his hands,* Jamal expresses the awe he feels at his daughter's birth. [The verbal phrase logically modifies *Jamal.*]

OR

Jamal, *thinking about the new life that he holds in his hands,* expresses the awe he feels at his daughter's birth.

Placement of Modifiers   Exercise 25–1

NAME _____ SCORE _____

DIRECTIONS   Below each of the following sentences is a word, phrase, or clause that, if inserted correctly in the sentence, could serve as a clear and logical modifier. Write *1* in the blank if the modifier can be inserted in only one place in the sentence and *2* if it can be inserted in two or more places. Then write the sentence with the modifier placed in all the positions where it will not cause an unclear or awkward sentence.

EXAMPLE

William Least Heat Moon's first book *Blue Highways* describes an auto-

mobile journey across America.

which was published in 1983   1

William Least Heat Moon's first book <u>Blue</u>
<u>Highways</u>, which was published in 1983,
describes an automobile journey across America.

1. These essays discuss Least Heat Moon's latest book.

   which were written in the Popular Culture class   _____

2. The students brought them to the library.

   where they were to make copies for everyone   _____

3. These papers count as twenty-five percent of the course grade.

   according to the syllabus   _____

4. Morgan will read her paper to the class.

   after we have completed discussion of *Blue Highways*   _____

5. The latest draft of her paper lies on my desk.

   awaiting revision   _____

6. We will submit it next fall to the Popular Culture Association.

   if she is happy with the revision   _____

7. One paper has already been accepted for that meeting.

   that Jamal submitted   _____

8. We will be pleased to have several papers accepted.

   however   _____

Placement of Modifiers   Exercise 25–2

NAME _____ SCORE _____

DIRECTIONS   Rewrite each of the following sentence bases so that the modifier that follows is clearly and logically related to a word or phrase in the sentence base. Or expand the modifier so that it is clear by itself when it is attached to the sentence base. (Include examples of both methods in your answers.) Be sure to capitalize and to punctuate the modifier correctly when you attach it to the sentence base (see **12b** and **12d**).

EXAMPLE

Peggy decided to write several drafts of this essay.

remembering her instructor's reaction to her last essay

Remembering her instructor's reaction to her last essay, Peggy decided to write several drafts of this essay.

1. This essay examines Maxine Hong Kingston's *Woman Warrior.*

    taking a very contemporary perspective

2. Peggy had been thinking about the term "the disappeared."

    used to describe victims of political assassinations

3. By unintentionally disgracing her family, Kingston's No-Name Woman loses her identity.

    having become one of the disappeared

4. No-Name Woman is an old story in Kingston's family.

    told by her mother

5. A woman becomes pregnant.

    having been raped

6. Her family disowns her and shuns her.

    refusing to say her name

7. Ultimately she dies.

    having been disgraced but being without fault

8. Kingston's mother told this story as a cautionary tale.

    intending to encourage her daughter to remember family honor

9. In her paper Peggy is focusing on No-Name Woman.

    hoping to reclaim her identity

10. Something in this story affected all of the women in the class.

    seeing their potential as nameless women

26

Use parallel structure to give grammatically balanced treatment to items in a list or series and to parts of a compound construction.

Parallel structure means that a grammatical form is repeated—that an adjective is balanced by another adjective, a verb phrase by another verb phrase, a subordinate clause by another subordinate clause, and so on. Although ineffective repetition results in poor style (see chapter **21**), repetition to create parallel structure can result in effective writing. The repetition of a sentence construction makes ideas clear to the reader, emphasizes those ideas (see chapter **29**), and provides coherence between the sentences in a paragraph (see chapter **32**).

Connectives such as *and, but* and *or* often indicate that the writer intends to use parallel structure to balance the items in a list or series or the parts of a compound construction.

LIST OR SERIES   We have read works by these three writers: a *collection* of stories by Zora Neale Hurston, one *volume* of Maya Angelou's autobiography, and Toni Morrison's *novel* SULA.

COMPOUND PARTS   Victoria *has interviewed* Angelou and *has ordered* taped interviews of Morrison and *has plans* to visit with two Hurston scholars.

26a To achieve parallel structure, balance a verb with a verb, a prepositional phrase with a prepositional phrase, a subordinate clause with a subordinate clause, and so on.

The following examples are written in outline form to make the parallel structure, or lack of it, more noticeable. Correct parallel structure is indicated by vertical parallel lines, repeated words are printed in italics, and connectives are printed in boldface.

AWKWARD   Victoria's committee recommends that she
       examine one writer in depth
rather than
       examining three writers superficially.

PARALLEL   Victoria's committee recommends that she examine
‖ *one writer* in depth
rather than
‖ *three writers* superficially.

AWKWARD   As she researches Morrison, all that she
       reads in the journals,
       learns from interviews,
and
       what her teachers tell her
convinces her to concentrate on SULA.

243

PARALLEL   As she researches Morrison, all that she
        ‖ *reads* in journals,
        ‖ *learns* from taped interviews,
        and
        ‖ *hears* from her teachers
        convinces her to concentrate on SULA.

26b To make the parallel clear, repeat a preposition, an article, the *to* of the infinitive, or the introductory word of a long phrase or clause. (Repeated elements of this type are printed in italics.)

Victoria's research has presented her
‖ *with an opportunity* to travel
as well as
‖ *with an opportunity* to meet Morrison.

However, she also has to spend her travel money wisely:
‖ *to use it for* research
  ‖ *of* Morrison
  or
  ‖ *of* Angelou
not
‖ *to use it for* entertainment.

The committee believes
‖ *that she will* conduct original research
and
‖ *that she will* be a fine representative of the school.

26c In addition to coordinating conjunctions, connectives like *both…and, either…or, neither…nor, not only…but also,* and *as well as*—and expressions like *not* and *rather than* which introduce negative phrasing—are used to connect parallel structure. (These connectives are printed in boldface below.)

Victoria's trip to interview Morrison is the result
  not only
‖ of careful planning
  but also
‖ of solid research.

Parallel Structure   Exercise 26–1

NAME _____ SCORE _____

DIRECTIONS   Make an outline, like the outlines used in this section, of the parallel parts of each of the following sentences.

EXAMPLE

Victoria says that her interview with Maya Angelou will focus on her poetry and that her interview with Marge Piercy will focus on her novels.

Victoria says
‖ that her interview...
and that
‖ her interview....

1. Three other students are also involved in research: Kim on Leslie Silko and Alice on Chaucer and Morgan on Jane Austen.

2. Unfortunately the material on those three authors is not concentrated in one library and is not easily accessed by computer.

3. The department has given Alice money to buy a modem, to have it installed, and to join Internet.

4. Her earlier efforts to do research by computer have been fragmented and ineffective rather than focused and productive.

5. Our former head librarian was neither interested nor helpful.

6. Alice needs not only a modem but also a CD-ROM player.

7. With the CD-ROM player she will be able to access the *PMLA Bibliography,* to search the ERIC database, and to look up words in the *Oxford English Dictionary.*

Parallel Structure   Exercise 26–2

NAME _____ SCORE _____

DIRECTIONS   Rewrite the following sentences to restore the parallel structure.

EXAMPLE

Our writing class is not so much a lecture but rather a workshop.

Our writing class is not so much a lecture as a workshop.

1. Every meeting is carefully planned, and it involves collaboration.

    Every meeting is carefully planned, which also involves collaboration.

2. Some people in the class believe that the work produced by the small groups exceeds the work of a single student.

3. Class today is devoted to Leslie Silko; it also is devoted to Louise Erdich and to Mourning Dove.

4. Unlike previous classes this is not so much about writing but rather reading.

    Unlike previous classes this one is more about reading than writing.

5. Some students think reading to each other seems more a luxury rather than a necessity.

6. Dr. Makeba believes reading aloud will teach us two things: to recognize the voices of the writers and identifying key passages.

7. Unlike my other classes this one forces me to be an active learner rather than passively watching.

8. Participation in the small groups was increased after the first two weeks and began to involve everyone.

9. We learned to rely on group judgment and relied on healthy disagreements.

10. Developed and named after our group leader, our group is called Sam's Group.

27

As much as possible, maintain consistent grammatical structure, tone or style, and viewpoint.

As you read the following paragraph, notice how many times you must refocus your attention because of an unnecessary shift in number, tense, voice, or discourse.

All my life I have been around strong women. My grandmother became my nurse,

tense

my nanny, my companion, and my guide when I am two. One of my earliest memories is of

tense

her giving me a bath in a number two wash tub in front of the rumbling coal oil heater. It is

cold, and I was shivering despite the warm water, but her soft voice and gentle words make

this a pleasant memory. Even in these earliest memories I do not recall thinking of myself

as timid or unsure of myself. I was more a watcher, a careful observer who would think

number

long before they acted. Even today I carry those same traits to work every day. My grand-

mother believed in the *Bible;* somewhere in the *Bible,* to her mind, lay the answer to every

question. So she knew right from wrong and was quick to set me straight. A typical child

number   *number*

who deludes themselves into thinking they are wiser than an adult, I resisted her teachings.

voice

Today I am grieved when I think of the times that I disobeyed her.

tense

My mother is a somewhat more distant figure during my childhood. As I think about

discourse   *person*   *person*

her I wonder can I really capture her in words. We want to be accurate in our representa-

person

tion of our parents, but my mother existed during my childhood at the periphery of my life.

I realize now, fortunately early enough to tell her, that I learned from her how to work—

how to bend my shoulder to a task and never quit.

27a Avoid needless shifts in tense, mood, or voice.

SHIFT   During the discussion of Andrew's new novel, he *listened* carefully but *said* nothing while his wife *listens* carefully and loudly *applauds* every compliment for the novel.   [shift from past tense to present tense]

CONSISTENT   During the discussion of Andrew's new novel, he *listened* carefully but *said* nothing while his wife *listened* carefully and loudly *applauded* every compliment for the novel.

SHIFT   Andrew insists that in his fiction women *be shown* as the strength of the family while men *are* less *committed* to the family.   [shift from subjunctive mood to indicative mood]

CONSISTENT   Andrew insists that in his fiction women *be shown* as the strength of the family while men *be shown* as less committed to the family.

SHIFT   Andrew *created* the character Molly from his grandmother; the best aspects of his grandmother *are represented* by Molly.   [shift from active voice to passive voice]

CONSISTENT   Andrew *created* the character Molly from his grandmother; Molly *represents* the best aspects of his grandmother.

Be especially careful in writing essays on literature or historical topics to maintain a consistent present tense while retelling a plot or an event.

SHIFT   Molly *is characterized* as the matriarch of the family who *kept* them together during hard times.   [shift from present tense to past tense]

CONSISTENT   Molly *is characterized* as the matriarch of the family who *keeps* them together during hard times.

27b Avoid needless shifts in person and in number.

SHIFT   When *we* read LOST LABORS, *one* realizes that Molly is the moral center of the novel.   [shift from first person to third person]

CONSISTENT   When *we* read LOST LABORS, *we* realize that Molly is the moral center of the novel.

SHIFT   A *reader* who is unfamiliar with Andrew's work will think that *they* are reading a contemporary version of Dickens.   [shift in number]

CONSISTENT   *Readers* who are unfamiliar with Andrew's work will think that *they* are reading a contemporary version of Dickens.

27c Avoid needless shifts between indirect and direct discourse.

SHIFT   Although Andrew has written for years, he still asks himself *if he is being true to his roots* and *would his grandmother approve.*   [shift from declarative word order to interrogative word order]

CONSISTENT   Although Andrew has written for years, he still asks himself *if he is being true to his roots* and *if his grandmother would approve.*

OR

As he writes, Andrew asks, *"Am I being true* to my roots? *Would my grandmother approve?"*

27d Avoid needless shifts in tone or style.

SHIFT The older characters in Andrew's fiction speak with a strong accent, are very mannered and courteous, and *interface with the church every Sunday.* [shift from formal style to doublespeak]

CONSISTENT …and *attend church every Sunday.*

27e Avoid needless shifts in perspective or viewpoint.

SHIFT Andrew's study looks like a well-kept library; books festooned with improvised bookmarks and floppy disks storing every word that he has written indicate his packrat tendencies. [shift from external perspective to internal perspective]

CONSISTENT Andrew's study looks like a well-kept library, but shelves of books festooned with improvised bookmarks and cartons of floppy disks storing every word that he has written indicate his packrat tendencies.

Shifts

Exercise 27–1

NAME _____ SCORE _____

DIRECTIONS   Indicate the kind of shift in each of the following sentences by writing *a* (tense, mood, voice), *b* (person, number), *c* (discourse), or *d* (tone, style) in the blank. Then revise the sentence to eliminate the needless shift.

EXAMPLE

Andrew White's fiction draws heavily on his biography and ~~was~~ *is* influenced

by his early reading.   *a*

1. White's parents were raised on farms and ~~come~~ *came* to live in town as

    young adults.   *a*

2. White's father worked with his three brothers to make a living on

    the farm, but he finally ~~realizes~~ *realized* that he must leave the farm.   *a*

3. He ~~asked~~ *asks* himself can all of us live off this farm.   *a*

4. A young man like his father is tied closely to the land, so when he

    ~~leaves~~ *left*, it was heartbreaking.   *a*

5. As one reads White's first novel, ~~we~~ *one* realize that Johnny is modeled

    closely after his father.   *b*

6. Johnny comes to the small town of Rhodes and ~~went~~ *goes* to work in the

    carpet mills.   *a*

7. Here one works long hours, and ~~he~~ *one* is paid low wages.   *b*

8. In the rooming house where he lives he ~~met~~ *meets* a young woman, also

    on her own for the first time.   *a*

9. ~~After a night of passionate osculation,~~ they realize they are in love.   *c*

    they realize they are in love after a night
    of passionate osculation

10. They immediately ~~wonder~~ wondered can they get married.   a

11. The novel is now being made into a film, and White ~~insists~~ insisted that his

    mother be shown as very mature and wise for her age and that his

    father is less settled.   a

12. His father was affected strongly by the move to town and ~~adjusts~~ adjusted

    only reluctantly.   a

13. Marilyn, his mother, seems more adaptable, more dependable and

    ~~quickly worked herself into~~ works quickly to find a better paying job.   c

14. She runs a cutting machine that ~~cut~~ cuts carpet to special lengths and

    widths.   a

15. It is a job that ~~required~~ requires a calm and intelligent operator.   a

Shifts   Exercise 27–2

NAME _____   SCORE _____

DIRECTIONS   The following paragraphs, which discuss one of Andrew White's novels contain thirteen shifts in tense, voice, person, number, and discourse. Correct each shift by marking through it and writing your revision above the line. Finally, if possible, read aloud the original version and your revision to compare the improvement in coherence when consistent tense, voice, person, number, and discourse are maintained.

When Johnny White leaves the farm to move to the little town of Rhodes, he came with carefully washed and ironed clothes folded neatly in a battered suitcase. Except for the deep tan on his wrists and neck he looks just like all of the other young men who is looking for work. And like them he wonders can he make a living here.

Johnny is accustomed to hard work, and the mill was hiring, so he gets on the second shift loading and unloading trucks. Before the end of the first day he has a job, and he finds a place to live. Mrs. Dabney on Troup Street rented him one of their back rooms. He has a room, a hot plate, and a shared bath. Out back he can see Mrs. Dabney's garden plot and row after row of flower beds. The crinnelated paths and the green upswellings bespeaking spring awaken in him joy eternal. It is spring and still a bit early to plant, but he can see day lilies putting up new green growth and the first sign of buds on the apple trees.

The first day at work is hard and long, but one works well and comes to his room feeling tired but proud. I wondered can I do this, he thinks. Now I know I can. He walks out in the back garden and picked up a hoe. With a few quick scrapes of the hoe several dandelions are uprooted, and the low burdock meets a similar fate. With the corner of the hoe he begins to define the rows that separate the perennials, carefully outlining the little plot for each plant. Soon he knelt down and began using his hands to mound the cool and moist soil. It smells rich and dark, a good soil that he recognizes. He works steadily, and just under his breath sings quietly to himself his mother's favorite hymn.

28

Make each pronoun refer unmistakably to its antecedent.

A pronoun depends on its antecedent, the word it refers to, for its meaning. If a pronoun does not refer clearly and logically to another word, then your reader will not know what the pronoun means. And if a pronoun refers to the general idea of the preceding sentence or sentences, the reader may have to reread a part or parts of the earlier material to determine the meaning of the pronoun.

> *They* claim that the fictional character represents the author's mother. *They* say *this* because of an interview that *they* had with the author.

There are three main ways to correct an unclear reference of a pronoun: (1) rewrite the sentence or sentences to eliminate the pronoun; (2) provide a clear antecedent for the pronoun to refer to; or (3) substitute a noun for the pronoun, or as in the case of *this*, add a noun, making the pronoun an adjective.

> *The members of the Craddock Club* claim that the fictional character represents the author's mother. *They* make *this claim* because of an interview that *they* had with the author. [Note in the second sentence that *this* has become an adjective modifying the noun *claim*.]

28a Avoid ambiguous reference.

AMBIGUOUS   Alberto told Ashley that *he* was innately aggressive.

CLEAR   Alberto told Ashley, "*You* are innately aggressive."
OR
                Alberto told Ashley, "*I* am innately aggressive."

28b Avoid remote or obscure reference.

A pronoun that is located too far from its antecedent, with too many intervening nouns, will not have a clear meaning; nor will a pronoun that refers to an antecedent in the possessive case.

AWKWARD   In the article "The Drums Continue," *it* discusses fiction by Native American writers. [The pronoun *it* refers clumsily to *article*.]

CLEAR   The article "The Drums Continue" discusses fiction by Native American writers.

AWKWARD   *One* may read this article for a good survey of the writers. *You* may also be surprised at how many of the writers are women.

CLEAR   One may read this article for a good survey of the writers. One may also be surprised at how many of the writers are women.

    257

Note: Some grammarians feel that *you* is both natural and correct as long as the writer does not shift person in the sentence or the paragraph; other grammarians feel that *you* should be avoided in formal composition.

Reference of Pronouns   Exercise 28–1

NAME _____ SCORE _____

DIRECTIONS   In the following sentences mark an inverted caret (V) through each pronoun whose reference is vague or awkward and write that pronoun in the blank. Then revise the sentence or sentences to clarify the meaning.

EXAMPLE

the article

It is interesting to read Bennett's article because V teaches much about

the Navajo way of life.   *it*

1. In Bennett's article it explains how *Bennett* she learned to weave like a

   Navajo.   *she*

2. Bennett's friends did not encourage *Bennett* her because this seemed inap-

   propriate to them.   *her*

3. Some of her friends believed that the Navajo would not teach it to
   Bennett
   her.   *her*

4. Bennett imagined finding a wise old weaver skilled in all aspects of

   the craft, which would be the ideal arrangement for *Bennett* her.   *her*

5. But it was proving impossible to find a person to teach it. *the craft*   *it*
   Tiana Bighorse
6. Tiana Bighorse was a master weaver, and she used this to teach

   Bennett.   *she*

7. Tiana taught her to make dyes from plants and yarn from wool.
   making dyer from plants and yarn from wool
   Bennett learned it eagerly.   *it*

8. It became important for Bennett to apply all of her skills, so she
   making dyes from plants and yarn from wool
   began it on her new cedar loom.   *it*

REFERENCE OF PRONOUNS

9. Navajo custom would have her [*Bennett*] weave a pattern of stripes which seemed to her to be too little of a challenge.

    her

10. She decided to use all of her colors of yarn and all of her designing skills to create a sampler. Only in a sampler could she [*Bennett*] display all of them.

    she

11. During this weaving she made a mistake. In it she [*Bennett*] wove the image of a snake.

    She

12. It is bad luck to weave a snake image, but she [*Bennett*] corrected it by weaving in a roadrunner about to eat the snake.

    she

29

Arrange the parts of a sentence, and the sentences in a paragraph, to emphasize important ideas.

Emphatic word order, used at the proper time, is an effective way to emphasize ideas and add variety to your writing. But emphatic sentence patterns should be saved for ideas that deserve special stress; if you use unusual patterns too often, your style will appear stilted.

29a Gain emphasis by placing important words at the beginning or the end of a sentence—especially at the end—and unimportant words in the middle.

UNEMPHATIC	America is the most wonderful of ideas according to Bharati Mukherjee.
EMPHATIC	America, according to Bharati Mukherjee, is the most wonderful of ideas.

Note: The beginning and the end (again, especially the end) are also the two most effective places to put important ideas in a paragraph or an essay.

29b Gain emphasis by using periodic sentences. (This rule is an extension of 29a.)

A sentence that holds the reader in suspense until the end is called *periodic;* one that makes a complete statement and then adds detail is called *loose.* The loose sentence, which is more common, is usually easier to follow. But the periodic sentence, by reserving the main idea until the end, is more emphatic.

LOOSE	America is a place that encourages dreams when it is observed romantically.
PERIODIC	When it is observed romantically, America is a place that encourages dreams.

29c Gain emphasis by arranging ideas in the order of climax.

In a series, place ideas in order beginning with the least important one. Present the most important or most dramatic idea last.

UNEMPHATIC	Mukherjee says America gave her an opportunity to reinvent herself, a place to study, and a profession.
EMPHATIC	Mukherjee says America gave her a place to study, a profession, and an opportunity to reinvent herself.

29d Gain emphasis by using the active instead of the passive voice.

UNEMPHATIC	Mukherjee was the author of the novel *Jasmine.*
EMPHATIC	Mukherjee wrote the novel *Jasmine.*

Note: When the receiver of an action is more important than the doer, the passive voice will make the emphasis clear.

> Mukherjee's offer to grant an interview was immediately accepted.

29e Gain emphasis by repeating important words.

> Bill Moyers began the interview with a question about home, about her definition of home. Had her definition of home changed, he asked. Growing up in India, Mukherjee said, home always had been a place. If someone asked her to name her home, she named the village where her father had been born. So home was a fixed, unchanging, inherited place. When she came to America that changed. Here she could shed the past and the fixed places and define home for herself—she could even define herself anew in this new home.

Caution: Repetition of a word produces only monotony unless the word is important enough to be emphasized. (See also **21c**.)

29f Gain emphasis by using inverted word order or by putting a word or phrase out of its usual order.

UNEMPHATIC	Large and various America attracted Mukherjee because it tempted her to dream.
EMPHATIC	America, large and various, attracted Mukherjee because it tempted her to dream.
UNEMPHATIC	Perhaps she could find a new life among its optimistic people.
EMPHATIC	Perhaps, among its optimistic people, she could find a new life.

29g Gain emphasis by using balanced construction. (See also chapter **26**.)

UNEMPHATIC	Perhaps dreams could live in America, but India is a sterile country.
EMPHATIC	Perhaps dreams could live in America; in India they could not.

29h Emphasize an important sentence in a paragraph by making it noticeably shorter than the others. (See also chapter **24**.)

> After Mukherjee completed college in Iowa, she and her husband, the writer Clark Blaise, immigrated to Canada. As a biracial, bicultural couple, they expected to be welcome in Canada. When they moved to Canada in 1966, they were well received by a very tolerant society. After some years the racial and cultural climate in Canada changed, and Mukherjee, like many other immigrants, began to experience prejudice. For her personally the racial intolerance forced a breaking point when she was spat upon, thrown to the back of a bus, and evicted from a posh hotel. *The couple immediately left Canada.*

Emphasis

NAME _____ SCORE _____

DIRECTIONS Rewrite each of the following sentences in emphatic word order. Use the rule indicated in parentheses after the sentence to guide you in revising for emphasis.

EXAMPLE

There are many taped interviews in our library in addition to the Bill Moyers interview of

Bharati Mukherjee. (**29b**)

There are many taped interviews, including the Bill Moyers interview of Bharati Mukherjee, in our library.

1. In India Mukherjee felt restricted and confined, but America was different. (**29g**)

2. Perhaps she could free herself by leaving India. (**29f**)

3. According to Mukherjee an immigrant survives by being disciplined, strong, and optimistic. (**29b**)

4. Mukherjee reveals her ideas about immigrants by writing in three genres: the novel *Jasmine*, her best work; *Middleman,* a collection of stories; and screenplays. (**29c**)

5. In 1988 *Middleman* was given the National Book Critics Circle Award. (**29d**)

6. *Jasmine* has been recognized by critics as a particularly complete portrait of America. (**29d**)

7. Confronted by America's capacity for evil, Jasmine refuses to think like a victim. (**29f**)

8. Jasmine does keep her integrity, and does murder, and does blackmail. (**29c**)

9. Unforgettable images of Jasmine's courage and optimism appear through the skill of Mukherjee's writing. (**29a**)

10. The attractive qualities of Jasmine may be caused by her thinking like a pioneer. (**29d**)

Emphasis

NAME _____ SCORE _____

DIRECTIONS   Write a paragraph in which you try to emphasize certain ideas by using three or more of the techniques explained in chapter **29**. When you have finished, number the sentences in your paragraph and analyze what you have done to achieve emphasis by answering the questions on the next page.

SUGGESTED TOPICS

your favorite movie or story about immigrants

your definition of home

your experience with racial or cultural prejudice

why you would like to live in a different part of the country/world

PARAGRAPH

ANALYSIS

1. Did you use a short, abrupt sentence to emphasize an idea? If so, which sentence is used in this way? _____

    _____

2. Why did you emphasize this idea?

3. Which sentences in your paragraph have loose structure? _____

    _____

4. Which sentences have periodic structure? _____

5. Did you use any other techniques to achieve emphasis—for example, inverted word order, balanced structure, repetition of an important word or words? If so, list each technique used and the number of the sentence in which it appears.

30

Vary the length, structure, and beginnings of your sentences to make your style pleasing.

On a few occasions, a series of short sentences that all begin with the subject is effective. In general, however, vary the length, structure, and beginnings of your sentences to achieve a fluid style.

30a Vary the length of sentences, using short sentences primarily for emphasis. (See also 29h.)

> All American writers, even those who are offering messages of hope and possibility, must be very clear-eyed about the potential for evil. I hope that the stories in *The Middleman and Other Stories* or *Jasmine* present a full picture, a complicated picture of America. But I like to think that I, as well as my characters, constantly fight evil. *We don't retreat from battle.*
> —BHARATI MUHKERJEE

30b Vary the beginnings of sentences.

Subordination is the key to a variation from subject-first word order.

(1) Begin with an adverb or an adverb phrase or clause.

ADVERB	*Eventually,* we will think of immigrants as pioneers.
ADVERB PHRASE	*In 1963,* her family came to America.
ADVERB CLAUSE	*After she married,* she decided to stay.

(2) Begin with a prepositional phrase or a verbal phrase.

PREPOSITIONAL PHRASE	*In the interview,* Muhkerjee proves wonderfully articulate.
VERBAL PHRASE	*Studying the interview,* I can see connections between her biography and her fiction.

(3) Begin with a coordinating conjunction, a conjunctive adverb, or a transitional expression when such a word or phrase can be used to show the proper relation of one sentence to the sentence that precedes it.

COORDINATING CONJUNCTION	Because she arrived in America as a minority immigrant, Muhkerjee had every opportunity to feel passive. *But* she, as she says, thinks like a pioneer which prevents her from becoming a victim.
CONJUNCTIVE ADVERB	*Indeed,* it is this same trait which makes Jasmine so powerful a character.
TRANSITIONAL EXPRESSION	Jasmine even becomes a criminal. *Indeed,* she is even involved in murder, but she never loses her dreams.

(4) Begin with an appositive, an absolute phrase, or an introductory series.

APPOSITIVE   *An intellectually challenging hour,* the interview made me think about my responses to immigrants.

ABSOLUTE PHRASE   *Their expressions intent,* the students leaned forward to better hear the interview.

INTRODUCTORY   *Idealistic, romantic, exotic*—Jasmine is well named.
SERIES

30c Avoid loose, stringy compound sentences.

To revise an ineffective compound sentence, try one of the following methods.

(1) Make a compound sentence complex.

COMPOUND   Muhkerjee came from a society where caste, gender, and class determined her identity, and she wanted freedom.

COMPLEX   Because Muhkerjee came from a society where caste, gender, and class determined her identity, she wanted freedom.

(2) Use a compound predicate in a simple sentence.

COMPOUND   Today immigrants arrive in America, and they have many of the same ambitions and fears of the earliest European settlers, and they are true pioneers.

SIMPLE   Arriving in America today, immigrants have many of the same ambitions and fears of the earliest European settlers and are true pioneers.

(3) Use an appositive in a simple sentence.

COMPOUND   The American mythology is called "romanticism," and it refers to the ability to dream.

SIMPLE   The American mythology, "romanticism," refers to the ability to dream.

(4) Use a prepositional or verbal phrase in a simple sentence.

COMPOUND   A dream is an expression of a desire for change, and it creates hope in us.

SIMPLE   By expressing a desire for change, a dream creates hope in all of us.

30d Vary the conventional subject-verb sequence by occasionally separating the subject from the verb with words or phrases.

Each subject and verb below is italicized.

SUBJECT-VERB   An immigrant's *home is* a place, but *it,* paradoxically, *is* a state of mind. [compound sentence]

VARIED   An immigrant's *home,* a place, *is,* paradoxically, a state of mind. [simple sentence]

SUBJECT-VERB   An *immigrant leaves* one home and *searches* for another.

VARIED   An *immigrant,* having left one home, *searches* for another.

30e Occasionally, use an interrogative, imperative, or exclamatory sentence instead of the more common declarative sentence.

What is the potency of Ellis Island for someone like me—an American, obviously, but one who has always felt that the country really belonged to the early settlers, that as J.F. Powers wrote in "Morte D'Urban," it had been "handed down to them by the pilgrims, George Washington, and others, and that they were taking a risk in letting you live in it." [a question followed by a declarative statement]

—MARY GORDON, *"More Than Just a Shrine"*

Close your eyes. Remember. Recall the first taste of water in a free country.   [three imperative sentences]   —GINA SHIN

Variety

NAME _____ SCORE _____

DIRECTIONS   Analyze the ways in which variety is achieved in the following paragraph by answering the questions on the next page.

[1]One of these tales was about the woman who was left at the altar. [2]Mamá liked to tell that one with histrionic intensity. [3]I remember the rise and fall of her voice, the sighs, and her constantly gesturing hands, like two birds swooping through her words. [4]This particular story usually would come up in a conversation as a result of someone mentioning a forthcoming engagement or wedding. [5]The first time I remember hearing it, I was sitting on the floor at Mamá's feet, pretending to read a comic book. [6]I may have been eleven or twelve years old, at that difficult age when a girl was no longer a child who could be ordered to leave the room if the women wanted freedom to take their talk into forbidden zones, not really old enough to be considered a part of their conclave. [7]I could only sit quietly, pretending to be in another world, while absorbing it all in a sort of unspoken agreement of my status as silent auditor. [8]On this day, Mamá had taken my long, tangled mane of hair into her ever-busy hands. [9]Without looking down at me and with no interruption of her flow of words, she began braiding my hair, working at it with the quickness and determination that characterized all of her actions. [10]My mother was watching us impassively from her rocker across the room. [11]On her lips played a little ironic smile. [12]I would never sit still for her ministrations, but even then, I instinctively knew that she did not possess Mamá's matriarchal power to command and keep everyone's attention. [13]This was never more evident than in the spell she cast when telling a story.

ANALYSIS

1. Which two sentences are shorter than the others? _____

    _____

2. What is the purpose of the short sentences? _____

    _____

3. How many simple sentences are there?_____

    How many compound sentences? _____

    How many complex sentences? _____

4. In which sentences is the subject preceded by an adverb?_____

    _____

5. In which sentences is the subject preceded by an adverb phrase?_____

    _____

6. In which sentences is the subject preceded by an adverb clause? _____

    _____

7. Which sentence begins with a transitional expression?_____

    _____

8. Which sentences vary from Subject–Verb–Complement word order by inserting a word or words between the subject and verb? _____

    _____

9. How many of the sentences are declarative sentences? _____

    _____

Variety   Exercise 30–2

NAME _____ SCORE _____

DIRECTIONS   Write a paragraph in which you use at least three of the methods for achieving variety explained in chapter **30**. Because most people are more likely to use varied sentence patterns when they write on subjects that they feel strongly about, traditional views that they can question, or topics that they can treat humorously, you may find one of the five beginnings suggested below useful. After you have finished your paragraph, number your sentences and analyze what you have done to achieve variety by answering the questions on the next page.

SUGGESTED BEGINNINGS

1. I have witnessed a clash of cultures while at work.

2. I have friends who are recent immigrants, and I admire them because....

3. If "home" is a state of mind, then I am most at home at... because....

4. Immigration laws should be more strongly enforced because....

5. My favorite woman character in a movie (or television series or book) is...
    because....

PARAGRAPH

PARAGRAPH CONTINUED

ANALYSIS

1. Have you used a sentence or two that is noticeably shorter than the other sentences in the paragraph? _____

2. What type of sentence structure have you mainly used: simple, compound, or complex? _____

3. Which sentences have you begun with something other than the subject? _____

   _____

4. Does any sentence have a word or words inserted between the subject and verb or between the verb and complement? _____

5. Have you used any kind of sentence other than the declarative sentence? _____

   _____

CRITICAL READING AND LOGICAL THINKING

31

Learn to be a critical reader and to apply critical thinking as you read and write. Avoid logical fallacies.

Learning to reason critically and logically and to judge the reasoning of other writers is an essential part of your preparation as a writer. In this section you will practice skills necessary for you to become an active and critical reader of your prose or of the prose of another writer.

31a Distinguish between fact and fiction.

Facts are pieces of information that can be verified through independent sources or procedures. Opinions are judgments that may or may not be based on facts.

FACT   The book was published in America.

OPINION   Paperback books are easier to read.

Facts, like opinions, can change. Curious and questioning readers are always prepared to examine facts with the same critical reading skills that they apply to opinions. They also are prepared to assimilate new ideas as the facts change.

31b Read for evidence.

As a critical reader you must expect writers to support their claims with appropriate evidence. You should expect evidence to be accurate, representative, sufficient, and verifiable.

31c Evaluate for credibility.

As you read, evaluate the credibility of the writer according to these criteria:

Has the writer supported claims with evidence?
Has the writer revealed the sources of the evidence?
Has the writer acknowledged the legitimacy of other points of view?
Has the writer maintained an appropriate tone and style?
Has the writer reached a conclusion that the evidence will support?

31d Learn how to use inductive reasoning.

Every day the little girl spoke Spanish at home to members of her family. When she went to school, however, she struggled with the new language, English. Gradually she learned it too and easily slipped from one language into the other. But in her mind, Spanish was the family language, the language of private, intimate lives. English was the language for the rest of the world.

Inductive reasoning, as in the above example, is based on evidence: people observe or otherwise acquire facts—or what they believe to be facts—and they make a generalization based upon them. But, as the example of the girl thinking that everyone outside her family speaks English demonstrates, our reasoning sometimes fails us. When we reason inductively, we must take certain precautions: we must

> make sure the evidence is sufficient;
> make sure the conclusion fits the facts;
> make sure we do not ignore evidence;
> make sure we do not present only evidence that supports our conclusion.

31e Learn how to use deductive reasoning in your writing.

If you know that you have new Japanese neighbors and you hear a group of Asians across the street speaking a language that you do not recognize, you are likely to conclude that they are your new neighbors.

The kind of reasoning used in this example is based on a logical structure called a *syllogism.*

SYLLOGISM

Major Premise (usually a generalization): Students who do well in high school go to college.
Minor Premise (a specific fact): Nadia did well in high school.
Conclusion: Nadia is going to college.

When the major premise and the minor premise are correctly related to form a conclusion, the syllogism is valid. Even if the reasoning is valid, however, the conclusion may be false if one of the premises is false. For instance, suppose that Nadia is not going to college. That makes your major premise false; therefore, your conclusion is false. Based on the evidence that you had, your reasoning was valid, but your conclusion was false.

As you use deductive reasoning in your writing, particularly in argumentative papers, think very carefully about your premises to be sure your argument is sound—both true and valid. Also, consider your reader as you frame your premises: how difficult will it be for the reader to accept your premises?

31f Learn how to use the Toulmin method.

Another way of viewing the use of logic is to see an argument as a progression from accepted facts or evidence to a conclusion by way of a statement.

All students are required to take the final exam, and since Omar is a student, Omar must take the final exam.

The conclusion (or *claim*) is that Omar must take the final exam. The evidence (or *data*) is that Omar is a student. The statement (*warrant*) is that all students must take the final exam. The warrant ties the two statements together, making the claim flow from the evidence.

The Toulmin method encourages writers to fully understand and to be able to refute contrasting points of view. It promotes a very thoughtful and civilized discourse about sometimes volatile issues. Consult your handbook for a fuller discussion of the method.

Deduction

NAME _____ SCORE _____

DIRECTIONS   Prepare for a class discussion of the premises and conclusions in the following:

1. Major Premise: All angels are immaterial beings.

   Minor Premise: All immaterial beings are weightless.

   Conclusion: All angels are weightless.

2. Major Premise: One must choose between learning to use a computer and making costly errors.

   Minor Premise: José has learned to use a computer.

   Conclusion: Therefore, he will not make costly errors.

3. Major Premise: It is impossible to be both rich and unhappy.

   Minor Premise: Rucker is not rich.

   Conclusion: Therefore, he must be unhappy.

31g Avoid fallacies.

Fallacies are faults in reasoning. They may result from misusing or misrepresenting evidence, from relying on faulty premises or omitting a needed premise, or from distorting the issues.

(1) Non sequitur: A statement that does not follow logically from what has just been said—a conclusion that does not follow from the premises.

> FAULTY   Of course Sharon Olds will speak at May Day exercises. Galway Kinnell spoke last year, didn't he? [That Kinnell spoke does not prove Olds will speak.]

(2) Hasty generalization: A generalization based on too little evidence or on exceptional or biased evidence.

> FAULTY   Two-year-olds are stubborn. [Undoubtedly, some two-year-olds are not stubborn.]

(3) Ad hominem: Attacking the person who presents an issue rather than dealing logically with the issue itself.

> FAULTY   Her response to the poem seems sensible, but how can we take seriously the ideas of someone who is still a freshman? [That she is a freshman does not necessarily invalidate her ideas.]

(4) Bandwagon: An argument saying, in effect, "Everyone is doing or saying this, so you (or we) should too."

> FAULTY   Everyone else is skipping class, so why shouldn't we? [That others do it does not make it right.]

(5) Red herring: Dodging the real issue by drawing attention to an irrelevant issue.

> FAULTY   Why worry about pollution of the river when we have homeless people on the streets? [Homeless people have nothing to do with pollution.]

(6) False dilemma: Stating that only two alternatives exist when in fact there are more than two.

> FAULTY   We have only two choices: Immigrate to New Zealand or become inner-city teachers. [Other possibilities exist.]

(7) False analogy: The assumption that because two things are alike in some ways, they must be alike in other ways.

> FAULTY   Since the novels are both paperback and cost the same, one is probably as good as the other. [The cost and paperback cover have nothing to do with quality.]

(8) Equivocation: An assertion that falsely relies on the use of a term in two different senses.

> FAULTY   The teacher has the right to set the attendance policy, so she should do what is right and give unlimited cuts. [The word *right* means both "a just claim" and "correct."]

(9) Slippery slope: The assumption that one thing will lead to another as the first step in a downward spiral.

> FAULTY   The ethnic strife in the former Soviet Union shows that we are headed for another world war. [The strife will not necessarily lead to such extreme results.]

(10) Oversimplification: A statement that omits some important aspects of an issue.

> FAULTY   Now that you know how to use the computer, you can write the paper. [Writing the paper is a far different activity than working with the computer.]

(11) Begging the question: An assertion that restates the point just made. Such an assertion is circular in that it draws as a conclusion a point stated in the premise.

> FAULTY   I did poorly on the test because I did not know the answers. [Doing poorly and not knowing the answers are essentially the same thing.]

(12) False cause: The mistake of assuming that because one event follows another, the first must be the cause of the second. (Also called *post hoc, ergo propter hoc,* or "after this, so because of this.")

> FAULTY   Hurricane Sarah hit last summer and two months later the whole pecan grove died. [The assumption is that the hurricane caused the death of the trees, an assumption which may not be true.]

Fallacies   Exercise 31–2

NAME _____   SCORE _____

DIRECTIONS   Identify the fallacies in the following sentences.

1. The Berlin Wall fell in 1989; now immigration rates
   have increased by ten percent.   _____false cause_____

2. Vinh is so inexperienced because he has not done this
   before.   _____

3. Why worry about the ozone layer when the inner-city
   crime rate is so high?   _____

4. The students are sick of hearing the administration's
   excuses about funding for the athletic team, but it is a
   sickness that we can cure by cutting the funds in half. _____

5. We have two choices: tear down the old gym or con-
   vert it into office space.   _____

6. His questions to the visiting speaker were not well
   received because we all knew about his drug problem. _____

7. The Lyceum has only women speakers, and so does
   the honors program. It is time for us to do the same. _____

8. The poem is brief and it rhymes; therefore, it will be
   good.   _____

9. The classes are taught in the same building by teachers
   from the same department, so they should be identical
   classes.   _____

10. Sophomores just do not understand *haiku*.   _____

281

32

Write unified, coherent, and adequately developed paragraphs.

We recognize the beginning of a new paragraph by the indention of the first word—about one inch when handwritten or five spaces when typewritten. A paragraph may range in length from 50 to 250 words, with an average length of about 100 words. The indention and length of a paragraph are signals to the reader that this unit of discourse will coherently and adequately develop an idea. As we read a paragraph, we expect to learn the controlling idea and to understand the relationship that each of the sentences has to that idea. And, finally, we expect the sentences to flow smoothly, so that we do not have to mentally fill in any words or phrases or stop reading at any point to refocus our attention.

32a Construct unified paragraphs.

(1) Make sure each sentence is related to the central thought.

In the following paragraph the controlling idea appears in italics. The words in boldface echo the controlling idea and help to unify the discussion.

> 1 *I want to be a modern woman.* I still have a nostalgic Afro, though it's **stylishly short.** I apologize to the hair industry, but frankly, I like both my kinks and my gray strands. Plus, being a sixties person, **glowing in the dark carries negative implications for me.** Most of my friends do wear **base, pancake, powder, eye makeup, lipstick, and always keep their nails in perfectly ovaled shapes with base, color, sealer, and oil for the cuticles.** Do I use these things? No. But neither do I put them down nor try to make my friends feel guilty for **not being natural.** There is something to be said for **improvement.** I've been known to comment: "Wow, you **look really good. Who does your nails**?" Why, I even have a dear friend who is a few months younger than I and uses a **night cream to guard against wrinkles.** Do I laugh? No, ma'am. I say, "Well, your **face is very, very, smooth,**" which (1) makes her feel good about her efforts and (2) keeps the friendship intact.
>
> —NIKKI GIOVANNI, *Sacred Cows...And Other Edibles*

Giovanni explains in a humorous tone her aspiration to be a modern woman. Every sentence in the paragraph relates clearly and directly to the controlling idea. The reader never has to fill in gaps in the ideas or suffer the momentary confusion caused by a sentence that does not continue to develop the main idea.

(2) State the main idea of the paragraph in a clearly constructed topic sentence.

A topic sentence embodies the central thought of a paragraph. Notice how the first sentence of paragraph 2 clearly signals the idea to be developed; obviously Woody Allen intends to define "spiffy."

2   Now, we all know when someone is dressed up, we say he looks "spiffy." The term owes its origin to Sir Oswald Spiffy, perhaps the most renowned fop of Victorian England. Heir to treacle millions, Spiffy squandered his money on clothes. It was said at one time he owned enough handkerchiefs for all the men, women, and children in Asia to blow their noses for seven years without stopping. Spiffy's sartorial innovations were legend, and he was the first man ever to wear gloves on his head. Because of extra-sensitive skin, Spiffy's underwear had to be made of the finest Nova Scotia salmon, carefully sliced by one particular tailor. His libertine attitudes involved him in several notorious scandals, and he eventually sued the government over the right to wear earmuffs while fondling a dwarf. In the end Spiffy died a broken man in Chichester, his total wardrobe reduced to kneepads and a sombrero.

—WOODY ALLEN, *Without Feathers*

Often the main idea of a paragraph is stated at the beginning, as in paragraphs 1 and 2, but it may occur anywhere in the paragraph. In paragraph 3 the topic sentence is in the fourth sentence.

3   I was thinking one day about recent deaths of some of the traditional people and how difficult it is to maintain tradition. I was also thinking how important oral tradition is in helping maintain the values of culture, and how in a sense oral tradition is also an art form. As the elders pass on, the young people fill their places. Even though we know no one lives forever, no one dies if what they have gained by living is carried forward by those who follow—if we as individuals assume the responsibilities. This is easy to talk and write about, but it is hard to practice.

—FRANK LAPEÑA, *News from Native California*

When a paragraph progresses from particulars to a generalization, the topic sentence is likely to occur at the end, as in paragraph 4.

4   So we have to remind ourselves that there are things that transcend generations, and the living force of that truth is carried by the person-to-person confidentiality of oral tradition. A lot depends upon the transmission of information from one person to another. Oral tradition is the educational tool of understanding the natural world.

—FRANK LAPEÑA, *News from Native California*

A single topic sentence may serve for a sequence of two or more paragraphs. The first sentence in paragraph 5 unites paragraphs 5 and 6.

5   We found the Americans as strange in their customs as they probably found us. Immediately we discovered that there were no *mercados* and that when shopping you did not put the groceries in a *chiquihuite*. Instead everything was in cans or in cardboard boxes or each item was put in a brown paper bag. There were neighborhood grocery stores at the corners and some big ones uptown, but no *mercado*. The grocers did not give children a *pilón*, they did not stand at the door and coax you to come in and buy, as they did in Mazatlán. The fruits and vegetables were displayed on counters instead of being piled up on the floor. The stores smelled of fly spray and oiled floors, not of fresh pineapple and limes.

6   Neither was there a plaza, only parks which had no bandstands, no concerts every Thursday, no Judases exploding on Holy Week, and no promenades of boys going one way and the girls the other. There were no parks in the *barrio;* and the ones uptown were cold and rainy in winter, and in summer there was no place to sit except on the grass. When

there were celebrations nobody set off rockets in the parks, much less on the street in front of your house to announce to the neighborhood that a wedding or a baptism was taking place. Sacramento did not have a *mercado* and a plaza with the cathedral to one side and the Palacio de Gobierno on another to make it obvious that there and nowhere else was the center of the town.

—ERNESTO GALARZA, *Barrio Boy*

Occasionally no topic sentence is necessary because the details clearly imply the controlling idea.

7 We were working at the laundry when a delivery boy came from the Rexall drugstore around the corner. He had a pale blue box of pills, but nobody was sick. Reading the label we saw that it belonged to another Chinese family, Crazy Mary's family. "Not ours," said my father. He pointed out the name to the delivery ghost [Kingston uses "ghost" to designate a non-Chinese person.], who took the pills back. My mother muttered for an hour, and then her anger boiled over. "That ghost! That dead ghost! How dare he come to the wrong house?" She could not concentrate on her marking and pressing. "A mistake! Huh!" I was getting angry myself. She fumed. She made our press crash and hiss. "Revenge. We've got to avenge this wrong on our future, our health, and on our lives. Nobody's going to sicken my children and get away with it." We brothers and sisters did not look at one another. She would do something awful, something embarrassing. She'd already been hinting that during the next eclipse we slam pot lids together to scare the frog from swallowing the moon. (The word for "eclipse" is *frog-swallowing-the-moon*.) When we had not banged lids at the last eclipse and the shadow kept receding anyway, she'd said, "The villagers must be banging and clanging very loudly back home in China."

—MAXINE HONG KINGSTON, *Woman Warrior*

32b Make paragraphs coherent by arranging ideas in a clear, logical order and by providing appropriate transitions.

(1) Arrange ideas in a clear logical order.

The paragraphs below illustrate several ways to arrange ideas in a paragraph. The choice depends on the context of the writing and on the writer's purpose.

TIME ORDER

8 There is a story about the way the first pipe came to us. A very long time ago, they say, two scouts were out looking for bison; and when they came to the top of a high hill and looked north, they saw something coming a long way off, and when it came close they cried out, "It is a woman!" and it was. Then one of the scouts, being foolish, had bad thoughts and spoke them; but the other said: "That is a sacred woman; throw all bad thoughts away." When she came still closer, they saw that she wore a fine white buckskin dress, that her hair was very long and that she was young and very beautiful. And she knew their thoughts and said in a voice that was like singing: "You do not know me, but if you want to do as you think, you may come." And the foolish one went; but just as he stood before her, there was a white cloud that came and covered them. And the beautiful young woman came out of the cloud, and when it blew away the foolish man was a skeleton covered with worms.

—BLACK ELK, *Black Elk Speaks*

Paragraph 9 demonstrates space order, an arrangement particularly useful for descriptions.

SPACE ORDER

9   The kitchen was dominated by a large Victorian china closet, and the built-in wall shelves were lined with oilcloth, trimmed with ruffle, both decorated by brilliant and miniature fruits. Prominent on a wall of the kitchen was a large reproduction of a still life, a harvest table full of produce, framed and under glass. From it, I learned to identify apples, pumpkins, bananas, pears, grapes, and melons, and "peaches without worms." A joke between my mother and me. (A peach we had bought in the city market, under the New Haven's elevated tracks, bore, like the trains above, passengers.)

—JACK AGUEROS, *The Immigrant Experience: The Anguish of Becoming American*

ORDER OF IMPORTANCE

10   The ethnic American is overtaxed and underserved at every level of government. First, he cannot afford fancy lawyers or expensive lobbyists getting him tax breaks on his income. Yet, being a homeowner he shoulders the burden of property taxes which are the primary revenue producers for the municipalities where he lives. Second, he knows that one major illness in his family can wipe him out financially. If he needs a nursing home for an elderly family member, he is not eligible for financial assistance—he earns too much. And last and most important to him, his children attend parochial schools which receive little government assistance. Thus his future, his children, are imperiled.

Sometimes the movement within the paragraphs is from general to specific or from specific to general—as paragraphs 11 and 12 demonstrate.

GENERAL TO SPECIFIC; SPECIFIC TO GENERAL

11   Today, eight years after my departure (from Mexico), when they ask me for my nationality or ethnic identity, I can't respond with one word, since my "identity" now possesses multiple repertories: I am Mexican, but I am also Chicano and Latin American. At the border they call me *chilango* or *mexiquillo;* in Mexico City it's *pocho* or *norteno;* and in Europe it's *sudaca.* The Anglos call me "Hispanic" or "Latino," and the Germans have, on more than one occasion, confused me with Turks or Italians. My wife Emilia is Anglo-Italian, but speaks Spanish with an Argentine accent, and together we walk amid the rubble of the Tower of Babble of our American post-modernity.

—GUILLERMO GÓMEZ-PEÑA, *"Documented/Undocumented"*

12   Discrimination means discernment; it means the ability to perceive the truth, to use good judgment and to profit accordingly. The Oxford English Dictionary traces this understanding of the word back to 1648 and demonstrates that for the next 300 years, "discrimination" was a virtue, not a vice. Thus, when a character in a nineteenth-century novel makes a happy marriage, Dickens has another character remark, "It does credit to your discrimination that you should have found such a very excellent young woman."

—ROBERT KEITH MILLER, *"Discrimination Is a Virtue"*

One common form of the general-specific pattern is topic-restriction-illustration. The writer announces the topic, restricts or qualifies it, and then illustrates it.

TOPIC–RESTRICTION–ILLUSTRATION

13   America is not a melting pot. It is a sizzling cauldron for the ethnic American who feels that he has been politically extorted by both government and private enterprise. The ethnic American is sick of being stereotyped as a racist and dullard by phony white liberals, pseudo black militants and patronizing bureaucrats. He pays the bill for every major government program and gets nothing or little in the way of return. Tricked by the political rhetoric of the illusionary funding for black-oriented social programs, he turns his anger to race—when he himself is the victim of class prejudice. He has worked hard all of his life to become a "good American;" he and his sons have fought on every battlefield, then he is made fun of because he likes the flag.

—BARBARA MIKULSKI, *Poles in the Americas: 1608-1972*

In the problem–solution pattern, the first sentence states a problem and the solution follows.

PROBLEM–SOLUTION

14   Unity is not automatically bequeathed to people of color. Racism translates the differences among us into *relatively* preferential treatment for some at the expense of others, promoting internalized racism and cross-racial hostility. Disunity among people of color due to the exploitation of differences is an inherent part of the system of racism. The potential for unity is there and the power is tremendous—witness the recent Civil Rights Movement. For unity to develop and continue to exist, the distrust and discord ever-present among us must be replaced.

—VIRGINIA R. HARRIS AND TRINITY A. ORDOÑA, *Haciendo Caras: Making Face, Making Soul*

In the question–answer pattern, the topic sentence asks a question and the supporting sentences answer it.

QUESTION–ANSWER

15   Where will the American Indian homeless go to avoid freezing to death this winter? Yes, that's right; it's hard for some people to believe, but it's true. There are a lot of American Indians who are homeless; as a matter of fact, 1 out of 18 homeless on skidrow is Indian.

—GARY TEWALESTEWA, *"American Indians: Homeless in Their Own Homeland"*

Many types of development exist, and you will have occasion to create types that combine or modify those represented in the preceding paragraphs. Remember, however, that your goal as a writer is to make your sequence of thought clear.

(2) Provide appropriate transitions.

Transitional devices such as pronouns, repetition of key words or ideas, appropriate conjunctions and other transitional expressions, and parallel structures help create a coherent paragraph. Paragraph 16 exhibits several transitional devices.

16   In individual interviews **we asked** each **woman** what **she thought** would stay with her about her experiences in the school or program she attended. **We asked her** to tell us about specific academic and non-academic experiences, about **good and bad** teachers, **good and bad** assignments, **good and bad** programs or courses. **We asked her** whether **she** thought that **her** participation in the program had changed the way **she thought**

about herself or the world. **We asked:** "In your learning here, have you come across an idea that made you see things differently?" "What has been most helpful to you about this place?" "Are there things it doesn't provide that are important to **you**? Things **you** would like to learn that **you** can't learn here?" **Finally, we asked,** "Looking back over your whole life, can **you tell us** about a really powerful learning experience that **you've had,** in or out of school?"

—BLYTHE MCVICKER CLINCHY ET AL, *"Connected Education for Women"*

In this finely crafted paragraph the authors use several devices to achieve coherence.

PRONOUN REFERENCE   Repetition of *we, her, she,* and *you.*

REPETITION OF KEY WORDS OR IDEAS   The repeated *we asked* and *she thought.*

PARALLEL STRUCTURE   The structure depends on repeated questions put to women students by women questioners. The repeated questions and pronouns make the paragraph strongly coherent.

The authors could have used conjunctions and other transitional expressions to link sentences, but they did not need them—except for *finally* near the end which helps provide closure.

You may find the following list of connectives useful:

1. *Alternative and addition:* or, nor, and, and then, moreover, further, furthermore, besides, likewise, also, too, again, in addition, even more important, next, first, second, third, in the first place, in the second place, finally, last.
2. *Comparison:* similarly, likewise, in like manner.
3. *Contrast:* but, yet, or, and yet, however, still, nevertheless, on the other hand, on the contrary, conversely, even so, notwithstanding, for all that, in contrast, at the same time, although this may be true, otherwise, nonetheless.
4. *Place:* here, beyond, nearby, opposite to, adjacent to, on the opposite side.
5. *Purpose:* to this end, for this purpose, with this object.
6. *Cause, result:* so, for, hence, therefore, accordingly, consequently, thus, thereupon, as a result, then.
7. *Summary, repetition, exemplification, intensification:* to sum up, in brief, on the whole, in sum, in short, as I have said, in other words, that is, to be sure, as has been noted, for example, for instance, in fact, indeed, to tell the truth, in any event.
8. *Time:* meanwhile, at length, soon, after a few days, in the meantime, afterward, later, now, then, in the past.

Clear writing demands clear transitions between paragraphs as well as between sentences. Notice the transitional devices used in the following paragraphs in which Allene Guss Grognet discusses second-language learning among older immigrants.

17   Taking adult learning theory, or andragogy, seriously can help build successes. Andragogy assumes that learning situations take into account the experiences of the learner, providing the opportunity for new learning to be related to previous experiences. Furthermore, the adult learner should be involved in analyzing both the new and the old experiences.

Andragogy also assumes that for the adult, readiness to learn is decreasingly the product of biological development or academic pressure, and increasingly the product of the desire to accomplish tasks required in work and/or social roles.

Finally, andragogy assumes that children have more of a subject-centered orientation to learning, whereas adults tend to have a problem-solving orientation to learning (e.g., The child wants to learn "arithmetic," while the adult may want to learn to add and subtract in order to keep a check book.) This means that language learning must incorporate strategies appropriate to adult learners. Learning situations which adults perceive as putting them in the position of being treated as children are bound to interfere with their learning.

—ALLENE GUSS GROGNET, *"Elderly Refugees and Language Learning"*

The transitional expressions—*furthermore, also, finally*—effectively signal the relationships between ideas; the content of the paragraphs bears out the signal. Other similarly useful expressions are

First...Then...Next...Finally...
Then...Now...Soon...Later...
One...Another...Still another...
Some...Others...Still others...
A few...Many...More...Most...
Just as significant...More important...Most important of all...

32c Develop the paragraph adequately.

Sometimes very brief paragraphs, even paragraphs of one sentence, are appropriate. But most very brief paragraphs are brief because their topics are not developed or because they are not paragraphs at all—they are fragments of paragraphs which actually belong elsewhere in the writing. Analyze the paragraphs below to decide how they are inadequately developed and what revision would improve them.

18   Now that I can have her only in memory, I see my grandmother in the several postures that were peculiar to her: standing at the wood stove on a winter morning and turning meat in a great iron skillet; sitting at the south window, bent above her beadwork, and afterwards, when her vision failed, looking down for a long time into the fold of her hands; going out upon a cane, very slowly as she did when the weight of age came upon her; praying.

19   I remember her most often at prayer. She made long, rambling prayers out of suffering and hope, having seen many things. I was never sure that I had the right to hear, so exclusive were they of all mere custom and company. The last time I saw her she prayed standing by the side of her bed at night stark naked to the waist, the light of a kerosene lamp moving upon her dark skin. Her long, black hair, always drawn and braided in the day, lay upon her shoulders and against her breasts like a shawl.

20   I do not speak Kiowa, and I never understood her prayers, but there was something inherently sad in the sound, some merest hesitation upon the syllables of sorrow. She began in a high and descending pitch, exhausting her breath to silence; then again and again—and always the same intensity of effort, of something that is, and is not like urgency in the human voice. Transported so in the dancing light among the shadows of her room, she seemed beyond the reach of time. But that was illusion; I think I knew then that I should not see her again.

—N. SCOTT MOMADAY, *The Way to Rainy Mountain*

These three paragraphs are paragraphs only insofar as indention denotes a paragraph. Together, however, they form a complete discussion of the idea stated in the first sentence. If you have difficulty developing paragraphs, study carefully the methods of development discussed in **32d**.

(1) Use relevant details to develop the controlling idea.

You always need to know the details that support the idea you are writing about. Occasionally you may not use those details, but knowing them will make it possible for you to write about the idea with confidence. All the types of development discussed in **32d** require that you know and use relevant details.

In the following paragraph the author explains some of the logic of Black English.

21   Black English also differs considerably from Standard English in the various ways in which negative statements are structured. The Black English *He ain't go* is not simply the equivalent of the standard *He didn't go.* The speaker of black English is not using *ain't* as a past tense, but rather to express the negative for the momentary act of going, whether it happened in the past or is happening right now. If the Black English speaker, on the other hand, wants to speak of someone who is habitually the kind of person who does not go, he would say, *He ain't goin.* *Ain't* also serves several other functions in Black English. *Dey ain't like dat* might be thought by speakers of Standard to mean *"They aren't like that"*— but it actually means *"They didn't like that,"* because in this usage *ain't* is the negative of the auxiliary verb *to do. Ain't* can also emphasize a negation by doubling it, as in *He ain't no rich.* And in what would be a negative *if*-clause in Standard English, the rules of Black English eliminate the *if* and invert the verb—with the result that the equivalent of the Standard *He doesn't know if she can go* is the Black English *He don't know can she go.*
       —PETER FARB, *WordPlay: What Happens When People Talk*

The first sentence suggests the purpose for the details—to illustrate Farb's contention that Black English structures negative statements differently from Standard English. With that in the reader's mind the details build a picture of a complex linguistic system.

(2) Illustrate a generalization using several closely related examples or one striking example.

22   Poverty is asking for help. Have you ever had to ask for help, knowing your children will suffer unless you get it? Think about asking for a loan from a relative, if this is the only way you can imagine asking for help. I will tell you how it feels. You find out where the office is that you are supposed to visit. You circle the block four or five times. Thinking of your children, you go tell her that you need help. That never is the person that you need to see. You go see another person, and after spilling the whole shame of poverty all over the desk between you, you find that this isn't the right office after all—you must repeat the whole process, and it never is any easier at the next place.
       —JO GOODWIN PARKER, *"What Good Is Poverty?"*

32d Learn to use various methods of paragraph development.

Writers do not often write paragraphs that perfectly exemplify a single method of development. Most paragraphs combine two or more of the methods as the writer adapts them to a particular audience and purpose. The models that are presented below will help you, however, to learn the characteristics of each type of development. By studying and imitating the models you are not simply restricting yourself for the moment to a particular type of writing; instead, you are learning to use that type of writing to make yourself a more flexible and confident writer. You will have that type of development in mind the next time you write and will almost unconsciously use it in paragraphs or parts of paragraphs because you know it fits your purpose, audience, and content.

(1) Narrate a series of events.

In paragraph 23, the writer narrates her mother's response to the job forced on her by the death of her husband.

23   She pulled on her girdle and her old gray suit, stepped into her black suede chunky heels, applied powder and lipstick to her face, and took the subway downtown to an employment agency where she got a job clerking in an office for twenty-eight dollars a week. After that, she rose each morning, got dressed and drank coffee, made out a grocery list for me, left it together with money on the kitchen table, walked four blocks to the subway station, bought the *Times,* read it on the train, got off at Forty-second Street, entered her office building, sat down at her desk, put in a day's work, made the trip home at five o'clock, came in the apartment door, slumped onto the kitchen bench for supper, then onto the couch where she instantly sank into a depression she welcomed like a warm bath. It was as though she had worked all day to earn the despair waiting faithfully for her at the end of her unwilling journey into daily life.

          —VIVIAN GORNICK, *Calling Home: Working-Class Women's Writing*

(2) Describe by presenting an orderly sequence of sensory details.

In paragraph 24 Annie Dillard describes in nearly microscopic detail some of the sights of a jungle. Notice the narrative structure and the active verbs.

24   When you are inside the jungle, away from the river, the trees vault out of sight. It is hard to remember to look up the long trunks and see the fans, strips, fronds, and sprays of glossy leaves. Inside the jungle you are more likely to notice the snarl of climbers and creepers round the trees' boles, the flowering bromeliads and epiphytes in every bough's crook, and the fantastic silk-cotton tree trunks thirty or forty feet across, trunks buttressed in flanges of wood whose curves can make three high walls of a room—a shady, loamy-aired room where you would gladly live, or die. Butterflies, iridescent blue, striped, or clearwinged, thread the jungle paths at eye level. At your feet is a swath of ants bearing triangular bits of green leaf. The ants with their leaves look like a wide fleet of sailing dinghies—but they don't quit. In either direction they wobble over the jungle floor as far as the eye can see. I followed them off the path as far as I dared, and never saw an end to ants or to those luffing chips of green they bore.

          —ANNIE DILLARD, *"Teaching a Stone to Talk"*

(3) Explain a process.

In a paragraph from his autobiography, Malcolm X explains how learning the dictionary guided his mastery of language.

25   I was so fascinated that I went on—I copied the dictionary's next page. And the same experience came when I studied that. With every succeeding page, I also learned of people

and places and events from history. Actually the dictionary is like a miniature encyclopedia. Finally the dictionary's A section had filled a whole tablet—and I went on into the B's. That was the way I started copying what eventually became the entire dictionary. It went a lot faster after so much practice helped me to pick up handwriting speed. Between what I wrote in my tablet, and writing letters, during the rest of my time in prison I would guess I wrote a million words.

—MALCOLM X, *The Autobiography of Malcolm X*

(4) Show cause and effect.

A paragraph of this type asserts a causal relationship; it must explain why one thing caused another and must do so convincingly. In paragraph 26 the author states the effect first—that she is a nudist from the neck up. Then she explains the causes for this decision not to wear makeup.

26   From the neck up, I am a nudist. No mascara for me. No eyeliner, no lipstick, no blush, no powder, foundation, eye shadow, highlighter, lip pencil or concealing stick. My nakedness is partly pragmatic and partly philosophical. Just getting my eyes open in the morning is a feat. I have neither the will nor the ability to apply makeup when I can hardly see straight. At night, the most I can manage is brushing my teeth. I'm afraid that removing makeup would go the same way as scrubbing the sink and cleaning the oven. Also I rub my eyes occasionally, which doesn't help the makeup. Neither does my baby daughter.

—KAREN RAY, *"The Naked Face"*

(5) Compare or contrast to develop a main idea.

Paragraph 27 demonstrates the analysis necessary for comparison and contrast. It is part of a larger discussion of communication between men and women, and in this paragraph the author analyzes the responsive sounds that we utter as we listen to another person talk.

27   Anthropologists Daniel Malz and Ruth Borker report that women and men have different ways of showing that they're listening. Women make—and expect—more listening noises, such as "mhm" and "uh-huh." So, when a man is listening to a woman telling him something, he's not likely to make enough noises to convince her he's really hearing her. And, when a woman is listening to a man, making more "mhms" and "uh-huhs" than he expects or would use himself, he may get the impression she's impatient for him to finish or exaggerating her interest in what he's saying.

—DEBORAH TANNEN,
That's Not What I Meant: How Conversational
Style Makes or Breaks Your Relations with Others

(6) Use classification and division to relate ideas.

Classification and division require grouping ideas or elements into categories. In paragraph 28 Martin Luther King, Jr., asserts that there are three ways for oppressed people to deal with their oppression. In the remainder of the paragraph he discusses one of these ways.

28   Oppressed people deal with their oppression in three characteristic ways. One way is acquiescence: the oppressed resign themselves to their doom. They tacitly adjust themselves to oppression, and thereby become conditioned to it. In every movement toward

freedom some of the oppressed prefer to remain oppressed. Almost 2800 years ago Moses set out to lead the children of Israel from the slavery of Egypt to the freedom of the promised land. He soon discovered that slaves do not always welcome their deliverers. They become accustomed to being slaves. They would rather bear those ills they have, as Shakespeare pointed out, than flee to others that they know not. They prefer the "fleshpots of Egypt" to the ordeals of emancipation.

—MARTIN LUTHER KING, JR., *Stride Toward Freedom*

(7) Formulate a definition.

Paragraph 29 is part of an extended definition essay in which Judy Syfers, a wife and mother, explains why she, too, would like a wife.

29   I want a wife who will take care of the details of my social life. When my wife and I are invited out by our friends, I want a wife who will take care of the babysitting arrangements. When I meet people at school that I like and want to entertain, I want a wife who will have the house clean, will prepare a special meal, serve it to me and my friends, and not interrupt when I talk about things that interest me and my friends. I want a wife who will have arranged that the children are fed and ready for bed before my guests arrive so that the children do not bother us. I want a wife who takes care of the needs of my guests so that they feel comfortable, who makes sure that they have an ashtray, that they are passed the hors d'oeuvres, that they are offered a second helping of the food, that their wine glasses are replenished when necessary, that their coffee is served to them as they like it. And I want a wife who knows that sometimes I need a night out by myself.

—JUDY SYFERS, *"I Want a Wife"*

(8) Use a combination of methods to develop the main idea.

Combining methods of development, the authors of the following paragraphs serve their readers well by writing clear, complete, and appropriate discussions. Notice how difficult it is to separate the methods of development in these paragraphs.

30   At Laguna Pueblo in New Mexico, "Who is your mother?" is an important question. At Laguna, one of several of the ancient Keres gynocratic societies of the region, your mother's identity is the key to your own identity. Among the Keres, every individual has a place within the universe—human and nonhuman—and that place is defined by clan membership. In turn, clan membership is dependent on matrilineal descent. Of course, your mother is not only that woman whose womb formed and released you—the term refers in every individual case to an entire generation of women whose psychic, and consequently physical, "shape" made the psychic existence of the following generation possible. But naming your own mother (or her equivalent) enables people to place you precisely within the universal web of your life, in each of its dimensions: cultural, spiritual, personal, and historical.

—PAULA GUNN ALLEN,
The Sacred Hoop: Recovering the Feminine in American Indian Traditions

31   Some are refugees from sad countries torn apart by war. Others are children of the stable middle class whose parents came to the U.S. in search of a better life. Some came with nothing, not even the rudiments of English. Others came with skills and affluence. Many were born in the U.S. to immigrant parents.

No matter what their route, young Asian Americans, largely those with Chinese, Korean, and Indochinese backgrounds, are setting the educational pace for the rest of

America and cutting a dazzling figure at the country's finest schools. Consider some of this fall's freshman classes: at Brown it will be 9% Asian American, at Harvard nearly 14%, the Massachusetts Institute of Technology 20%, the California Institute of Technology 21% and the University of California, Berkeley an astonishing 25%.

By almost every educational gauge, young Asian Americans are soaring. They are finishing way above the mean on the math section of the Scholastic Aptitude Test and, according to one comprehensive study of San Diego-area students, outscoring their peers of other races in high school grade-point averages. They spend more time on their homework, a researcher at the U.S. Department of Education found, take more advanced high school courses and graduate with more credits than other American students. A higher percentage of these young people complete high school and finish college than do white American students. Trying to explain why so many Asian-American students are superachievers, Harvard Psychology Professor Jerome Kagan comes up with this simple answer: "To put it plainly, they work harder."

—DAVID BRAND, *"The New Whiz Kids"*

Unity, Coherence, and Development

Exercise 32–1

NAME _____ SCORE _____

DIRECTIONS Discuss the unity, coherence, and development of the following paragraphs by answering the questions that follow them.

PARAGRAPH ONE

[1]Our schools and our institutions of higher learning have in recent years begun to embrace what Catherine R. Stimpson of Rutgers University has called "cultural democracy," a recognition that we must listen to a "diversity of voices" in order to understand our culture, past and present. [2]This understanding of the pluralistic nature of American culture has taken a long time to forge. [3]It is based on sound scholarship and has led to major revisions in what children are taught and what they read in school. [4]The new history is—indeed, must be—a warts-and-all history; it demands an unflinching examination of racism and discrimination in our history. [5]Making these changes is difficult, raises tempers, and ignites controversies, but gives a more interesting and accurate account of American history. [6]Accomplishing these changes is valuable, because there is also a useful lesson for the rest of the world in America's relatively successful experience as a pluralistic society. [7]Throughout human history, the clash of different cultures, races, ethnic groups, and religions has often been the cause of bitter hatred, civil conflict and international war. [8]The ethnic tensions that are now tearing apart Lebanon, Sri Lanka, Kashmir, and various republics of the Soviet Union remind us of the costs of unfettered group rivalry. [9]Thus, it is a matter of more than domestic importance that we closely examine and try to understand that part of our national history in which different groups competed, fought, suffered, but ultimately learned to live together in relative peace and even achieved a sense of common nationhood.

—DIANE RAVITCH, *"Multiculturalism: E Pluribus Plures"*

QUESTIONS

1. Which sentence states the controlling idea? _____

2. What are the keys words in the controlling idea? _____

3. What transitional expressions help achieve coherence? _____

4. What is the main method used to develop the controlling idea? _____

THE PARAGRAPH

PARAGRAPH TWO

¹The Flint Hills are the last remaining grand expanse of tallgrass prairie in America. ²On a geologic map, their shape something like a stone spear point, they cover most of the two-hundred-mile longitude of Kansas from Nebraska to Oklahoma, a stony upland twenty to eighty miles wide. ³At their western edge, the mixed grass prairie begins and spreads a hundred or so miles to the shortgrass country of the high plains. ⁴On the eastern side, settlement and agriculture have all but obliterated the whilom tallgrass prairie so that it is hardly visible to anyone who would not seek it out on hands and knees; although the six million acres of the Flint Hills—also called the Bluestem Hills—were once a mere four percent of the American long-grass prairie, they are now nearly all of it. ⁵The grasses can grow to ten feet high, high enough that red men once stood atop their horses to see twenty yards ahead; that wasn't common, but it occurred, and, even today in moist vales protected from development and cattle, I've found big bluestem and sloughgrass, the grandest of the tallgrasses, eight feet high. ⁶In season these and their relatives make the Flint Hills an immense pasturage nutritionally richer than the Bluegrass country of Kentucky. ⁷During the warm season, a big steer will gain two pounds a day, and the 120,000 beeves in the uplands will put on twenty-two million pounds.

—WILLIAM LEAST HEAT MOON, *PrairyErth*

QUESTIONS

1. Which sentence states the controlling idea? _____

2. What transitional devices are used in sentences 3 and 4? _____

_____

3. What type of order is used? _____

4. What is the main method used to develop the controlling idea? _____

_____

Paragraph Practice: Details   Exercise 32–2

NAME _____ SCORE _____

DIRECTIONS   Using *details* as the method of development (see **32c[1]**), write a paragraph on one of the subjects listed below or on one of your own or your instructor's choosing. First, plan the paragraph, writing out a controlling idea. Then compose the sentences in your paragraph. You may use details from this book (rephrased in your own words, of course), details from your own knowledge, or, if your instructor permits, details gathered from research.

SUBJECTS

1. a scene from nature
2. a memory of a family member
3. a family tradition in which you participate
4. a sporting event in which you participated
5. an automobile for which you hold strong feelings

CONTROLLING IDEA

DEVELOPMENT

1.

2.

3.

4.

5.

PARAGRAPH

Paragraph Practice: Examples   Exercise 32–3

NAME _____ SCORE _____

DIRECTIONS Using several closely related *examples* or one striking *example* as the method of development (see **32c[2]**), write a paragraph on one of the subjects listed below or one of your own or your instructor's choosing. First, plan the paragraph, writing out the controlling idea and making a list of three or more examples that will develop the controlling idea. Then compose the sentences in your paragraph. You may use examples from this book (rephrased in your own words, of course), examples from your own knowledge, or, if your instructor permits, examples gathered from research.

SUBJECTS

1. a typical day of work at a fast-food restaurant
2. your typical composing process for a writing assignment
3. a successful date
4. an unsuccessful date
5. a good adult/child relationship

CONTROLLING IDEA

DEVELOPMENT

1.

2.

3.

4.

5.

PARAGRAPH

Paragraph Practice: Process Analysis Exercise 32–4

NAME _____ SCORE _____

DIRECTIONS   Using *process analysis* as the method of development (see **32d[3]**), write a paragraph on one of the subjects listed below or one of your own or your instructor's choosing. First, plan the paragraph, writing out the controlling idea and making a list of three or more examples that will develop the controlling idea. Then compose the sentences in your paragraph. You may use examples from this book (rephrased in your own words, of course), examples from your own knowledge, or, if your instructor permits, examples gathered from research.

SUBJECTS

1. how to make work easier
2. how you learned to dance, to fish, to play soccer, etc.
3. how you research a family tree
4. how to arrange a surprise party
5. how to choose friends

CONTROLLING IDEA

DEVELOPMENT

1.

2.

3.

4.

5.

PARAGRAPH

Paragraph Practice: Cause and Effect   Exercise 32–5

NAME _____ SCORE _____

DIRECTIONS   Using *cause and effect* as the method of development (see **32d[4]**), write a paragraph on one of the subjects listed below or one of your own or your instructor's choosing. First, plan the paragraph, writing out the controlling idea and making a list of three or more examples that will develop the controlling idea. Then compose the sentences in your paragraph. You may use examples from this book (rephrased in your own words, of course), examples from your own knowledge, or, if your instructor permits, examples gathered from research.

SUBJECTS

1. the effects of movies on popular views of American Indians
2. the effects of Cuban immigrants on Florida
3. the effects of Chinese immigrants on America in the nineteenth century
4. the causes of Irish immigration to America in the nineteenth century
5. the effects of using only English (or only bilingual) teaching on education in America

CONTROLLING IDEA

DEVELOPMENT

1.

2.

3.

303

4.

5.

PARAGRAPH

Paragraph Practice: Comparison or Contrast

Exercise 32–6

NAME _____ SCORE _____

DIRECTIONS   Using *comparison or contrast* as the method of development (see **32d[5]**), write a paragraph on one of the subjects listed below or one of your own or your instructor's choosing. First, plan the paragraph, writing out the controlling idea and making a list of three or more examples that will develop the controlling idea. Then compose the sentences in your paragraph. You may use examples from this book (rephrased in your own words, of course), examples from your own knowledge, or, if your instructor permits, examples gathered from research.

SUBJECTS

1. compare or contrast a date in your parents' day to a typical date now
2. compare or contrast men's and women's attitudes toward food
3. compare or contrast the portrayal of a particular ethnic group on television or in the movies to what you know about that ethnic group
4. compare or contrast two sides of a contemporary social issue (such as public funding of AIDS research)
5. compare or contrast 1960's hippies to today's counter-culture crowd

CONTROLLING IDEA

DEVELOPMENT

1.

2.

3.

4.

5.

PARAGRAPH

Paragraph Practice: Classification   Exercise 32–7

NAME _____ SCORE _____

DIRECTIONS   Using *classification* as the method of development (see **32d[6]**), write a paragraph on one of the subjects listed below or one of your own or your instructor's choosing. First,
plan the paragraph, writing out the controlling idea and making a list of three or more examples
that will develop the controlling idea. Then compose the sentences in your paragraph. You may
use examples from this book (rephrased in your own words, of course), examples from your own
knowledge, or, if your instructor permits, examples gathered from research.

SUBJECTS

1. methods for making friends
2. ways of reacting to aggressive people
3. types of "untidy" roommates
4. types of friendships
5. types of racism

CONTROLLING IDEA

DEVELOPMENT

1.

2.

3.

4.

5.

PARAGRAPH

Paragraph Practice: Definition   Exercise 32–8

NAME _____ SCORE _____

DIRECTIONS   Using *extended definition* as the method of development (see **32d[7]**), write a paragraph on one of the subjects listed below or one of your own or your instructor's choosing. First, plan the paragraph, writing out the controlling idea and making a list of three or more examples that will develop the controlling idea. Then compose the sentences in your paragraph. You may use examples from this book (rephrased in your own words, of course), examples from your own knowledge, or, if your instructor permits, examples gathered from research.

SUBJECTS

1. the slang words popular today
2. the meaning of being an *adult*
3. the meaning of the term *husband* or *wife*
4. the meaning of *racism*
5. the meaning of being *educated*

CONTROLLING IDEA

DEVELOPMENT

1.

2.

3.

4.

5.

PARAGRAPH

Paragraph Practice: Combination of Methods

Exercise 32–9

NAME _____ SCORE _____

DIRECTIONS   Write a paragraph on one of the subjects listed below. First, plan the paragraph, writing out the controlling idea and making a list of three or more examples that will develop the controlling idea. Then compose the sentences in your paragraph, list in the margin the type or types of development you have used. Underline the controlling idea of your paragraph, and make a list of the transitional devices you have used to achieve coherence.

SUBJECTS

1. a book or television program that has changed the way you think about minorities or women
2. a theme in a story by your favorite writer
3. the meaning of family
4. an aspect of male/female relationships
5. an aspect of relations between generations (such as between your generation and that of your grandparents')

CONTROLLING IDEA

DEVELOPMENT

1.

2.

3.

4.

5.

PARAGRAPH

TRANSITIONAL DEVICES

33

450 – 600 words
(4–6 pages)

Learn to plan, draft, and revise your compositions effectively.

The principles that you studied for writing effective paragraphs—unity, coherence, and adequate development—are equally important for writing a whole composition. But even more than for a paragraph, the writing of an essay requires a series of activities—planning, drafting, and revising—that is seldom linear or neat. Usually composing will require you to engage in the three activities several times as you discover, develop, and create the final form of a composition. Whatever repetition or messiness you experience, you must learn to be patient with yourself at the same time you work to improve. The more aware you become of the conventions of writing and of what works well for you, the better and easier your writing will become.

33a Consider the purpose and audience of your composition.

PURPOSE

Although it is sometimes difficult to identify, writing always has a purpose. Once you know what a given composition is supposed to accomplish, the composing process will begin to proceed smoothly.

The purposes of nonfiction writing may be classified as *expressive, informative,* and *persuasive.* Very seldom will you write an extended composition that has only one of these purposes, but the terms will help you describe what you wish to write or analyze what you have written.

Expressive writing emphasizes a writer's feelings and reactions to the world. If you keep a diary or journal or write personal letters in which you recount your responses to your experience, you are engaging in expressive writing.

Informative writing focuses a reader's attention on the objective world, not on the writer's responses to that world. This textbook is a good example of informative writing as it leads you to think about the ideas and actions that help you learn to write. News articles, encyclopedia articles, science reports, and other technical writing that transmits information to a specific audience—all are good examples of informative writing.

Persuasive writing attempts to affect a reader's opinions and/or actions. It relies specifically on evidence and logical reasoning. And as you attempt to persuade, you are likely to employ expressive and informative writing. Whatever final purpose you decide on, you must have a clear picture in your mind of what you intend to accomplish. Only then can you begin to control your writing.

AUDIENCE

In recent years many authors have written books that make challenging subjects available to the general public—Richard Selzer's *Confessions of a Knife* and Stephen Jay Gould's *Wonderful Life* come to mind. Selzer and Gould are highly trained scientists who can write very specialized articles or books for equally specialized audiences. Both writers are comfortable in the jargon or technical language that is appropriate to their specialized audiences. Fortunately for us, however, they are also comfortable writing for readers who understand little about such technical training and subjects. When they write to us—a general audience—they simply assume that we are curious, interested, attentive readers. They either omit the jargon or translate it into diction we can understand; they explain ideas in terms that we know.

Selzer and Gould are particularly good at infusing dry, technical information with a human element. Selzer describes a parasite that has entered the human body in terms that make it seem supernatural, perhaps even demonic. Gould manages to incorporate technical language into his prose, and to define it, so that we can understand what he says. He describes a worm known to us only through fossils. It is named Pikaia and is "an attractive species, a laterally compressed ribbon-shaped creature some two inches in length." Furthermore, "It is a chordate, a member of our own phylum...with a notochord, the stiffened dorsal rod that gives our phylum, Chordata, its name."

Selzer and Gould succeed as writers—in large part—because they know their audiences. They bring us information in a language that we find both vivid and accessible; as a result we as general readers get to see and know what they see and know.

33b Find an appropriate subject.

In college writing, an "appropriate subject" is one that meets the needs of the writing assignment. Sometimes your writing instructor assigns a topic, in which case you can immediately begin considering the needs of the audience (**33a**), what aspects of the topic you want to emphasize (**33c**), and how the composition (should be organized (**33d**). Many times, however, you will be allowed to choose a topic; for some students this freedom feels more like an obstacle to successful writing than an opportunity. In this case, your personal experience, knowledge, and interests are a good place to start looking for subject matter. You can write an interesting, stimulating paper on almost anything you care about.

Sometimes you will need to choose a topic outside your own experience. For example, a history professor who asks you to write a composition on some aspect of nineteenth century Russia will want you to demonstrate your command of certain information rather than your personal experience or feelings. But, again, you can write a better paper if you find an aspect of the topic that interests you.

And, of course, two other vital practical considerations are time and length. If you have to write a paper in a few hours, choose a subject you already know about—not one that requires research. If you have to write a paper of 500–600 words on Kate Chopin, do not choose "Kate Chopin's Writing Career" as your subject. Choose

"Chopin's Fiction and Victorian Morals" or "Chopin's Views on Marriage." Find a subject appropriate to the amount of time you have and the length the instructor has asked for.

33c Explore and focus the subject.

(1) Explore the subject.

Once you have a general subject in mind, the following methods, used singly or in combination, will help you explore it.

Listing Write down everything that comes to mind. Disregard grammar, spelling, and diction—just write. Here is a typical list one student made as she thought about a very broad subject: Home.

> Georgia
> Tennessee
> parents and siblings
> my cats
> homesickness
> friends
> what I miss when I am away
> where they have to take me when I return
> how to make a home
> is it a place
> is it also something in my mind
> what do I want from a home
> it gives me security and comfort—any place could do that
> it lets me be me
> it is where I am free to be me
> I carry home with me—this is it

who?
what?
why?
where?
when?

The list demonstrates the student's discovery of a possible subject—the idea that being at home is the same as feeling the freedom to be yourself and that you carry home with you.

Questioning Journalists typically ask *who? what? when? where? how?* and *why?* Answering those questions about a topic may help you find your subject. Look at the preceding list and consider the benefit of asking these questions about *home.* Simply asking why you need a home will stimulate ideas.

Strategies for Development Think about the subject home from three different approaches—*static, dynamic,* and *relative.* A *static* approach focuses on what a home is or on an example of a home. A *dynamic* perspective focuses on action and change: How does a home affect us? How do we create a home? Can a home change? A *relative* perspective examines relationships within a system. Think about the connection between home and family. Or between home and our sense of identity.

The development strategies discussed in **32d** suggest ways of thinking about a topic. For example,

Narration   What is a story that focuses on home?

Process   How can you create a home?

Cause and Effect   How does home change you?

Description   What does home look like?

Definition   What is home?

Classification and Division   What does one lose by not having a home?

Example   What are some benefits?

Comparison and Contrast   How is a home different from a house? Where is an immigrant's home?

(2) Limit and focus the subject.

During the previous discussions of exploring the subject, we also have examined limiting and finally focusing the subject—getting a clear idea of what you want to accomplish for a certain audience in a paper of a certain length. Suppose, for example, we move from the very broad topic, *Home*, to topics that are more limited.

home→place→state of mind→people who seem at home anywhere→immigrants→the psychology of creating a new home

The last topic—What must immigrants do psychologically to create a new home?—focuses the subject. You now know the limits of your discussion, and you know what kind of information you must research.

33d Construct a focused, specific thesis statement containing a single main idea.

In **33c** we suggested a variety of ways to limit and focus a subject. We finally narrowed the broad subject, home, into a single specific question: What must immigrants do psychologically to create a new home? The question demonstrates a limited, focused subject. The paper we write will answer the question for ourselves and our reader. At some point in the composing process we need to condense that answer into a single statement that clearly suggests the thesis of the composition—the idea that binds together the discussion. For example,

VAGUE THESIS   It is difficult for immigrants to feel at home.

IMPROVED THESIS   An immigrant must embrace the future, and to some extent reject the past, if he is to construct a new home.

The vague thesis statement is as true as the improved one, but it helps neither the writer nor the reader. The word "difficult" expresses no clear focus for the writer; therefore, the reader is not sure what to expect. The improved thesis statement focuses by explaining "difficult": an immigrant must reject the past if he is to embrace the future.

The thesis statement helps a writer decide how to construct the essay. For example, a series of brief case studies of immigrants could illustrate the two halves of the thesis: (1) rejecting the past, and (2) embracing the future. And, of course, a reader will interpret a thesis statement as an indication of the form and content of the discussion.

Depending on the method of development, the thesis statement may occur anywhere in the essay. Or it may not need to be stated at all. For the reader's benefit, however, the thesis statement usually appears at or near the beginning of the essay. At other points in the discussion the writer may repeat the thesis entirely—although in different terms—or in part. The repetition helps to guide the writing and reading process.

33e Choose an appropriate method or combination of methods of development for arranging ideas and prepare a working plan.

The strategies for developing paragraphs and possible essay topics also work very well for developing longer pieces of writing. *Exemplification, narration, process, cause and effect, classification, definition, description, analysis,* and *comparison and contrast—*one of these or a combination of them can be used for organizing your paper effectively. Review **32d**.

Eventually every writer develops a working plan; if you intend to write successfully, you must find one that works well for you and master it. Some writers use a very informal plan; perhaps a list (see **33c**) is sufficient for them. They jot down ideas, cross out some, move others to another location in the list, draw lines to suggest connections or overlap. They are comfortable with this relatively imprecise kind of plan, knowing that they will write, revise, write some more, and finally clarify what to say and how to say it. The plan remains extremely flexible.

An informal plan may begin with a list and evolve into an informal outline. The earlier list about home could evolve into this informal outline.

Informal Outline

Thesis statement: An immigrant must embrace the future and, to some extent, reject the past if he is to create a new home.

1. Why the Shin family left Korea
2. Gina's description of arriving in America
3. The Shin family business and the freedom it gives them
4. The Chan family leaves Thailand
5. Why they chose to come to America
6. How the family business helped them create a home

A formal outline uses indention and numbers to indicate levels of subordination.

Formal Sentence Outline

Thesis statement: An immigrant must embrace the future and, to some extent, reject the past if he is to create a new home.

I.   Mr. Shin decides the family must leave Korea.
    A. The unstable political climate oppresses the people.
    B. He wants to be in business for himself.
    C. He believes in America as the place of individual liberty.
II.   Mr. Chan plans to leave Thailand.
    A. Political unrest makes him fear for his safety.
    B. He has relatives already in America.
III.   Both immigrants start businesses in America.
    A. Shin starts a computer business.
    B. Chan starts a restaurant.
    C. The businesses buy them freedom to grow and change.
IV.   Both have integrated into their communities.
    A. They live in nice houses.
    B. They are active in church and in civic activities.
    C. Both even are proud to pay taxes.

Formal Topic Outline

Thesis statement: An immigrant must embrace the future and, to some extent, reject the past if he is to create a new home.

I.   Shin leaves Korea
    A. Political instability
    B. Business
    C. American mythology
II.   Chan leaves Thailand
    A. Political unrest
    B. Relatives in America
III.   Both in business
    A. Shin and computers
    B. Chan and restaurant
    C. Freedom to grow and change
IV.   Identity with community
    A. Houses
    B. Church, civic activities
    C. Americanized, taxes

33f Write the first draft.

Writers often handicap themselves by assuming that they should write a composition in a certain order—that they should write the first word of the composition first and the last word last. Those writers mistake the order of the words in the completed composition (a product) for the order of the words as they come out in the actual writing (a process). Writing—including all the preliminary steps that we have discussed—usually is anything but straightforward and linear. So the best advice you can give yourself as you begin writing is to begin anywhere you can. Only after you get words on the page can you begin making decisions about revising and altering the content or form of the composition as you wish.

(1) Write effective introductions and conclusions.

Introductions and conclusions occupy strategic locations in a composition and strongly affect a reader's reaction to the composition. In general they are also harder to write because they differ in function from the rest of the composition. An introduction is the point of entry that arouses a reader's interest and indicates the subject and strategy of the composition. A conclusion satisfactorily completes the essay; it may summarize, restate certain ideas, contain the conclusion of an argument, or point to the other subjects that could be discussed.

The introductory paragraph below grabs the reader's attention and indicates the content, and to some extent the tone (the writer's attitude toward the subject) of the discussion that will follow.

> Broadway, west side, a storefront window, and painted on the plate glass a cup of steaming coffee; morning, Cottonwood Falls, the Emma Chase Café, November: I'm inside and finishing a fine western omelet and in a moment will take on the planks of homemade wheat bread—just as soon as the shadow from the window coffee cup passes across my little notebook.
>
> —WILLIAM LEAST HEAT MOON, *PrairyErth*

In the body of the essay the author explores the effects of the café on the town and on the women who have worked there. But this introductory paragraph does not indicate the theme of the essay—only the subject and the author's attitude toward that subject. He concludes the essay with a conversation with one of the women who tells what the café taught her and who states one of the themes that has been building in the essay.

> "…because of the Emma Chase, I see my femaleness differently; now I think feminism means being connected with other people, not just with other feminists."

This is a dominant theme in the essay—connectedness to land and to other people, often achieved by work.

In the following introductory paragraph the author clearly signals subject and theme. The concluding paragraph restates in different language that theme and points to the future.

INTRODUCTION   In middle-class circles these days, one can hardly drop into a conversation or pick up a magazine or skim through a book without encountering sentences that begin: "The trouble with men is…" These are not exclusively women's sentences; this is not a sexual class war, with Amazonian feminists launching guerilla raids upon men. More and more, the accusations also come from men themselves.

CONCLUSION   The winds of change blew for years before women won the vote, another half-century before the modern feminist movement began. They will have to blow far into the next century, no doubt, before men will have outgrown their troubles.

> —PETER FILENE, *"Between a Rock and a Soft Place"*

The purpose of Filene's essay is to explain and to persuade. By announcing his thesis in the beginning, he establishes his point of view immediately. At the conclusion, he restates the thesis because part of his point is the fact that change will come slowly and incrementally. He means, the reader may assume, to encourage patience and vigilance.

As you read essays in magazines, textbooks, or newspapers, look carefully at the introductory and concluding paragraphs. Examine the strategy involved in writing them and try to discover methods that you are comfortable using.

Caution: Avoid using clichés in your introductions. Also avoid unnecessary definitions, such as "Webster defines an emigrant as...." Finally do not apologize in either your introduction or your conclusion ("Although I am no expert on this subject, I..."). Apologies undermine the effectiveness of your paper.

(2) Develop a good title.

Good titles help establish good first impressions. But they can do much more. They can indicate the tone and content of a composition, and they can pique a reader's interest. The introductory and concluding paragraphs in **33f(1)** give one particularly good example. Filene's essay is titled "Between a Rock and a Soft Place." In the introductory paragraph he describes the rock that men are up against and begins to suggest the softer "feminine" side of men that is being encouraged. The title is accurate and a little lighthearted, as if not to take this problem overly seriously. The concluding paragraph revisits these soft and hard images which describe the paradox of being a man in contemporary society. The first and last paragraphs and the title work well together to indicate to the reader the content, the tone, and the shape of the discussion, and the reader is pleased with the symmetry that the writer has achieved.

33g Revise and edit the composition.

Do not think of revision as simply the last stage of composing. Revision plays an important part in every stage of composition—from the first vague notions about the subject to the last proofreading. During the composing process you will often pause to rethink or to see in a different way some aspect of the paper; each of these acts is a part of revision.

There is, however, some danger of being overly conscious of the need to revise as you write. Some writers become so impressed with the inadequacy of what they have written or are about to write that they freeze up, fall victim to a writer's block, and cannot continue. The best advice to give yourself is to write, to get words on the page that you and your instructor can assess. Until you get the words out of your head and onto a piece of paper, there is very little anyone can do to help you as a writer.

Below is a list of questions that you will find useful as you revise your papers. Apply them systematically to the final draft of the paper before you submit it for grading. Use the questions on the essay as a whole and on individual paragraphs to help you assess your writing during composition.

REVISER'S CHECKLIST

The essay as a whole

1. Does the whole essay stick to the purpose (**see 33a**) and the subject (**see 33b**)?
2. Have you kept your audience clearly in mind? Is the tone appropriate and consistent? See **33a**. Do any terms require definition?
3. Is the focus consistent (**33c**)? Do the ideas in the essay show clear relationships to the central idea, or thesis?
4. Is the central idea or thesis sharply conceived? Does your thesis statement (if one is appropriate) clearly suggest the position and approach you are taking? See **33d**.
5. Have you chosen an effective method or combination of methods of development? See **33e**.
6. Is the essay logically sound both as a whole and in individual paragraphs and sentences? See **31**.
7. Will the introduction arouse the reader's interest? Does it indicate what the paper is about? See **33f**.
8. Does the essay come to a satisfying close? See **33f**.

Paragraphs

1. Are all the paragraphs unified? Are there any ideas in any paragraph that do not belong? See **32a**.
2. Is each paragraph coherent? Are sentences within each paragraph in a natural and effective order? Are the sentences connected by repetition of key words or ideas, by pronoun reference, by parallel structure, or by transitional expressions? See **32b**.
3. Is the progression between paragraphs easy and natural? Are there clear transitions where needed? See **32b**.
4. Is each paragraph adequately developed? See **32c**.

Sentences and diction

1. Have you used subordination and coordination to relate ideas effectively? See **24**.
2. Are there misplaced parts or dangling modifiers? See **25**.
3. Do you find any faulty parallelism? See **26**.
4. Are there any needless shifts in grammatical structures, in tone or style, or in viewpoint? See **27**.
5. Does each pronoun refer clearly to its antecedent? See **28**.
6. Are ideas given appropriate emphasis within the sentence? See **29**.
7. Are the sentences varied in length? in type? See **30**.
8. Are there any fragments? comma splices or fused sentences? See **2** and **3**.
9. Do all the verbs agree with their subjects? pronouns with their antecedents? See **6**.
10. Have you used the appropriate form of the verb? See **7**.
11. Are any words overused? used imprecisely? vague? See **20**.
12. Have all unnecessary words and phrases been eliminated? See **21**. Have any necessary words been omitted? See **22**.

EDITING CHECKLIST

Punctuation, spelling, mechanics

1. Are commas (see **12**) and semicolons (see **14**) used where required by the sentence structure? Have superfluous commas been removed (see **13**)?
2. Is any end punctuation omitted? See **17**.
3. Are apostrophes (see **15**) and quotation marks (see **16**) placed correctly?
4. Are all words spelled correctly? See **18**.
5. Are capitalization (see **9**), italics (see **10**), and abbreviations used correctly?
6. Is your manuscript in an acceptable form? Have all words been divided correctly at the ends of lines? See **8**.

33h Write well-organized answers to essay tests; write effective in-class essays.

(1) Write clear, concise, well-organized answers on essay tests.

The best preparation for an essay test is to ask yourself questions that might be on the test and then to formulate responses to those questions. You may want to write out those responses before you take the test to make sure they are unified, coherent, and clear.

If you get in the habit of identifying potential test questions before you take tests, you will improve not only as an essay test writer but as a student in general. You will become better at identifying what is important and you will get good practice at formulating essential concepts.

Before you begin writing, plan how you intend to spend the time in prewriting, writing, and revising. Just a few moments of planning will probably prevent your being caught at the end of class furiously trying to scribble one last paragraph.

Be sure you read the instructions and questions on the test carefully. And as you write, be sure you carefully follow the guidelines that are stated or implied in the instructions or questions.

(2) Write well-organized, clear in-class essays.

In-class essays require you to use time well. Plan your time: jot down a brief outline of your essay; then quickly decide how much time you will need to allow to prewriting, to writing, and to revision.

If you have in mind the essentials of the Reviser's Checklist (**33g**), you can use them to help you analyze your writing as you write and after you finish.

Limiting a Topic

NAME _____ SCORE _____

DIRECTIONS   Point out the problems that you might have in writing about the following topics. Evaluate each topic on the basis of its suitability for an essay of 300–500 words written for readers like those in your English class.

TOPICS

the melting pot theory

the mosaic theory

a theme in Kate Chopin's "The Awakening"

what I have learned from an immigrant

DIRECTIONS   Choose one of the general topics listed below and plan a limited essay of 300–500 words. Consider your classmates as the audience for your essay. To limit the general topic that you choose, use one of the techniques discussed in **32a** or some other technique that you have found useful. Save the work that you do in limiting the topic because your notes will be useful in future exercises.

TOPICS

1. changing gender roles

2. women writers

3. Black Elk

4. Mourning Dove

5. Ellis Island

6. Maxine Hong Kingston

7. travel literature

8. education

9. work

10. nature literature

PLAN

PLAN CONTINUED

Planning the Composition: The Thesis Exercise 33–2

NAME _____ SCORE _____

DIRECTIONS   Point out the weaknesses of the following thesis statements. Then use the space below to write your own thesis statement for the limited topic that you chose in Exercise 33–1 or on another topic that your instructor approves.

THESIS STATEMENTS

1. We should participate in Women's History Month activities for three main reasons.

2. We should participate in Black History Month activities for three main reasons.

3. There are three main benefits from having a large Asian community in our city.

4. People who read love poetry are jerks.

THESIS STATEMENT

Planning the Composition: The Outline   Exercise 33–3

NAME _____ SCORE _____

DIRECTIONS   Read the following essay carefully and make a topic outline of it.

The story "Friend and Protector" by Peter Taylor invites the reader to decide which character best fits the title. A cursory reading could assign friend and protector status to the family servant Jesse because of his devotion to Uncle Andrew. One also might give the status to Uncle Andrew because of his care of Jesse. Although both are possibilities, Aunt Margaret most accurately portrays the role of friend and protector of Jesse Morton.

Although Margaret and Jesse differ in race and social status, she is his friend. Not only has she known him for many years, but she is well acquainted with his shenanigans. During his many years of service to the family, Jesse's encounters with trouble have become routine. The narrator and nephew says, "By the time I came along, Jesse's escapades and my uncle and aunt's reactions to them had become a regular pattern" (139). Aunt Margaret knows Jesse, but she remains loyal to him despite his past.

Jesse is the only one of the black servants to move with the family to Memphis. Because he receives a suspended sentence for his involvement in a murder, everyone assumes that Uncle Andrew has reached an understanding with the judge. Nevertheless, taking him displays a great deal of allegiance from both Mr. and Mrs. Nelson.

Jesse rewards their loyalty with devoted care to both of them but especially to Uncle Andrew. Despite his devotion to the family Jesse continues to get into trouble with the law and has to be bailed out. On one occasion Jesse has become involved in the "numbers gang" and has his life threatened. Uncle Andrew has to "rescue him from some room above a pool hall where the rival gang had him cornered" (144).

On the other hand, Aunt Margaret behaves like a mother to Jesse. She wants to know when he is going out for an evening. Perhaps she simply means to control him, but it seems more likely that she desires to shield him from harm. After all, he had come into their employment as little more than a boy and had grown up among them.

The Nelsons differ in their attitude toward Jesse as his troubles continue. Uncle Andrew dismisses him as a "mere nothing" (144). Margaret seems to expect more of Jesse and in some ways to marvel at him The narrator perceives Aunt Margaret as severe with Jesse. He learns her severity when he too misbehaves and is reprimanded by his aunt. She clearly expects better behavior out of him and Jesse. In a critical scene Aunt Margaret watches Jesse as he works in the garden. She stands immobile and upright, staring intently. "Then she would shake her head sadly—exaggerating the shake so that he wouldn't miss it—and turn her back to the window."

In the climax scene of the story Jesse has become ill and has lost his mind. He is frightened and nearly violent and tries to hide in Uncle Andrew's office. Much to everyone's surprise he continually calls Aunt Margaret's name. Margaret comes and with "Moist Eyes" speaks to Jesse in a voice "utterly sweet and beautiful" (156). As the narrator recognizes, this is an occasion like death, and he is witnessing one old friend saying good-bye to another.

Seeking to get a better look at Jesse, Margaret kneels and peers through the door, and when she sees him, her body goes "perfectly rigid" (157). She has not seen what she hoped to see; but she has seen what she feels compelled to see.

In this last scene her role as friend and protector comes clear. One is lead to characterize Margaret in this last scene in terms she used to describe herself: she is "true blue" (152).

OUTLINE

Writing the Whole Composition:
Introductions and Conclusions   Exercise 33–4

NAME _____ SCORE _____

DIRECTIONS   Using the outline that you completed for Exercise 33–3 as a guide, make notes for a new introduction and conclusion to the essay. Write the new introduction and conclusion in the space below.

INTRODUCTION

CONCLUSION

Writing the Composition

NAME _____ SCORE _____

DIRECTIONS   Write an outline for an essay of 300–500 words on the limited topic you selected earlier or on a topic that your instructor approves. Remember that your outline is only a guide and that you can change it, add to it, or subtract from it whenever you have reason to do so. When you have finished the outline, write a rough draft and evaluate your composition using the checklist below. Make any changes that are needed. Then make a final neat copy of your work. Be sure to give your essay a title that is suitable to the contents of your essay and that will make your audience want to read it.

CHECKLIST FOR A COMPOSITION

1. Is the title both provocative and appropriate?
2. Does the introduction include the thesis statement or a sentence that suggests the thesis? Is the rest of the introduction appropriate, and does it lead smoothly into the statement or the suggestion of the thesis?
3. Is the relationship of each paragraph to the thesis clear?
4. Is each controlling idea in each paragraph developed fully enough?
5. Is the essay coherent—that is, does each paragraph flow smoothly into the one that follows it? (Compare the first sentence of a paragraph with the last sentence of the preceding paragraph.)
6. Does the conclusion make you feel that the composition is complete, that the essay has ended where it began, with a restatement of the thesis?
7. Are both the grammar and the punctuation of the composition correct? (Proofread the paper at least once for any error that you tend to make frequently.)
8. Are all the words spelled correctly?
9. Is there any wordiness that needs to be eliminated?
10. Does the style seem fluid and clear?

COMPOSITION

THE WHOLE COMPOSITION

COMPOSITION CONTINUED

Writing the Composition

COMPOSITION CONTINUED

COMPOSITION CONTINUED

Parts of Speech	Uses in the Sentence	Examples
1. Verbs	Indicators of action or state of being (often link subjects and complements)	Tom *hit* the curve. Mary *was* tired. He *is* a senator.
2. Nouns	Subjects, objects, complements	*Kay* gave *Ron* the *book* of *poems.* *Jane* is a *student.*
3. Pronouns	Substitutes for nouns	*He* will return *it* to *her* later.
4. Adjectives	Modifiers of nouns and pronouns	*The long* poem is *the best.*
5. Adverbs	Modifiers of verbs, adjectives, adverbs, or whole clauses	sang *loudly* a *very* sad song *entirely too* fast *Indeed,* we will.
6. Prepositions	Words used before nouns and pronouns to relate them to other words in the sentence	*to* the lake *in* a hurry *with* no thought *beside* her
7. Conjunctions	Words that connect words, phrases, or clauses; may be either coordinating or subordinating	win *or* lose in the morning *and* at night We won today, *but* we lost last week. Come *as* you are.
8. Interjections	Expressions of emotion (unrelated grammatically to the rest of the sentence)	*Woe* is me! *Ouch!* *Imagine!*

Common auxiliaries (helping verbs)

am	do	might
am (is, are, *etc.*)	does	must
going to *or*	had	ought to
about to	had to	shall
are	has	should
be	has to	used to
been	have	was
can	have to	were
could	is	will
did	may	would

Forms of the verb to be

am	have been	will *or*
are	is	shall be
had been	was	will *or*
has been	were	shall have been

Common indefinite pronouns

another	everybody	nothing
anybody	everyone	one
anyone	everything	somebody
anything	neither	something
each	nobody	
either	no one	

[Usually considered singular]

all	more	none
any	most	some

[May be considered singular or plural]

Relative pronouns

that	who	whomever
what	whoever	whose
which	whom	

Subordinating conjunctions (or subordinators)

after	if	until
although	in order that	when
as	since	whenever
as if	so that	where
as though	that	wherever
because	though	while
before	unless	

Common prepositions

across	for	over
after	from	through
as	in	to
at	in front of	under
because of	in regard to	until
before	like	up
beside	near	with
between	of	
by	on	

Conjunctive adverbs

accordingly	hence	moreover
also	henceforth	nevertheless
anyhow	however	otherwise
besides	indeed	still
consequently	instead	then
first, second, third, *etc.*	likewise	therefore
furthermore	meanwhile	thus

Common transitional phrases

as a result	in addition	on the contrary
at the same time	in fact	on the other hand
for example	in other words	that is
for instance		

Principal Parts of Some Troublesome Verbs

Present	*Past*	*Past Participle*
begin	began	begun
blow	blew	blown
burst	burst	burst
choose	chose	chosen
draw	drew	drawn
drink	drank	drunk
drive	drove	driven
eat	ate	eaten
fly	flew	flown
freeze	froze	frozen
give	gave	given
lay	laid	laid
lie	lay	lain
raise	raised	raised
ring	rang	rung
rise	rose	risen
speak	spoke	spoken
steal	stole	stolen
swim	swam	swum
take	took	taken
wear	wore	worn

Individual Spelling List

Write in this list every word that you misspell—in spelling tests, in themes, or in any other written work. Add pages as needed.

NO.	WORD (CORRECTLY SPELLED)	WORD (SPELLED BY SYLLABLES) WITH TROUBLE SPOT CIRCLED	REASON FOR ERROR*

*See pages 173–92 for a discussion of the chief reasons for misspelling. Indicate the reason for your misspelling by writing *a, b, c, d, e, f,* or *g* in this column

a = Mispronunciation
b = Confusion of words similar in sound and/or spelling
c = Error in adding prefixes or suffixes
d = Confusion of *ei* and *ie*
e = Error in forming the plural
f = Error in using hyphens
g = Any other reason for misspelling

Individual Spelling List (cont.)

NO.	WORD (CORRECTLY SPELLED)	WORD (SPELLED BY SYLLABLES) WITH TROUBLE SPOT CIRCLED	REASON FOR ERROR

Individual Spelling List (cont.)

NO.	WORD (CORRECTLY SPELLED)	WORD (SPELLED BY SYLLABLES) WITH TROUBLE SPOT CIRCLED	REASON FOR ERROR